FROM TAYLORISM TO FORDISM

This is a history of 'scientific management' and workers' alienation, written by a psychiatrist.

From its origins in Frederick W. Taylor's 'time-and-motion studies' in early twentieth-century America, Taylorism has come to define our epoch's organization of work and even the time spent in recovering from it. Aimed at supplanting the worker's skills and authority, 'scientific management' has fragmented the work process, dividing workers from each other and from their creativity.

Henry Ford took the assault a step further by turning workers into appendages of machines, thus pioneering the Fordist system which was soon embraced throughout the industrialized world. Although automation has since reduced the numbers employed on the traditional assembly line, such models are increasingly applied to clerical and intellectual labour.

From Taylorism to Fordism arose from the author's experience as a psychiatrist dealing with workers' sense of alienation. He roots this psychopathology of work in the production system that treats the worker's body as a machine. Drawing on his surveys of French industry and on the Marxist classics, Doray's book sheds new light on the persistence of Taylorism/Fordism as a 'rational madness'.

FROM TAYLORISM TO FORDISM
A Rational Madness

By Bernard Doray

Translated by David Macey

Foreword by Maurice Godelier

'an association in which the free development of each
is the condition for the free development of all'

Free Association Books / London / 1988

English language edition first published 1988 by
Free Association Books
26 Freegrove Road
London N7 9RQ

Originally published in French under the title
Le taylorisme, une folie rationnelle? © BORDAS 1981

Translation © David Macey 1988

The publisher gratefully acknowledges the financial assistance
of the French Ministry of Culture in defraying part of the
cost of translation.

British Library Cataloguing in Publication Data

Doray, Bernard
  From Taylorism to Fordism: A Rational Madness
  1. Employment. Labour
  I. Title   II. Le taylorisme, une folie
  rationnelle? *English*
  331

  ISBN 1 85343 010 2
  ISBN 1 85343 011 0 pbk

Typeset by Input Typesetting Ltd, London

Printed and bound in Great Britain by
Bookcraft Ltd, Midsomer Norton, Avon

CONTENTS

FOREWORD

For half a century, Taylorism dominated the world of production, and was both its motor and its symbol. Is it already a thing of the past, an outdated way of organizing industrial labour? Whilst there can be no doubt that the world of Taylorism and Fordism is breaking up and that its cohesion and efficacy are now being seriously challenged, we must, like Bernard Doray, face facts. He reminds us that the employment statistics for 1978 showed that over 600,000 of the 7,400,000 workers in France – almost one-tenth – were still working on assembly lines, and that a high proportion of them were women. It also appears that many people who do not actually work on an assembly line still describe their productive activities as 'assembly-line work'. This shows the extent to which Taylorism – and its successor, Fordism – has become a symbol of the modern way of working, and that it is still that symbol that is branded on the body and consciousness of the worker.

Bernard Doray is a doctor and a psychiatrist. His professional experience has made him sensitive to the frustrations and anxieties of work, and his personal history led him to try to understand the various forms in which it existed. Going further still, he worked on two surveys carried out in two factories, one producing textiles and the other making electronic equipment. There, he learned at first hand what is meant by the fragmentation of labour, by the breakdown of jobs into tasks, and of tasks into simple movements to be performed at a set speed. He could have simply chosen to write an eye-witness 'journalistic' account of what he saw (and I am not using the word 'journalistic' pejoratively). But he chose instead to stand back and to investigate the birth and historical development of Taylorism.

He therefore turned to the past, to the age of manufacture and to capitalism's first great attempts to reorganize production under its own control. He began to trace Taylorism's ancestry and the genealogy which leads, with some interruptions, from the 'table system' to the automated 'line'. Despite major differences in the characteristic use made of labour-power in each period of capitalism, one feature remains constant from the age of manufacture to that of large-scale mechanized industry: labour-power is a reality, and every available resource provided by modern science is used in an attempt to measure it, break it down and reconstitute it, to make it serve the valorization of value and the accumulation of capital.

Doray then owed it to himself to pursue a second line of investigation and to go on to examine how in the nineteenth century physiology and mechanics helped to give men like Taylor the means and the desire to discover a 'law of human fatigue' which would allow them to extract everything possible from living labour short of killing the individual who performed it.

These attempts to break down, fragment and reconstitute human labour-power have resulted in a mode of work and production which splits the individuality of the worker in two. Part of his individuality is alienated in production, but another part is not directly involved in production, and may even have no involvement at all. It is a third dimension which Doray explores, by taking up the themes of alienated labour, the body as machine, and the body as mercenary, and then the theme of the Taylorist worker who becomes a slave to a machine-system, subject to the actions of automata which he cannot control either technically or socially.

These are some of the major themes explored in this book. I would now like to look at them in rather more detail. In the age of manufacture, capital ceased to be simply a means of acquiring wealth by buying and selling commodities or by lending money. Those older forms of capital usually allowed the processes that produced commodities to continue to exist alongside them, in their own social forms and on their own technical basis. A move to capture both labour processes and labour-power began. They were set to work under the direct control of the capitalist and became 'productive' capital. By analysing factory regulations, Doray shows how labour-power was imprisoned in a closed world and became tightly controlled by norms dictated from above. A military-style discipline was established and detailed regulations were laid down as to who could move around the factory, and at what times and for what reasons they could do so. Other regulations prescribed respect for and obedience to higher authorities in all circumstances. And so, in a society where it was about to be proclaimed that, as a general principle, all men were equal, labour and production constantly reconstructed a local world of social hierarchies and inequalities.

But these rules had yet to penetrate every part of the labour process. It took a further two hundred years and the emergence of Taylorism for capital to be able to control every aspect of labour-power 'in detail'. For that to come about, the great movement which had begun in the age of manufacture had to develop further, and the individual worker had to begin to disappear from production, only to reappear as an interchangeable fragment of a collective worker, of a collective labourer who had become an appendage to a machine-system. But even before the appearance of machines, the figure of the automaton began to emerge with the 'table system'. A number of workers sitting at a table carried out operations which gradually transformed raw materials into a manufactured product. This obviously resulted in increased productivity but, as Doray, following Marglin (1973) and others notes, the system also provided a convenient and direct way of supervising and controlling the workforce. The foreman could see at a glance what was happening and which worker was stopping or slowing down production. But the activity which propelled objects down the table still originated in the workers. They set the speed of the table. A century later, when the mechanized assembly line was introduced, the movement of the automaton was regulated in advance; it was external to the worker and it became the expression, the mode of existence of a machine-system whose rhythms

3

existed independently of human beings. At this point the line itself became 'a technically based and technologically repressive mechanism that kept workers at their task', to cite Edward's (1979, p. 118) eloquent description.

There is therefore both a break and a continuity in the history of forms of industrial labour. The fragmentation of labour in the factory made it possible to break down work into simple operations which gradually came to require new and specialized tools, and those tools were finally combined to form a machine-tool which rapidly displaced the worker to the periphery of productive labour.

With this transformation, a fundamental change occurred. The capitalist mode of production, which had gradually come to dominate labour processes inherited from the past and had pressed them into service without revolutionizing them, now began to destroy its own starting point and to construct a base of its own: mechanization, which was the precondition for large-scale industry. It is this long-term process which Marx, using a rather curious vocabulary, describes as the transition from the 'formal subsumption' of the labour process by capital to its 'real subsumption'. By describing it as 'real', Marx means that, with mechanization, capital at last found the material conditions which would allow it to flourish. It had found a productive body of its own. From the outset, capitalism meant production and commerce on an increasingly large scale; small capitalists do exist, but the capitalist system cannot remain small. Thanks to machines, capitalism was able to become mass production and could replace or dominate all other forms of production.

The appearance of machines made it both possible and necessary to pursue the tendency to fragment and reconstitute labour-power, a tendency which had begun long before machines appeared and which reaches its exemplary apotheosis with Taylorism. Taylorism took the analysis of labour processes to its logical conclusion by breaking them down into jobs which could themselves be broken down into tasks that in turn could ultimately be reduced to a limited number of simple movements. This process meant that, although human labour retained its concrete characteristics in that it was bound up with the particular tasks each worker performed in the labour process, it immediately acquired an *abstract* character. Once it had been isolated and identified, each productive movement was immediately assigned a quantum of time;

4

it therefore became equivalent to all sorts of other productive tasks which had nothing in common but the time taken to execute them. All industrial labour gradually became abstract labour which was both socially equivalent and socially necessary.

As a result of a paradox which is not really surprising, capitalism in practice implements processes which confirm Marx's hypothesis to the effect that in a competitive system of advanced commodity production, the value of commodities is, in the last instance, reduced to the socially necessary labour-time required for their production. At the level of theory, capitalism has of course always rejected this thesis.

It is less surprising to learn from Doray's study that the earliest experiments on the physiology of labour were not carried out directly on workers involved in a production process, but on prisoners and soldiers, or in other words on human guinea-pigs who were both obedient and malleable. It was only towards the end of the nineteenth century that direct observations were made in the factory.

The central point of Doray's analysis emerges, however, from the convergence of all his remarks and his investigations into the past. Basically, he reveals how the new division of labour leads to a division within the worker himself, by splintering both his concrete individuality, his relationship with himself and his relationship with his work. Doray shows that the viewpoint of the worker and that of the owner of capital can never coincide. For the latter, labour-power is something which he *has* the right to use, and he must employ it to his best advantage. For the former, labour-power is what he *is* in his innermost being, and it provides him with his means of existence. The viewpoint of 'having' and that of 'being' may be superimposed, but they can never coincide.

Doray does not turn this into a general philosophy or a metaphysical account of how humanity lost its 'essence'. He simply shows how Taylorism reflects and develops in exemplary fashion a contradiction which is central to the reality of our form of society: the contradiction between the objective *socialization* of labour and production and the objective *desubjectivization* of the worker. For Doray, the alienation of labour is not a philosophical category. It is a way of expressing the fact that, in our society, labour acquires a *social* meaning only if it *loses* its meaning *for the worker* who sees it only as a way of making a living. Alienated labour is not alienated simply because it belongs to *someone else*, but because it becomes *alien* to a worker who has no social or technical control over its meaning.

There is an element of madness in Taylorism in that, more so than any previous formula, it regards wealth as being the product of 'the reduction of human beings to a mechanical assemblage of partial functions and parts of organs', carrying out standardized operations, to use another of the author's striking formulations. There is therefore method in Taylorism's madness. There are historical and social reasons for its emergence, and their rationality can be reconstructed. Doray suggests that it is a 'rational madness' because it reflects the contradictory fact that the creation of human wealth has usually meant the exploitation and destructuring of the producers of wealth. This has nothing to do with individual madness, and Doray reminds us that Taylor's biographers emphasize his rationality and stress that his few eccentricities could be interpreted as signs of genius. But, being a doctor, Doray also knows that the permanent divisions labour produces within the individuality of the worker inevitably leave painful scars. At several points he outlines an almost psychoanalytic approach to working-class discourse. But he does not go far enough. One suspects that he would like to pursue this line of investigation and to give a systematic account of the effects of these divisions on the worker's id, ego and superego. He also describes psychoanalysis as being distorted by industrial psychology and human relations as being manipulated; once again, one would like to know more about this. A number of other questions also have to be raised.

Towards the end of his book, the author uses union newsletters, house journals and the Communist press to paint a sketch of working-class attitudes towards Taylorism and Fordism. He shows both that working-class attitudes were divided and that the unions fell into the trap that had been laid for them. American unions initially rejected these new methods of work organization and denounced them as new forms of exploitation, but they gradually allowed themselves to be won over and helped to promote them. Doray shows that Ford management and the unions developed along parallel lines. Initially, both Ford and Taylor banned unions from their factories. They promised much higher wages and a wide variety of material benefits to the workers who accepted the new working methods; that is, they adopted the old policy of giving workers 'shares' in the company's success. Fordism and Taylorism then realized that they could not expand and develop unless they worked with the big unions. Perhaps Doray should have analysed in greater detail the mechanisms behind this parallel development and done more to explain why the unions did to some extent fall into the trap.

The capitalist system could not expand simply by playing the 'high wages' card in a few ultra-modern factories. At the same time it also had to extend its production processes and generate forms of mass consumption by agreeing to guarantee all workers a minimum wage which would ensure a steady flow of mass consumption. Increasingly, it found itself involved in general negotiations with partners who, by the very nature of things, represented collectivities of workers: the unions. The unions, it seems, rapidly found themselves divided as to what attitude to adopt towards offers of higher wages linked to a Fordist transformation of working conditions. Doray's study outlines these divisions and these almost unavoidable traps, but his analysis needs to be pursued much further.

A study of Soviet Taylorism, which is barely touched upon here, would have far-reaching implications. Remarkably enough, French Communist newspapers from the period 1925–35 perpetrated what is in effect a mythology about the virtues of introducing Taylorism in the Soviet Union. They *assumed* that the Soviet Union was the land of economic and political democracy, and that the introduction of Taylorism would *immediately* lead to an improvement in the living conditions of the workers. This mythology did, of course, express the hopes and the faith the working class placed in the virtues of socialism. But it raises a question which is still relevant today.

Doray suggests that the answer to this question can never be purely technological, since the subordination of workers to machines and to the mechanical body of capitalism also implies their cultural, social and political subordination to the owners of capital, to those who valorize capital and 'exploit' it to their own advantage. In order to put an end to their subordination, we must, according to Doray, develop an economic and political democracy – which, whilst it still does not exist in the USSR, does exist in mutilated form in capitalist countries. The hope has of course already been expressed that the transition to automation will make it possible to sweep away Taylorism and Fordism, which were once the basis for industrial development, and construct a more supple universe of semi-autonomous units of production, and some people dream of bringing them under workers' control. But – and here Doray is right to be prudent, as there can be no purely technological solutions to problems involving such major social, political and economic issues – it would seem wise to avoid sensational prophecies and catchy but inaccurate slogans.

It is time for me to conclude my remarks. Doray's study is in general sober and modest. But he will certainly be criticized over his allusions to the mercantilists and the physiocrats. Here, he seems to be on shaky ground, as we can see from his interpretation of the identity of Quesnay's 'sterile' and 'productive' classes. For Quesnay, both factory workers and their masters were 'sterile', whilst both capitalist farmers and the agricultural labourers who co-operated with them in furthering the productive work of nature were 'productive'. Masters and workers therefore do not form antagonistic classes, one of which is the subject and the other the object or instrument of the production process.

That, however, is not the important point. The important point is that Doray has attempted to write a further chapter in the history of the French working class, and we badly need that history. We have many histories of the making of sectors of the working class in England and America, but it is only recently that the same trend has developed in France, where it is represented by the pioneering work of Michèle Perrot, Alain Cottereau, Jean-Paul de Gaudemar and others who follow in the footsteps of Georges Friedmann and Pierre Naville, who were its founding fathers.

Maurice Godelier
February 1981

INTRODUCTION

Now one of the very first requirements for a man who is fit to handle pig-iron as a regular occupation is that he shall be so stupid and so phlegmatic that he more nearly resembles in his mental make-up the ox than any other type . . . He is so stupid that the word 'percentage' has no meaning to him, and he must consequently be trained by a man more intelligent than himself into the habit of working in accordance with the laws of this science before he can be successful.
F. W. Taylor, *The Principles of Scientific Management*

People who experience themselves as automata, as robots, as bits of machinery, or even as animals . . . are rightly regarded as crazy. Yet why do we not regard a theory that seeks to transmute persons into automata or animals as equally crazy?
R. D. Laing, *The Divided Self*

Many of the modern myths that have grown up around mechanization and work on the assembly line express the view that there is an element of madness in the Taylorist reduction of human beings to a mechanical assemblage of partial functions and parts of organs. And yet the word 'madness' seems rather too strong. Taylor himself never displayed anything more than a few minor eccentricities, and his biographer Copley tends to ascribe them to the peculiarities of the exceptional mind. His 'System' survived for decades; whilst, as we will argue here, it is probably true that it has had its day as a coherent system, it was for a very long time a real phenomenon, and it was used to bring about an extensive rationalization of productive structures. Its effects went far beyond the organization of tasks and, fifty years after Taylor's death, an enthusiastic admirer could still write:

The improvement in our standard of living and the subsequent modification of our way of life that was made possible by the accumulation of material goods result, in my view, from Taylor's attitude of mind, and from that of the thousands of people who were involved in the search for new ways to transform matter and to manage the human societies that put those means to use. (Maury, *1967, p. 9*)

A curious conception of history . . . but it does make the point that Taylorism now affects every aspect of our way of life. And it is far removed from the apragmatic delusions of Jules Amar (1927), a contemporary of Taylor's and the founder of the 'physiology of labour' school who, late in life, dreamed up a physiological system for the management of social life.

Taylorism did not drive its inventor mad, nor does it always drive mad those who are its object. Working-class culture displays a wealth of wiles, forms of irony, withdrawals and revolts which real people use to negotiate the autonomy of their being and to reject subjectively a system which invades their productive bodies:

My working life certainly does not correspond to the life I would like to lead. It corresponds to something I accept, that's all. Well, really I put up with it rather than accepting it . . . You have to be here at 7.15 in the morning, not at 7.30; that's one of the things you have to put up with. You have to be here at 1.00, not at 1.15, so I put up with it . . . I don't really care, so I put up with it. They tell me: 'That thing over there is black.' Personally, I would say it's white, but I'll come round to their way of thinking and say that it's black. I'll take my time about it, but I'll come round to seeing it their way. Bosses are good at training people to be that way . . . What I really mean is that my professional life is one thing, and that my personal life is another. (electrician in a machine-tool assembly plant)

Saying something is black when your own eyes tell you it is white, losing face, but knowing what you think . . . the alienation of industrial work involves the subordination of the 'viewpoint' of the actors in the labour process to the dominant 'viewpoint'. In this mode of production, the dominant viewpoint is that of the valorization of capital, and the history of its productive structures is articulated around the subordination of the labour process to the process of valorization. In our investigations into the roots of Taylorism, we must therefore bear in mind the fact that its technical mechanisms imply a social contradiction. They bring the producers into certain relationships with one another and with capital; they signify both a certain productive order and a relationship between the producers and that order.

During the period that preceded the great move to rationalize labour which began in the early years of this century, productive structures presented what was essentially a composite picture.

Julien Turgan's valuable monographs (1860–85) on the great factories of France give us some idea of the diversity that existed in the second half of the nineteenth century:

The Gobelins tapestry workshop (1860 – the dates in parentheses correspond to the date of publication of the relevant monograph) handled only 1,500 kilograms of wool per year, but the master-dyers there could consistently differentiate between twenty-four different shades of a single colour. *Manufactures d'art* such as this were the exception rather than the rule.

Traditional establishments like the Bepterosse factory which made ceramic buttons in Briare (1865); here, operations were mostly carried out manually, but they had already been broken down and were executed by teams of twenty-five women sitting at long tables. Other examples included the Berteil factory (1878) which made silk hats. Almost every operation required a particular knack or skill, and the only tools that were used were at the same time very simple and highly specialized.

Workshops organized on the old 'manufactory' basis inside factories that had already been largely mechanized, such as the packing shop in the Trébucin coffee-roasting plant (1885), the sheds where cocoa was graded at the Compagnie Coloniale's factory (1880), and the sheds where tablets of chocolate were packed at the Usine Menier (1870), the rag-picking shed which supplied the paper-making machines at the Papeterie d'Essonne (1860), or the shop where watch glasses were cut by hand at the Manufactures des Trois Fontaines (1854).

Factories in which activities were still mainly manual but were subordinated to an industrial automaton or a mechanized shop.

Examples included partly mechanized mills like the Davin worsted mill (1862), which still employed three hundred workers to operate mule jennies (semi-mechanized looms) and where the speed of the looms set the speed for all the preparatory operations (sorting, scouring and drying fleeces, carding, and winding on the yarn), and the modern tile factory at Montchanin near Le Creusot (1886), where a press gave a constant supply of clay sufficient to make five tonnes of pressed, trimmed and dried tiles in a day.

Largely mechanized factories in which all that survived of the old manufactory system was a certain type of division of labour. The great Pleyel piano factory (1865), for instance, housed a saw-mill, a woodwork shop, storerooms (in which 300,000 oak boards and 90,000 beech boards were being dried out at any one time, together with supplies of pine, mahogany, lime, pear and cedar), a shop for copperwork, a smithy and an assembly shop. At the Belvalette coachworks in Boulogne-sur-Mer, most operations were mechanized, but the coachpainter still plied his craft, as the outside of each vehicle required twenty coats of varnish. The Usine Godillot in the rue Rochechouard in Paris (1880) prided itself on its ability to supply the Army with one million pairs of boots a year, whilst at the Usine Pernod (1884) sixty workers, men and women, could wash, fill, seal, label and box sixteen bottles per minute. At the Usine Japy (1870), a host of small specialized machines made it look as if the shop floor worked 'by clockwork'. The Usine Mercier (1865), which made carding-engines, was equipped with no fewer than two hundred machine-tools housed in workshops organized on the old craft basis (carpentry, casting, metal-turning, smithcraft, etc.). In Lille, the Ateliers de Construction Fives (1866) produced five or six locomotives per month, as well as cranes, light engines and metal scaffolding, and employed 2,500 workers, and Ateliers de Construction Derosne et Cail (1862) employed over 1,000 (including boilermakers, casters and lathe operators) in its Grenelle plant alone.

Large steelworks, like the La Providence plant in Hautmont (2,000 workers in 1884) and, above all, the 'Empire of Iron' in Le Creusot. This was an industrial complex where both iron-ore and coal were mined; it also had blast furnaces, rolling mills, machine shops and assembly shops.

The Manufacture de Glaces at Saint-Gobain (1863) employed

both craftsmen and women and children. Here, forms of co-operation requiring physical strength (as when ten workmen had to carry a sheet of glass weighing 300 kilograms with perfectly synchronized movements) existed alongside a highly mechanized system for circulating raw materials. In fact, so highly mechanized was it that the description Turgan gives of the factory in 1863 could almost be a description of the 'special glass' section in the modern Boussois glassworks.

And there we have it: the overall picture of productive capital in the second half of the nineteenth century is primarily one of a complex tangle of heterogeneous productive structures which have, in a sense, a historical consistency of their own. The temporality of the material structures of production does not have the smooth linearity of chronological time.

We will therefore follow the example set by the classical analysts in order to identify the structures that emerged from primitive forms of industrial capital, beginning with the structures of the age of manufacture.

CHAPTER ONE

MANUFACTURE

As impassioned series consist simply of groups, we
must first of all learn how to form groups. 'Ah, groups.
A fascinating subject. Groups must be amusing!' This
is how the wits react when one speaks of groups:
one has to endure a stream of insipid equivocations.
Whether or not the subject is amusing is open to debate,
but one thing is certain: we know nothing about groups,
and we do not even know how to shape three people
into a proper group, let alone thirty.
C. Fourier, *Le Nouveau Monde industriel*

The structures of the age of manufacture, which survived into the nineteenth century either in the shape of anachronisms like the Gobelins or in degraded forms scattered across a mechanized universe, had begun to develop three hundred years earlier. In a sense, they can be seen as products of the *verlagsystem* and the putting-out system. These were hybrid systems for controlling domestic labour. They were no longer forms of merchant's capital, but they had yet to develop into industrial capitalism (on all these points, see Kellenbenz, 1970; Valleroux, 1885 and Unwin, 1904).

As supplies of certain raw materials (such as wool, cotton, silk and metals) came to depend upon large-scale trade, the guilds which controlled the market found themselves in a position to dominate the artisans they supplied. In eighteenth-century Paris, for example, the cloth merchants who were at the top of the guild hierarchy could employ weavers on their own terms, and both supplied them with raw materials and sold their products (fine textiles from Sedan, Abbeville and Elbeuf, quality goods from the Dauphiné and Rouen, broadcloth from the Berry, and so on).

The *verlagsystem* and the putting-out system developed and systematized the employer–employee relationship by reorganizing the division of labour, by bringing together 'free workers' and members of craft guilds, and by introducing a distinction between work carried out in the towns and work carried out in the countryside.

Relations between the *canuts* of Lyons [silk-workers] and capitalist merchants provide a particularly long-lived example of this model. The *canuts* owned their own looms and controlled their own family units of production, whilst the merchants acted as intermediaries between them and the suppliers of silk on the one hand and the trade in silk goods on the other.[1]

This was certainly an employer–employee relationship, but it was not wage-based:

Merchant's capital was transformed into things (wool, silk, metals, silk goods or cloth). It followed their economic progress and increased as their market-value increased. In order to generate more money, money must be temporarily transformed into things.

Systems for collecting the products of home-working began to dominate the social division of labour, and to impose their own market conditions (and working conditions) on handicraft workers. In short, they began to invade the social sphere of labour.

As the factory system emerged, capital became fixed. It now took the form of walls, roofs, tools and raw materials, and of brain and brawn. In their turn, those elements were transformed into finished goods. The merchant appropriated the *canut*'s labour by imposing his own conditions. The factory-owner did not need to appropriate the finished product, as it was already an extension of his productive capital. And to ensure that there was no misunderstanding about that, he inscribed his trademark on objects, just as he inscribed his name on the walls within which they were produced. It was only then that the object of labour became a commodity or a marketable product.

In what sense was the new wage-system superior to the home-working system? In what sense did the enclosing and concentration of labour in special and expensive structures (factories) benefit the capitalist who paid for them?

In a seminal article, Stephen A. Marglin (1976) strongly challenges the received view that the capitalist benefited simply from the increase in technical efficiency and the potential for further rationalization that resulted from the concentration of the labour force.

The main lines of his argument are as follows. Marglin attaches crucial importance to the fact that the capitalist acquired a monopoly over the market, whereas 'The guild workman had no intermediary between himself and the market' because 'he generally sold a product, not his labour, and therefore controlled both product and work process' (p. 16). From this point of view, there is far from being a schism between the factory system and home-working systems such as 'putting out'.

As we have already said, factories can be regarded as an *extension* of something that had already been established by more primitive relations between capital and labour. Under the putting-out system, the specialization and division of tasks that the merchant had begun to introduce put him in the position of becoming an essential intermediary in the circulation of both raw materials and finished products. It was, so to speak, a more refined version of the system which had already subordinated handicraft workers to the merchant guilds. And so, 'the capitalist division of labour, as developed under the putting-out system, embodied the same principle that "successful" imperial powers have utilized to rule their colonies: divide and conquer' (Marglin, p. 20).

The world of the handicraft worker had been brought under control, but it had yet to be permanently occupied, as 'the worker still had complete control over the labour process; the worker was free to choose how long and how intensely he worked' (p. 28).

What, then, was the point of the factory system? If any real and effective subordination was to come about, two things had to happen. On the one hand, the capitalist had to impose upon the workers productive structures which expressed his objectives. On the other hand, those structures had to circumscribe the activity of labour as closely as possible. In short, when labour is 'interned' (a hackneyed expression, but at least it is accurate), the 'viewpoint' of capital is no longer separated from that of labour, and the process of valorization can control the labour process more closely than ever.

Marglin's thesis, then, is as follows:

The agglomeration of workers into factories was a natural outgrowth of the putting-out system (as a result, if you will, of its internal contradic-

tions) whose success had little or nothing to do with the technological superiority of large-scale machinery. The key to the success of the factory, as well as its inspiration, was the substitution of capitalists' for workers' control; discipline and supervision could and did reduce costs without being technologically superior. (p. 29)

To support his argument, Marglin cites Andrew Ure. Ure was a keen observer of human nature, and he understood perfectly well that the quality that distinguished Arkwright, who was the first great English mill-owner, was not so much the technological imagination which led him to invent the water frame (which was superior to the hand-operated mule jenny of the day) as his extraordinary passion for being in command and the pugnacity with which he succeeded 'in training human beings to renounce their desultory habits of work, and to identify with the unvarying regularity of the complex automaton' (Ure, 1835, p. 15).

Marglin also stresses – and this is the strong point of his argument – that the agglomeration of workers into factories often predated technological advances (and there is sometimes a contradiction between the two developments). Benjamin Gott, the great Yorkshire mill-owner, used only human energy in his mills; hand-weavers were brought together in his weaving sheds long before power looms were introduced.

The advantage of Marglin's approach is that it enables us to grasp the contradictory nature of the process; on the one hand, industrial activity became organized, but on the other the workers' ability to organize was destroyed. In a sense, we see here the seeds of Taylorism. In order to illustrate the negative side to the organization of discipline, Marglin gives the contrasting example of a sector which survived these changes. Traditional forms of self-organization (a team system) continued to exist in British mines until the 1950s, when the extraction of coal was mechanized, because capitalism could 'conquer without dividing'. Attempts to Taylorize the work of the miners resulted in such a loss of efficiency, so much absenteeism and so many disputes that a new solution had to be found, and the role and autonomy of the teams had to be reestablished. Thanks to the work of Trist and Bramforth (1951), this was to become a famous example. It was also the occasion for a major intervention on the part of the Tavistock Institute and was to give birth to the socio-technical movement (see Ortsman, 1978a, pp. 94–5).

WORKERS' CONTROL?

Marglin gives his article a nicely provocative title: 'What do bosses do?' Serge Bonfilou takes a less intellectual view. In 1979, he took part in the occupation of the printing works where he was employed in an attempt to prevent its closure. In the fourth year of the occupation, he had these comments to make on this collective appropriation of the instruments of labour. Many of the references are to an occasional publication put out by the workers themselves.

In the old days, you were never really sure what you were doing. It was always 'Do this, do that'. I worked on lay-out. I never needed to take any initiative. Everything was mapped out in advance. The only room for initiative I had was in the way I organized my own work. I would take my lay-out sheet to the boss, and if it was wrong, he would hand it back to me and say, 'Change that, that, and that' . . . Now, someone brings in copy, and we decide which typeface to use, and set it ourselves. We do the foreman's job. We have to; all the foremen have left (laughs).

Q. *Did you have much trouble learning?*

A. *Trouble? (shrugs) There's not much to casting off.*

Q. *What were you doing when I came in just now?*

A. *Printing on cellophane, not that it's my trade.*

Q. *Does the strike committee organize the work?*

A. *Yes, two or three people are in charge of that . . . 'the print-makers', we call them. They do the art-work and the paste-up. That's only on complicated jobs. On smaller jobs, we usually get by on our own. We all know each other. We work things out, and decide things for ourselves. We share out the work and decide which machines to use. (In 'the old days', the linotype operators worked under one foreman, and another foreman was in charge of lay-out. All communications had to go through the foremen.)*

Q. *Why was the work divided up like that?*

A. *Why? To stop us talking to each other. It was a kind of repression to stop us taking the initiative, to divide our ranks. To stop us realizing that, basically, we could do the boss's job . . .*

(continued over page)

To stop us realizing that we didn't need him. That might not be true of everything, but it is true of a lot of things. The bosses had to feel important. If something went wrong, they treated you like dirt. And if you turned up late . . . even if the work was already done. But you never got any compliments for doing good work. They just set you something else to do. I'd say that the bosses we had here were like sergeant-majors. The occupation makes you realize that they did have a job to do . . . No need to go to a military academy, is there?

Following Marglin, we may regard the period of manufacture as a significant moment within the broader spectrum of the subordination of the labour process to the objectives of the valorization of capital. It was primarily in terms of the organization of labour that the factory-system proved superior to earlier systems. The subordination of the labour process took the form of the gradual incorporation of the productive space within the cycle of capital, as guild-masters, merchants and then factory-owners gradually acquired a monopoly over the trade in both raw materials and finished products.

The factory was initially structured by the most basic elements of the mode of production which gave birth to it. It represented a break with all earlier systems in that no exchange took place inside it. When the *canut* handed over his piece to the merchant, it became a complete and autonomous commodity once more; it was both a use value and an exchange value, and its price was determined by a process of bargaining in which the object was assessed in monetary terms, in terms of general equivalents within the commodity system. Between the point at which the cloth-merchants' guild supplied a mill in Paris with raw wool and the point at which the piece left the dyers' shop, the labour process was punctuated or interrupted by several monetarized exchanges involving cloth-merchants, spinners (who suppled, carded and spun the wool), weavers, fullers (who scoured and thickened the wool), croppers and dyers.

The factory surrounded the labour process. An object which was being manufactured followed two simultaneous routes, which diverged when the raw materials came on to the factory floor and which converged only at the end of the manufacturing process, when the product was marketed. Only the factory-owner saw them converge.

In so far as it was an object of concrete labour, the product went through all the technical phases of its manufacture (and in some cases, as in a carriage works, there could be many such phases) and they were virtually all carried out in the same place. Tasks were carried out in parallel or serially, and they were technically articulated, but at no point was the through-put of the object of labour interrupted by commodity relations.

As it followed its technical route, the object gradually took on a physical shape as traces of labour were imprinted on it. It thus became a value-bearing object, an object for the valorization of capital. But the process was invisible to the actors involved in the labour process, as it took place at a certain remove from them. It took place in a different social space: the space in which a monopoly had been established over the function of the market. That social space dominated the factory; it included it in its plans, but it never merged with it.

From the master's point of view, the flow of production objectified the cycle of production, of its consumption and of its extended reproduction: 'If we look at the workshop as a complete mechanism, we see the raw material in all stages of production at the same time . . . The different stages of the process, previously successive in time, have become simultaneous and contiguous in space' (Marx, 1976, p. 464).

Basically, the factory internalized the through-put of traces of labour. The wage-earner left traces of his activity within the space it delineated, but those traces never took on a monetary form in his eyes. In other words, modern capitalism is based upon the wage-system and upon a transgression of the general laws of equivalence. And it is that transgression which makes labour-power an economic issue.

According to Marx's definition, labour-power consists of the physical and intellectual abilities which men and women mobilize as they work: there is no a priori reason why it should have a commodity value (and even in a commodity society, not all the physical and intellectual abilities that are exploited to useful ends give rise to an exchange of commodities, most housework being the obvious example). In fact labour-power becomes central to the economic struggle between employers and employees only when manufactured objects are no longer a direct object of struggle.

When capital itself becomes directly productive, part of the existence of the wage-earner also becomes a form of capital's existence (together with raw materials, it forms productive circulating capital). What is exchanged between employer and employee is certainly a thing, because physical strength and intelligence have a material reality, but it is not simply a thing in the sense that wool cloth or flour are things. It is a thing, but at the same time it is part of the individuality of the wage-earner, and it does not exist outside his existence.

The appropriation of labour-power, or the transformation of capital into brain and brawn (the productive body of the worker), is not then a simple process (and here we obviously touch upon the fundamental question of economic exchange; we will return to this point later). It is mediated by social relations and it implies that the capitalist has the right to use the worker's labour-power.

These social relations are structured primarily by the fact that wage-earners and capital do not measure the value of labour-power by the same standard:

For the wage-earner, labour-power is above all part of his existence, and he parts with it in exchange for a wage which permits him and his family to live: his criterion for the value of labour-power is supplied by his conditions of existence.

Labour-power is also a modality of capital's existence: it is productive circulating capital which is consumed in production and which enables money to generate more money. Capital buys labour-power more or less at its value (by remunerating wage-earners), but it uses it to produce more value, and its criterion is the rate of profit. From the point of view of capital, labour-power is an economic abstraction. It is part of productive capital, and its value is transferred to the objects it produces. For capital, the value of living labour is the dead labour it will come to represent. We thus have a cycle of labour-power and a cycle of capital, a view from below and a view from above. For the wage-earner, capital is a necessary intermediary which turns his personal labour-power into a means of making a living; for capital, the use of abstract labour-power is a precondition for extended reproduction.

THE USE OF LABOUR-POWER AND THE WORKING DAY

We know that Marx formalizes the relationship between the two by describing a division (which is obviously fictitious) of the working day: part of it belongs to the wage-earner, and during this part of the day he produces a quantity of labour equal to the value of the means of subsistence he and his family require (if his labour-power is bought at its value, he receives his share of the value he produces in the form of wages). During the second part of the day, he produces more value: the surplus value which is appropriated by his employer. This now seems obvious. In fact it represents a structural discovery on the part of Marx; no one before him had formalized things in this way. In Chapter 10 of *Theories of Surplus Value* (1969b), he himself asks why it is that David Ricardo, whose *Principles of Political Economy and Taxation* (1817) is the finest product of classical political economy, could not present matters so clearly. The question is all the more legitimate in that Ricardo, unlike Adam Smith, had all the means to do so. He had realized that the value paid to the wage-earner does not correspond to the value he produces during the working day, and that the average wage is determined by the value of the necessary means of production. He had also realized that wage bargaining centres on the division between wages and profits. But he did not focus his theory on surplus value because he did not investigate the social relations implicit in this highly specific form of bargaining (which concerns the employer's right to use the worker, and not merely a thing). And, Marx goes on, he did not investigate those social relations because, for him, they were self-evident; a natural and a historical fundamental. Ricardo did in fact grasp the principle of relative surplus value (he recommended lowering the cost of corn in order to reduce workers' living costs, the value of labour, and to increase profits), but he did not investigate the basis of relative surplus value, and therefore failed to grasp the principle of absolute surplus value. I shall not dwell on the effects of this ideological blind-spot. Basically, it relates to the problem of seeing the process

(*continued over page*)

of the valorization of capital as a specific economic cycle, and not merely as an effect of the labour process. It has to be seen, that is, as the motor behind production, as a force which adapts the labour process to its own purposes. Ricardo therefore confuses the rate of profit and the rate of surplus value; in fact he postulated only the rate of surplus value, as though valorization could be understood purely in terms of its immediate relationship with the labour process. This explains why he had no theory of the organic composition of capital, and no real understanding of the law of the tendency of the rate of profit to fall.

The factory was, then, a productive space whose structures can be read in terms of the history of relations between capital and labour. If we wish to read them in that way, we cannot ignore the general conditions of the mobilization of labour. Before the factory could come to life, it had to find powerful outside recruiting agents which could make it seem to be a necessary intermediary between the working masses and their conditions of existence. Two elements combined to provide it with an abundant and willing labour-force: poverty and the law.

In mid-nineteenth-century England, the law's answer to poverty was the workhouse. It took the 1834 amendment to the Poor Laws for the obligation to work to become part of the life of the poor. Outdoor relief was surgically removed, and the only element of earlier legislation to be retained was the administration of charity on a local basis. This facilitated the systematic building of workhouses.[2] These institutions looked pleasant, and they did not spoil the urban landscape for the bourgeoisie,[3] but they were, as Buret (1839) puts it, 'like bogymen for the poor'. He cites the example of the new workhouse in Cuckfield (Sussex), where 149 paupers applied to the parish guardians for relief on the day of the first snowfall of the year: only six were prepared to face the horrors of working the crank. Three of the six who accepted relief on this basis admitted defeat after two days.

The effects of the change were not slow to be seen. In 1837, Buret tells us, the budget for the relief of paupers was reduced to its 1803 level (in other words, it was cut by half). 'As soon as the law came into effect, pauperism disappeared as if by magic. The poor either emigrated or found work; they accepted wages which they would previously have scorned to accept, and they were willing to let their children work for a pittance' (Buret).

In France, the *ancien régime* had set up a charity administration which was not always coherent, and had introduced charity legislation which was only irregularly applied. As we know, the turning point came with the Revolution.[4]

The workhouse is a useful introduction to the internal law of the factory in that it reveals the workings of the reformist imagination. Workhouses were truly utopian institutions, as they were not really included in any economic cycle.[5] They represented both the symbolic presence of the law ('No pauper can escape the obligation to work') and a hideous caricature of the real sites of social production. Every feature of the factory was accentuated to a caricatural degree: paupers were detained in the most literal sense (they could not even go to church); the sexes were totally segregated; different age-groups were also segregated, and the healthy were segregated from the sick. The regime was one of 'purely mechanical' forced labour. This digression is not, however, without its dangers, as it may lead to undue emphasis being placed on the intentionality that is at work, for example, in the factory regulations we are about to examine, rather than on the non-intentional structures which shape industrial space. Others before us have confused the history of industry with the history of industrialists, and the productive order with its representation.

We shall therefore take factory regulations at face value: they are rules which are primarily intended to organize and legitimize a mode of private domination based upon the inequality of the rights of individuals, as opposed to the common law which defines all individuals as being free and equal. In practice, they represent a form of legislation which is unilaterally imposed by the masters, and which is concealed behind a juridical fiction (the fiction that employers and employees freely enter into a contractual relationship which is to their mutual advantage). This legislation is specifically directed against the customs of the craft guilds, and it is designed to protect employers from the possibility of their employees appealing to the *conseil des prud'hommes* [an industrial tribunal with extensive powers] or to common law.[6] French jurisprudence in fact 'accepts that regulations posted inside a workshop constitute a contract which has been freely entered into . . . and that every clause therefore has the full force of the law for both the courts and the parties concerned' (Cailleux, 1901).

France, unlike Germany, Austria-Hungary, Switzerland, Russia and other countries, lived through the whole of the nineteenth century under a regime of so-called 'freedom of contract' (which meant that there was no law compelling companies to make their internal rules comply with any detailed labour legislation); French factory regulations are therefore of particular interest in that they express employers' preoccupations with remarkable clarity.

The Bibliothèque Nationale holds a number of nineteenth-century factory regulations (catalogued at fo. V 182). Few of them deal with the structures of the factory as such, but for our purposes they are highly significant reminders of the broad tendency to enclose and control labour which was inaugurated in the age of manufacture.[7]

Most of the regulations begin by stating that the very fact that they have been posted inside the factory gives them the status of an internal law, and that they apply to all. They then specify the terms of the worker's contract: conditions of employment, terms of dismissal, rates of pay, modes of payment, and so on. These general conditions are accompanied by clauses referring directly to the customs of the craft guilds and establishing qualitative and quantitative work norms: 'Any worker whom the masters judge to be incapable of carrying out the task with which he has been entrusted may be dismissed immediately and without compensation' (Tissage Mécanique Willot, Article 3); 'Any worker whose work is found to be unacceptable by the master or his appointed representative . . . may be dismissed immediately' (Tissage Mécanique de Cholet, Article 7, 1888); 'The manager may dismiss any workman who is incapable of earning 2.5 francs per day, or whose work is faulty, immediately and without giving a fortnight's notice' (Tissage Mécanique C. Piat, Article 9, 1866); 'The workman undertakes to produce well-made bolts of cloth which conform in every respect to the measurements given; failure to do so will result in a reduction of wages' (Fabrique L. Nicolas, Bar-le-Duc, Article 2, 1867).

This is only one aspect of a system of regulations designed to establish a minutely detailed and authoritarian system of control and to suppress 'minor dishonesties' (petty thefts, clumsiness, 'fiddling' and minor damage). Its primary purpose, however, is to impose the master's criteria for the intensity and quality of work: 'The workman does not have the right to pass any comments on the work he is given. He is responsible for any mistakes he may make' (Ulrich-Vivien corset factory, Article 5, 1867); 'Any work that is badly done or spoiled is punishable by a fine proportional to the extent of the fault, and the masters also have the right to demand compensation proportional to the extent of any damage caused' (Tissage Mécanique Willot, Article 6). Fines were also levied if goods were damaged at the O'Delant et Dupont linen mill (1835), whilst the Usine de Tissage Mécanique C. Piat fined anyone who cut material badly.

Many regulations provided for fines in the event of machines or tools being damaged, and in many cases such fines could be heavy. In most cases, the fine was equal to the cost of replacing the damaged machine. Examples included the Tissage Mécanique Willot (1873), the Manufacture d'Horlogerie (1873), Etablissements J. Meny (1863), the Mathon cotton mill (1872), the Filature Naegely et Cie (1846), Tissage Mécanique C. Piat (1866), Papeterie de la Roche, and Construction de Machines à Vapeur Rosser et Bressant (1856).

Workers were often obliged contractually to clean their tools, their machines and even the shops in which they worked. In some cases, this was compulsory work to be carried out at a specific time – on Saturday, during the midday break, or before leaving work, as at the Filature Mathon (1872). At Rosser et Bressant, a factory which built steam-engines, labourers, apprentices and assistants even had to clean the plant on Sunday mornings. Minor damage to the fabric of the building was covered by a special scale of fines. Workers could be fined for 'writing on the walls or doors' (Usine de Persan, 1853), and for 'leaving rubbish in workrooms, or writing or scribbling on the doors or walls of the establishment' (Etablissements J. Meny, 1863). In more general terms, they were forbidden not only to 'damage any object belonging to the factory' (Tissage Mécanique C. Piat, 1866), but also to interfere with the heating, lighting or water supply (Filature Naegely, 1846). Such prohibitions obviously distanced the workers still further from their working environment. Regulations concerning control over machinery – an even more strategic object – made it even clearer that the factory belonged to the employer.

The work of the engineman was the object of special legislation which stipulated when he had to report for work ('at 3 a.m. precisely'; Typographie Panckouke) and when the driving engines had to be started up ('at the blast of the whistle, repeated at three-minute intervals'; Papeterie de la Roche). At Rosser et Bressant, 'the engineman must start up the engines when the bell is rung for the first time; this applies whenever the factory opens'. If a mechanized factory was to start work on time, the engineman obviously had to be punctual, and the machinery for which he was responsible had to be in good working order (and here we touch upon the relationship between the subordination of the labour process and mechanization). Being the only workman to come into contact with the motive forces of the factory, the engineman thus enjoyed a relatively privileged status, but he was also subject to special forms of discipline ('If one or more machines slow down or cease work as a result of negligence on the part of the engineman, he is liable to a fine of 50 centimes'; Typographie Panckouke, Article 5) and was obliged to carry out maintenance work on Sundays. This has to be read against a background of collective and sometimes organized resistance on the part of the workers. Resistance could, for example, take the form of minor acts of sabotage, and the masters attached great importance to this: 'Do you not feel nauseous when you hear these social reformers ("*les sublimes*") singing the praises of someone who has put emery in the stuffing-box of the steam-engine, or congratulating the machine-man who stuffed a rag into the donkey pump's feed pipe before he left work?' (Poulot, 1980, p. 200).

A further set of rules was designed to prevent workers from interfering with the speed of the machines or, in more general terms, with their controls (Tissage Mécanique de Cholet, 1888; Tissage Mécanique Valentin et Claudel, 1836; Tissage Mécanique C. Piat, 1866; Filature Vinchou, 1864; Filature Naegely, 1846; Manufacture de Corsets Ulrich-Vivien, 1867; Papeterie de la Roche). The fines for breaking these rules were often heavy, and dismissal was possible. Responsibility for the adjustment of machinery usually lay with the foremen.

All these regulations specified the terms of workers' contracts. They were designed to legalize authoritarian checks on the work they did. They were not, however, particularly detailed. They asserted, in repetitive fashion, the principle of the employer's authority over an unspecified range of activities. As we have already noted, it was only when factory-owners had to protect themselves against legislation on industrial accidents that concrete activities became the object of a codified body of duties and prohibitions.

In four areas, the regulations were, however, remarkably detailed. They were designed to bring the labour process under tight control.

1. The delimitation of time: time could be punctuated in a variety of ways:

The opening of the factory gates will be announced by a bell, which will be rung twice. They will remain open until the second bell. Workmen must be at the factory and ready to begin work when the second bell rings. They will be liable to fines of 0.05 francs for every five minutes they are late. Anyone who is more than half an hour late may be laid off. (the Vieux Jean d'Heurs et Rénesson ultramarine factory, Article 3, *1867*)

Movement in and out of the factory was also controlled by bells at the Horlogerie de Montbéliard (1873), at the Salaignac factory in Tarbes (1853), at the Raffinerie Massion-Rozier (1869), at the Ateliers Naegely et Cie (1846) and at a variety of other mills. Similar rules applied in many mechanized weaving sheds.

Regulations specifying starting times, and the corresponding sanctions for late arrival, are an expression of the employers' attempts to impose a rigid working day; workers who were five minutes late were often fined, and in no case could they be more than fifteen minutes late without being fined. Repeated late arrival led to heavier fines and eventually to dismissal (at the Usine de Persan in 1863, for example, any worker who was five minutes late on more than three occasions was liable to dismissal).

A number of regulations explicitly give management the unilateral right to modify the length of the working day in accordance with the overall needs of production. The regulations of both a chintz factory and a corset factory stipulate that: 'The factory works a twelve-hour day in normal circumstances. If necessary, the masters may modify the length of the working day as circumstances demand, or according to the time of year.' Similar conditions applied at the Oehl et Huser power mill. At Naegely et Cie, the working day could be extended if mechanical failures occurred, and night shifts were compulsory in the event of breakdowns, if the factory had surplus goods to be processed, or 'in any other circumstances'. Even when they had worked the hours for which they were paid, workers could be detained 'for as long as necessary', to be searched as they left the factory (J. Meny, 1863).

Finally, several regulations provide for Sunday working to maintain machinery and to clean workshops.

2. The delimitation of space: one of the earliest sets of regulations in the Bibliothèque Nationale's collection simultaneously reflects both the need to control movement in and around the factory and capital's uncertainty as to how to define its own space: 'Although offences against rural property do not relate in any strict way to factory discipline, they may give rise to disorder or to complaints which could be avoided, and workers are specifically instructed to refrain from entering gardens, vineyards or other properties' (Oehl et Huser, Article 6, 1845). Almost all regulations specify which doors workmen are to use, and define the role of the porter in checking who enters or leaves the factory. Fines were levied against workers who used doors other than those provided for their use (Usine de Persan, 1853; Ateliers Meny Bulh, 1863; Ateliers Naegely et Cie, 1846; Oehl et Huser, 1845), against anyone caught climbing a fence (Usine de Vieux Jean d'Heurs et de Rénesson), and against anyone who left the factory without permission. The porter was responsible for opening and closing outside doors, and in some cases for opening up workshops in the morning and for collecting the keys from the foreman when the factory closed in the evening (J. Meny Buhl, 1863).

These were not the only rules controlling movement between the interior and the space outside the factory. Many articles prohibited outsiders or workers' wives and families from having access to its territory. At Naegely et Cie anyone who allowed outsiders to enter the factory was fined the equivalent of eight days' wages, and the regulations stated that 'if anyone asks for a workman, the porter must call him, and the visitor must wait at the door' (Article 8). At Rosser et Bressant (1856), the concierge was forbidden to 'admit anyone if he did not know the reason for their presence in the factory, and must take them to the office, if need be. On no account should he interrupt workmen to take them to see anyone who asked for them' (Article 11).

Changing-rooms acted as airlocks between the factory gate and the shop floor. Personal belongings, baskets and shopping baskets had to be left there, and it was forbidden to enter either changing-rooms or dining-rooms other than at mealtimes.

Supervision of movement between the inside and the outside also gave rise to a ban on bringing 'wine', 'spirits', 'liquor', *eau de vie* or 'beer' into the factory.

3. Regulation of productive space and control over movement inside the factory were the object of specific rules which went against the customs of the old guilds by asserting that employers had the right to tell workers where to work inside the factory: 'Every workman must remain at the position assigned to him in the shop, and must not leave it for any reason unconnected with his work without permission from the masters, the foremen or the overseers' (Mille cotton mill, Article 9, 1859). They therefore also had the right to allocate different work to different teams ('Spinners may not change piecers or spindles without permission from the foreman'; Naegely) and to define the nature of tasks ('As workmen are not taken on for any specific trade or job, they must work at any trade or task set them; lack of familiarity with that trade or task does not constitute grounds for refusal. Differences in the type of cloth involved, differences in width of cloth, and differences in wage rates are not taken into account' (Tissage Mécaniques Willot; Tissage L. Nicolas)). In some mills, the regulations stated that management had the right to ask a spinner to mind two looms; in other factories, workers were fined if they used tools other than those provided.

In more general terms, regulations asserted the right of the employer to forbid all random movement; it was forbidden 'to wander from one room to another' (J. Meny), 'to go from room to room' or to 'loiter in any room other than that housing one's loom' (Ulrich-Vivien). Certain areas were subject to special rules: dining-rooms were usually out of bounds except at mealtimes, and at Oehl et Huser staying in the toilets 'longer than necessary' was punishable by a fine of 50 centimes. Access to the factory yard was similarly restricted.

4. Factory regulations usually dealt in great detail with sanctions that applied to acts of insubordination, disrespect or disobedience. Heavy fines or dismissal were the rule in such cases: 'Any act of insubordination or impoliteness will result in immediate dismissal. The manager's decision is final' (Tissage L. Nicolas). At César Piat, anyone found shouting, whistling or singing was fined 30 centimes.

Anyone who insulted a foreman was fined two francs, but the fine for insulting a director was three francs.

The role of floorwalkers ('who are responsible for the management of the workshop, within their own sphere of competence'), of overseers (who often had no technical skills) and especially of foremen, was often spelled out in great detail; they were vested with some of the employer's authority, and intervened in the pyramid structure of the factory at the appropriate level and on the basis of their respective skills. Foremen were usually responsible for supervising the movement of workers, for adjusting machines and for taking decisions concerning repairs.

In certain factories, the regulations included much more specific clauses to stamp out resistance, rejection of discipline and worker solidarity. Those found guilty of 'inciting rebellion or combination' were subject to immediate dismissal at Oehl et Huser. Weavers who formed combinations and 'united to put forward demands' were heavily fined (five francs) at C. Piat, whilst in 1853 the regulations in force at the Usine de Persan stated that all combination would immediately be denounced to the courts.

In many cases, spying was encouraged, either openly ('Any worker who discovers that another worker is disloyal and who informs the office of that fact will be rewarded; his name will not be made public', Filature Naegely), or by the threat of collective punishment ('Any man or any woman who notices broken panes in the vicinity of their loom will be fined at point five of the scale (the highest point) unless he or she is willing to name the person responsible for the damage', O'Delant et Dupont, 1853).

In other cases, disciplinary sanctions were applied to a whole range of activities and attitudes. 'Laziness' is an obvious example, but in one linen mill, children could also be fined for laughing, playing games or chattering. Elsewhere, singing, whistling and reading were all punishable by fines or dismissal. Sanctions were also applied to forms of behaviour indicating a lack of concentration, or which might distract others from their work: 'No worker, male or female, is allowed to talk to his or her neighbour; everyone must give the task in hand their full attention' (Usine A. Sourd).[8] Shouting, fighting, brawling, or anything else that might interfere with the smooth running of the factory led to heavy fines, at the very least. Drunkenness usually resulted in immediate suspension as well as a fine, and to dismissal in the event of recidivism.

'Laziness', 'drunkenness' and 'insubordination' are all special terms which transpose phenomena of working-class resistance and the rejection of discipline on to the plane of morality and of individual self-discipline.

These documents shed considerable light on the trend to enclose labour, a trend which has also been identified by authors inspired by the work of Foucault (see Murard and Zylberman). Studies in industrial architecture (Barros and Virnot, 1975) have revealed that the principles of closure and control, and a functionalization of time and space on a hierarchical basis, are also at work within this trend. Although he too uses the categories of closure, control and functionalization to describe the role given to time, Gaudemar insists that the process was slow, and returns to the question of productive space:

One thing seems clear: in the early stages of its development, capital was not in control of its own relationship with space. To be more accurate, it inherited a relationship with space which was predetermined by other activities, if only because the earliest factories were usually set up in premises designed for very different purposes, such as the châteaux and convents which were sold off cheaply when the property of the nobility and the clergy was disposed of during the Revolution. Smaller factories were set up in barns, lofts and even cellars. (1979, pp. 175–6)

Factory regulations, industrial architecture and other traces of productive structures studied by historians reveal the weight of the most general structures of capitalist authoritarianism rather than any truly productive function. This is simply because capital had to free itself from the heritage of the past before it could establish structures which were truly expressive of the needs of its valorization. From this point of view, Taylorism may be a significant moment in the belated appearance of a new productive order. With Taylorism, capitalism finds a truly apposite order in that it no longer has to pacify the shop floor by using blindly repressive measures, and can run the factory in accordance with the objectives of valorization.

However, this must not be allowed to conceal the fact that the practical organization of the productive base in the age of manufacture also implied prodigious structural transformations, even though they remain almost silent about their own history. We will now begin to look at those structures.

The factory was, as we have said, a sort of economic island where traces of work were accumulated in objects of labour without immediately giving rise to any commodity exchange. It was the precondition for an extensive reshaping of the division of labour in that it destroyed the traditional rhythms of the labour process, but it was also a precondition for the liberation of the technological imagination (Smith (1970, p. 115) speaks of the new role of 'those who are called philosophers or men of speculation, whose trade it is not to do anything, but to observe everything; and who, upon that account, are often capable of combining together the powers of the most distant and dissimilar objects'). Finally, it gave access to the labour process as it took direct control of the object of labour as it circulated in the workshop. The handicraft worker carried out a sequence of operations and brought the object of labour a stage nearer to completion. In the factory, the object was no longer an attribute of any one producer, and circulated from one work station to the next. Mobility became a characteristic of the object; it was identified with the abstract flow of production, and that flow appeared to be external to the workers, who were no longer associated with a particular object but with a fragmentary task.[9]

The initial effect of the fragmentation of work into serial tasks was to make it seem that each individual task had been naturally simplified. The whole working day seemed to be taken up with the repetition of a sequence of simple movements. This is how Julien Turgan (1862) describes the Manufacture Impériale de Tabac, which supplied Paris with five- and ten-centime cigars and which employed 1,500 women (each of whom made between 350 and 400 cigars in the course of a ten- or twelve-hour day):

This is what their work consists of: each woman is given a certain weight of inner leaves and 260 wrappers, with which she makes 250 cigars. The wrappers are prepared and cut in a special workshop. The woman makes a sort of large cigarette with the inner leaves, wraps it in a leaf called a binder, and then wraps everything inside a wrapper. She then cuts off one end with a knife, and shapes the other into a cone, and then gums it with a paste darkened with tincture of chicory. Once the cigars have been made, they are placed in packets of twenty-five; they are then submitted for approval to the woman in charge and to a foreman who examines them one by one, and are dispatched to the drying room.[10]

33

The second effect was that the overall process appeared to be unified by the regularity of the flow of production, by a movement which had nothing to do with individual activities. On the other hand, every activity could be measured against the flow of production itself; in practice, this meant the application of the principle of the abstract quantitative equivalence of different serial tasks. To take only one example (Turgan, 1884): in the Pernod factory in Pontarlier, a continuous flow of production was ensured by (a) four women who washed and dried the bottles; (b) one man who operated the machine which filled the bottles; (c) two women who operated the corking machine; and (d) eight other workers who labelled the bottles. Finally, the cases were sealed by a machine operated by two men. In terms of the flow of production, we thus have the equation:

$$4 \times \text{task A} = 1 \times \text{task B} = 2 \times \text{task C} = 8 \times \text{task D}$$

(this is not in fact a truly typical example, as the factory was quite highly mechanized, but that makes little difference for our purposes).

The fragmentation of the labour process also had a third effect. As tasks were broken down, and as the cycle of each task became shorter, the activity of labour became increasingly subject to the rate of flow of production; this provided the basis for the banalization of the labour process, and for a much stricter subordination of the activity of labour to the demands of production.

As the labour process became increasingly fragmented and began to take the form of stereotypical small tasks to be carried out with a regular rhythm dictated by external forces, the range of skills became more restricted. Skills were still craft-based, but it would be more accurate to say that they represented elements of the old crafts. In some cases, craft skills were reduced to mere gestures involving the use of a specialist instrument narrowly adapted to one particular function.

The women who worked on piece-rates in the nineteenth century had little in common with the craft workers of the past. Even though Turgan describes the workers he saw making silk hats in the Berteil factory in 1878 as 'craft workers', their skills were very restricted: the *monteur* merely used a special iron to fix the plush to the frame, and simply applied a mixture of laurel-water and wax, whilst the *tourneur* merely shaped the hat and trimmed the brim.

Skills were, then, degraded, but their very degradation led to the emergence of new skills based upon the development of mechanical reflexes and acquired automatic gestures, and these became more pronounced as work became more narrowly defined and more repetitive:

In order to make a watch, 700 separate operations have to be carried out on its component parts. This great division of labour has the effect of making the workers exceptionally skilled and dextrous. In the course of a single day, two young girls can make 400 or 500 steel screws of such small dimensions that 880 of them can be packed into one cubic centimetre. Moreover, these screws, which are the size of a grain of sand, must have grooved heads so that they can be turned with a screwdriver and correctly positioned inside the watch.

The groove is made by placing one screw at a time in a hole in the end of an oval flange; a small mill with barely perceptible teeth cuts the groove and, as soon as one screw is expelled from the hole, another takes its place. It takes incredible manual skill to pick up a screw, separate it from the rest, and place it the right way up with its head facing the mill. I held seven or eight dozen screws in my hand; it was like holding a pinch of the sand one uses for blotting ink, but every screw was threaded and grooved. (Turgan, *1870*)

To the outside observer there was something enigmatic about this virtuosity. The factory-owner captured it, trained it and organized it, but it still seemed to be imprisoned within the worker's body. Indeed, it was easy to imagine it being handed down from generation to generation by some mysterious link: 'The Boulogne factory enjoys the advantage of having an excellent team of workers who have been attached to the Etablissements Belvalette for generations, and who form a core that can be relied upon' (Turgan, 1874). (For an account of the factory-owner's need to retain a core of skilled workers, see Gaspard's account of the Fabrique Neuve de Cortaillot in the period 1752–1854; the factory, which was near Neuchatel, produced printed calico.)

The major characteristics of the age of manufacture were as follows. Capital established its hold by acquiring a monopoly over trade and by appropriating traces of labour rather than labour-power itself. The activity of labour was still a compact entity. Although craft skills had been broken down, they were often still an essential part of the labour process. The mechanisms of the productive body of the worker seemed obscure to the outside observer: the work of the body and the economic work of capital did not seem to belong to the same space or the same time. The multiple trials of strength that took place every day centred on the need to surround and pacify the territory of the worker rather than on an attempt to appropriate every aspect of its functions.

It might also be said that the factory system represented the first real attempt to subordinate the labour process to the process of valorization. In the factory, the productive functions of the human body entered the cycle of capital. But neither the technological structures of the factory nor the factory-owner's representation of human labour allowed a direct or significant link to be established between the potential and abstract capacities that go to make up the substance of capital which has been transformed into labour-power (into a dimension of the 'productive body of capital') and existing forms of human labour, which were still enigmatic for the factory-owner. Capital could ensure its own extended reproduction by consuming that part of itself which had become labour-power, but the nature of the transformation that took place still seemed alien to the social forces of capital. Because it could not accurately picture that transformation, capital resorted to extensive authoritarianism (Marx's 'barrack-like discipline'; Marx, 1976, p. 549), and to a codified separation of powers combined with archaic forms of social experimentation in an attempt to win the loyalty of a core of essential skilled workers. Poulot (1980, p. 225), for instance, speaks of the *grosses culottes* or the skilled élite craftsmen who, until the middle of the nineteenth century, enjoyed a privileged status and often controlled the recruitment of the workforce: 'without anyone realizing it, machines sounded the death knell for these proud men'.

ECONOMIC THOUGHT AND THE 'REALISM' OF THE FACTORY-OWNER

It was difficult to see the element of valorization in a labour process which still seemed to be alien to the social universe of capital. Even the greatest political economists were intellectually inhibited by the realism of the factory-owner. Adam Smith, for instance, broke with the doctrines of the physiocrats and established a clear theoretical

(*continued over page*)

---

distinction between producing commodities (exchange-values) and producing useful objects (use-values). That is, he identified the economic abstraction implicit in the production and circulation of objects, and he discovered that labour-power is the only source of exchange-values. But when he came to look at concrete acts of labour as economic signifiers, he abandoned the abstract point of view.

When Marx (1969a, p. 156) speaks of Smith's 'contradictory definitions' of productive labour, he correctly notes that Smith has difficulty in getting away from a concrete and non-economic image of the cycle of capital. The cycle of capital (which is transformed into labour-power, that is, into productive circulating capital which is consumed during production so that its value is reproduced on an extended scale) is temporarily alienated in the concrete activity of artisans who are in control of their own skills and who produce useful objects:

> There is one sort of labour which adds to the value of the subject on which it is bestowed: there is another which has no such effect. The former, as it produces value, may be called productive; the latter, unproductive labour. Thus the labour of a manufacturer adds, generally, to the value of the materials which he works upon, that of his own maintenance, and of his master's profit. The labour of a menial servant, on the contrary, adds to the value of nothing . . . The labour of some of the most respectable orders in the society is, like that of menial servants, unproductive of any value, and does not fix or realize itself in any permanent subject or vendible commodity, which endures after that labour is past, and for which an equal quantity of labour could afterwards be procured. The sovereign, for example, with all the officers of both justice and war who serve under him . . . are unproductive labourers . . . Their service, how honourable, how useful, or how necessary soever, produces nothing for which an equal quantity of service can afterwards be procured . . . In the same class must be ranked, some of the gravest and most important, and some of the

(continued over page)

most frivolous professions: churchmen, lawyers, physicians, men of letters of all kinds; players, buffoons, musicians, opera-singers, opera-dancers, etc. . . . . Like the declamation of the actor, the harangue of the orator, or the tune of the musician, the work of all of them perishes in the very instant of its production. (Smith, 1970, pp. 429–31, emphasis added)

Like the factory-owner, Smith had an acute but partial vision of society. In theory, there was no reason why he should not have reached the conclusion that the work of a clown or a doctor could produce profits for some shrewd capitalist. No reason at all . . . except that the age of manufacture delimited the respective territories of capital and labour in a specific way and assigned different attributions to them. Capital had conquered the world of the artisan by becoming productive capital, but it still had to depend on traditional forms of the supply of labour in order to conceptualize its own activity. It was rather as though it had made a crude picture by putting together images that had been torn from their true context.

CHAPTER TWO

THE TABLE SYSTEM

In order to form a phalange of impassioned series, at
least 50,000 *discors* must be broken up. Workers with
contradictory views about their art must be recruited;
masters capable of founding schools must be found;
and competitive rivalries must be created.
C. Fourier, *Le Nouveau Monde industriel*

She is perfectly calm, steady and hard-working. She
does not appear to be alienated, unless her claim to be
the daughter of General Duvivier is a sign of madness.
La Salpêtrière, register of admissions and discharges,
1844

The factory-owner sees the flow of production as a material
accumulation of traces of labour . . . The work of each productive
worker appears to consist of a repetitive series of simple actions
. . . The overall process is unified by the regularity of the flow of
production . . . As tasks are broken down, they are increasingly subject
to the flow of production . . . It is now time to make a more concrete
analysis of the structural features we have identified.

One of the most interesting structures of the age of manufacture was
the table system, which was often found in workshops in which most
work was carried out on a manual basis. In certain cases, tasks were
extremely fragmented, taking the form of identical or serial operations.[1]
This system was often found in packing or bottling plants. The Usine de
Torréfaction Industrielle Trébucien in Versailles, for example, employed
no fewer than seventy women, who worked in teams of fourteen at five
different tables. The engraving which illustrates Turgan's description
(1885) shows that each foreman supervised two tables, with a team of
seven women sitting on either side. The first woman took coffee from a

tub which was regularly filled by workmen, and she weighed out 250 or 500 grammes, and filled jars. A second had a supply of lids with which to seal each jar. A third stuck on labels, and so on. The women sat opposite each other and carried out the same partial tasks. The table system thus organized two parallel and symmetrical flows of production, resulting in a finished product which was taken away by teams of workmen.

This is an elaborate form of the fragmentation of work. It is similar to certain present-day forms of work organization. In electronics plants, for example, the 'line' is not mechanized; it is basically a long table, and the women workers pass along, say, transistor radios as they are assembled. The table system represented the application of two principles on a small but significant scale:

      1. The identification of tasks: the total number of operations to be carried out is broken down into seven small groups of related operations, corresponding to seven work stations. In the case of the Trébucien plant, the identification of tasks corresponded to the technical structure of the table system (one woman at the scales, one fitting lids, and so on).

      2. A regular flow of production can be guaranteed only if the women's work is synchronized; each task must be carried out in the same space of time as the other six. In other words, the principle of the identification (and differentiation) of tasks is combined with the principle of the equivalence (and non-differentiation) of time. The same principles are now applied in the highly developed study of time-and-motion methods.[2]

The sub-division of tasks, and their serial organization, implied a form of work analysis: the requisite operations had to be identified and the time taken to perform them had to be evaluated in terms of each other. This system of dividing up tasks offered industrialists certain major advantages. The 'virtuosity' (Marx, 1976, p. 460) acquired by the workers allowed them to carry out their tasks more quickly. But this system also made it easier to supervise and control them; it became very easy for the foreman to check the work rate of the twenty-eight women working under him, to see if anyone was slowing down the table or was working erratically. The output of one set of seven women could be compared with that of the women sitting opposite them; one foreman could compare the output of the two tables he controlled with those controlled by another foreman; daily output could be compared with average output, and so on. In short, the principles of identification and equivalence provided the basis for constant observation of the workforce, and the abstract became divorced from the concrete. For the workshop supervisor, the abstract element was obvious, but the individual worker could see the quantitative dimension of her work only in terms of her personal relationship with a norm, and the reality of the workshop appeared to be an expression of that relationship.

The table itself had a very special position within this structure. On the one hand, it was a simple and practical means of ensuring that an object circulated in a logical and stereotypical way (filling, sealing, labelling . . .). In that sense, it was an instrument in an operational process, and was no different from any other instrument. The women workers' mental image or operational image of their work provided further material support for the serialization of operations. On the other hand, the mode of circulation established by the table was external to the operational process itself. The table system recombined tasks that had been broken down by the division of labour; the table itself merely conveyed dead traces of living labour, and it was external to the activity of labour itself. In that sense, the table system was the ancestor of the assembly line; their structures are the same.

What is the significance of the inclusion of the productive space within the cycle of capital? We can take the Trébucien packing plant as an example. Fixed capital transfers part of its value to the product. The materials used passively convey the value of the labour that is crystallized in them, and that value simply moves through the productive space as they move through it. Everything revolves around the mobilization of labour-power, which is both the motor force behind the labour process and a central element in the process of the valorization of capital. As labour-power is consumed during production, it produces 'more' value or, in other words, surplus value.

Capital is therefore in a highly specific situation. If it is to perform its own economic 'labour' (extended reproduction), it must necessarily be alienated in the concrete and, in a sense, voluntary activity of the women.

We will deal with this point in more detail in Chapter 8. For the moment, we can describe the process as follows: to say that the labour-power of the seventy women in the plant 'belongs to Monsieur Trébucien, the Parisian industrialist' no more implies that he *becomes* 'his' women workers than it means that he is transformed into a table, a pair of scales or roasted coffee. It simply means that their productive bodies are at his disposal, just as if they were commodities. This has nothing to do with the body of Monsieur Trébucien himself; we are dealing with the register of 'having', and not with that of 'being'.

The women workers' relationship with the labour-power they own is not so purely symbolic (or amenable to symbolization). They certainly sell their labour-power, and in that sense it is an external object. But they must also make that object part of their individuality, and in a sense they have to *be* labour-power. As they have no control over the economic signifiers which give their labour a meaning (this implies taking the viewpoint of the valorization of capital), the dimension which does most to socialize their labour remains hidden from them.

We have, then, two viewpoints: that of being and that of having. At one level, the entire social relationship conveyed by labour-power revolves around the question of relations between these viewpoints. The wage-earner *is* labour-power; from her point of view, her relationship with labour is a concrete, personal, physical and immediate relationship (immediate in the sense that it is set in time) with an object and with tools. Every gesture she makes is fixed in time and in the immediacy of her existence; even if her work is repetitive, each gesture is performed only once (because the time of its existence is not cyclical) and it has no equivalent (precisely because it is unique).

The capitalist *owns* social labour-power in the form of living productive capital; from his point of view, labour is part of the cycle of accumulation. It is a natural form of value, and he regards it primarily as an accumulation of *traces* of living activity. To put it another way, living activity is meaningful only in the sense that value clings to its traces. It is only by becoming a trace that labour can endure through time (rather than being instantaneous), that it can *represent* an accumulation of social labour time (rather than being *fixed* in time), that it can 'have value', leave the social space of production and enter the space of commodity exchanges in the form of an object.

Traces are appropriated, and gestures become divorced from the objects they leave behind. Traces of labour obviously belong to a dimension that can be symbolized; they indicate the moment of the objectification of activity, the moment when an object that has been produced can take on a meaning within a system of representations that exists outside it.

This dispossession is not simply economic; it is also technical, cultural and political, and it involves a loss of subjective existence.[3] Ultimately, activities appear to have a purely operational meaning. Productive operations are, so to speak, 'hyper-concrete' and are introverted. They are so bound up with the immediacy and singularity of physical movement (which is in fact part of the operational process) that in some cases workers find it impossible to describe what they do without resorting to mime.[4]

But we have to go beyond the well-known phenomenon of the dissolution of subjectivity, because the fragmentation and practical articulation of tasks socialize labour in such a way as to create conditions that result in a profound modification of social consciousness. I refer to the relationship between the collectivization of the operational image and the subjective appropriation of the overall process. The contemporary implications of this relationship will be discussed below.

The table system organized space. Contemporary prints show workers separated by strict lines of demarcation, and a sharp division between the space of circulation and the space of labour. There is something mechanical about this division of space, about these specialist functions and instruments, about these stereotyped movements and regular rhythms. Adam Smith was not mistaken when he described machinery as the logical outcome of the division of labour to be found in the age of manufacture.[5] The table system can be seen as anticipating mechanization. One could, for example, see each row of women in the coffee-packing plant as a sort of human machine prefiguring the modern robots that now carry out the same operations. They form a homogeneous, coherent and relatively autonomous ensemble.[6] This underlines the fact that the replacement of human labour by machines involved forms of human labour which already had some of the characteristic features of the movements of machines (a rigid sequence of stereotyped movements). There was, however, one major difference. The factory-owner organized his women workers on a rational basis, saw to it that they were regularly supplied with raw materials, and synchronized and fragmented their tasks. He demanded attention, docility and dedication from them. But the motor principle which governed their movements still lay inside their productive bodies.

The division of labour inside the factory therefore regularized the flow of production, and both synchronized and constrained its rhythms. But each woman was still in control of her own movements. The sequence of tasks may have seemed to be the motor force behind her (just as the rails seem to drive the train), but it was simply a reflection of a collective rhythm which could not be imparted by any external source of movement.

Capital 'became labour-power' during the age of manufacture, but it had yet to come to terms with its own productive body. It had simply begun to control it from the outside.

CHAPTER THREE

SPLENDID VALUE-MACHINES?

From the nature of human power it must be concluded
that it is not, like the power of brutes, confined to any
particular organ of the body, or to any instrument,
natural or artificial. Neither the forehead, as in the
bull, nor the shoulder, as in the horse, nor the digital
members, as in the feline tribe, can be pointed out in
man as the seat of his power . . . We are authorized to
suppose that the mind of man is capable of devising
means to overcome all physical obstructions. We must
concede that the exercise of power, when raised to its
highest pitch, must have a field of action that lies
beyond the conflict with difficulties. We must then
acknowledge that the true sphere in which human
power ought to be exercised is enjoyment.
T. C. Banfield, *Four Lectures on the Organization of
Industry*

The Manufacture Impériale de Tabac and the packing room in the
Trébucien factory were examples of labour without machinery.
At the opposite extreme we have the 'La Foudre' mill, as
described by Turgan:

*The self-acting mule is one of man's strangest and most successful
creations. This is how this intelligent slave works: as soon as the
transmission belt begins to drive the pulley of the loom, the draught
begins to work; the carriage, which is mounted on flanged wheels, begins
to move away from the draught at a slow, steady rate. As it advances,
1,000 spindles, driven at a rate of 6,000 revolutions per minute, twist
the 1,000 threads of yarn as they emerge from the draught . . . The
spindles stop in their turn, as though at some mysterious signal. The
spindles wind back a little; a wire stretched the full length of the loom*

above the spindles descends across the threads; the carriage moves back and, as it does so, the spindle winds on the length of yarn it has twisted as it moved; the wire winds the yarn around the spindle, as though it were guided by an invisible hand, and gradually shapes the spool, layer after layer, spiral after spiral. The carriage moves back to its starting point, the yarn reaches the top of the spindle, and the process begins again. The worker standing in front of this enormous machine appears to be taking his rest; matter works docilely and by itself. The only function of the weaver – if we can still apply that term to a man who minds a mule – is to reattach a few broken threads from time to time, to clean his mule, and to replace the spools when they have been fully wound. English workmen are quite right when they say that the iron spinner is 'self-acting'. One man, two youths and two children are all that is required to operate two looms with 100 spindles each . . . Five splendid steam-engines, each with an actual driving power of 500 horsepower, do all the work; they are magnificently housed, and drive the harmonious machinery of the factory with mathematical precision. The factory thus becomes one of the most beautiful and most powerful of all the automata created by man in this age of industrial daring.
(1863)

The site of the mystery has been displaced from the human element to the mechanical element; it is as though matter were copulating with itself, and its activities, which are at once 'mathematical' and enigmatic, become something that approximates to the primal scene of the technological imagination.

We can get some idea of the massive upheavals brought about by the introduction of machinery from the surviving testimonies of the worker delegates who attended the 1867 Exposition Universelle in Paris (*Rapport des délégations ouvrières*, 1867). Machines began to compete with the skills of the workers, which were becoming obsolete,[1] but they also brought about a cultural upheaval and an identity crisis which were bitterly resented. Machines seemed to be an alien power in the world of work. They were at once the motor force behind an industrial system, the repository of a technical patrimony,[2] and representatives of a new industrial order in which subjectivity was doomed to be destroyed:

Being eminently cosmopolitan, the machine abolishes the distinctive techniques of different nations. In the case of shoemaking, we have noted the significant fact that the division of labour results in uniformly mediocre work, and we no longer see the masterpieces which could be held up as models for young workers to emulate. The only purpose of this manufacturing process is production on a large scale. A curious phenomenon! At the very time when the machine, a modern Briareus with thousands of iron arms, places itself at industry's service, at the very time when it is doubling and tripling its strength and should therefore be leaving workmen more time to perfect their craft, they are attempting to make man himself into a sort of machine by taking away part of his intelligence and responsibility. All this is being done simply to produce more. (shoemakers' delegation)[3]

Thanks to mechanization, then, the craft worker lost his position in the social hierarchy because his position in the labour process had been modified.

As we have already noted, both in handicraft industries and in the new forms of the division of labour introduced by manufacture, the primary active agent was the human body, and tools were no more than an extension of the human body. For the most part, they were small and simple, had no power of their own, and were used to impart skilled movements to the object of labour. The artisan who had 'learned his trade' used a battery of miniature tools; the 'specialist' worker used a more restricted range of tools which were more closely adapted to the task or, in some cases, only one tool. In both cases, a tool was, in technical terms, a direct extension of a function of the human body (in the simplest of cases a handle adapted to fit the human hand transmitted energy to a head which had been adapted to the task for which the tool was designed). In many cases, no special tools were required. In order to harness sources of energy which were much more powerful and reliable than human muscles, energy had to be channelled into paths which were, in technological terms, analogous to human movements. The movement of machines had to reproduce the movements of human beings who may or may not have been equipped with tools.

The self-acting iron spinner brought about this revolution in the weaving industry. The steam-engines at the La Foudre mill constantly transmitted 500 horsepower to the drive-shafts, belts and pulleys, and finally to the delicate mechanisms of the spindles. The self-acting loom connected a blind (non-human) source of energy with the spool around which the yarn was wound.[4]

The industrial revolution brought about by mechanization was initially based upon a host of inventions, some minor,[5] and some much more important. But they all tended to transfer skills to machines; the automaton became the worker's double, and its mechanical movements were equivalent to the skilled movements of the human body. In some cases, human movements were simply copied ('They have succeeded in controlling the movements of the machine with such accuracy that they can reproduce an infinite number of carriage wheels which are both identical to the model and mathematically identical to one another; no human hand could do this with the same precision' (Carrosserie Belvalette; Turgan, 1874); but other inventions resulted in the most complicated contrivances, like those dreamed up by Monsieur Carmoy, a manufacturer of brass-headed nails who was fortunate enough to find a way of making nails by machine, rather than casting them. He thus reduced his manufacturing costs by a factor of four; at the same time, France's consumption of nails rose by a factor of ten.

Monsieur Carmoy's Inventions

The problem that is to be solved if the following operation is to be carried out can be posed in the following terms: given, on the one hand, a circle of brass which is depressed in the centre and, on the other, a wire nail; place the wire on the brass, perpendicular to the plane of the metal, and crimp the head by pressing the brass around it, and shape into a section of a sphere.

That is the first part of the operation; the second consists of removing the nail, which is now complete, from the depression into which the brass has been moulded, and of transferring it to the chute.

This, then, is what happens. A woman sits in front of the tool. To her left, she has a supply of brass roundlets; to her right, a handful of nails. The brass roundlets are in a chute which pushes them forward towards the central press, where they will be swaged.

(continued over page)

The woman picks up a nail and positions it with the point upper-most; constant work has given her such wonderful dexterity that she can place nails so accurately that they do not fall over, but remain vertical for the short space of time it takes them to reach the centre of the tool. At the precise moment when they reach its centre, a punch descends; its lower extremity is rounded and recessed, and the nail is forced into the recess. The punch also houses a steel rod with a spring coiled around it. The rod acts like a finger pressing on the nail so as to hold it vertical.

The tension of the spring is so calculated as to allow the steel rod inside the punch to rise when pressure from the nail is applied to its tip. The purpose of this combination is to keep the nail truly perpendicular to the brass while it is being swaged.

The iron and the brass have now been joined together. But they have now to be removed from the depression into which they have been forced . . . This is perhaps the strangest and most successful of all Monsieur Carmoy's inventions. A fork advances from the rear of the automaton. The tine closest to the point of the nail is curved and, when it reaches it, it does not strike it violently but pushes it gently in the direction of the curve. The pressure causes the point to sway, and the head of the nail topples over. The nail is now horizontal, and its head is perpendicular to the pile. The fork now takes the head of the nail between its tines and, with a sharp movement from left to right, removes the nail and places it in a chute. In the meantime, the woman places another nail on a brass roundlet, and it takes the place of the nail that has just been removed.

Once the speed of the machine has been set, the woman is obliged to keep up with it, and she therefore produces between 25,000 and 30,000 complete nails in a single day (Turgan, 1882).

In some cases, a single invention gave birth to an entire factory. In that sense, the history of the Mercier factory is exemplary. In 1865, it was producing machine-tools, most of them for carding wool. In 1810, a Belgian mill-owner sold Hache et Piéton in Louviers a new type of carding-engine. Dubois, who had been employed at the Belgian mill, helped to assemble the machine. He was familiar with its workings, and set up in business with Mercier, who was a carpenter. Dubois and Mercier then marketed a machine of their own invention: a carding-engine combined with a Bely (a machine for roving the wool) and a spinning jenny. They prospered, and sold their first self-acting machine in 1818. Their partnership came to an end in that same year. At the same time, other mill-owners in Louviers were perfecting a machine which could nap cloth (it 'imitated the work of a man who held a small board covered in teasels in each hand; with the boards, he brushed pieces of cloth which were suspended vertically from top to bottom', Turgan, 1865; the machine in question was invented by Mazeline in 1809), a cropping machine (invented by Place in 1808), and mechanized fulling mills based on modified equipment imported from England.

Certain factories became veritable laboratories for experiments in applied mechanics, like the Japy factory, which launched France's first 'democratic watches' in 1870, and where a system of rewards was used to assist the workforce in the recuperation of their skills:

It is in the interests of anyone connected with the firm to make inventions and to simplify operations; anyone who does so will certainly be rewarded. The fact that everyone at Beaucourt is striving towards the same goal has made it possible to create, import and perfect all the automatic machines which fill the workshops; some of them can perform such extraordinary movements that they could be mistaken for real people. (Turgan, 1870)

The Godillot factory was another example. In order to produce shoes on a mass scale, it was necessary to rethink every phase of the manufacturing process in terms of the principles of mechanization. Soles were cut and moulded with a steam press rather than with the shoemaker's trimming knife; the process of attaching the heel to the shoe was mechanized; shoes were polished mechanically, as this was 'cheaper than polishing them by hand'; the vertical side of the heel was trimmed by a machine, and so on.

In all these cases, the aim was to release human skill, and to replace the human body – an integrated set of motor and operational functions – with a system in which a passive machine would be set in motion by an external motor. From now on, the machine was in charge.

Supplies of motive power were no longer restricted by the limitations of the human body (or by those of the bodies of animals). Motive power could be supplied constantly and without interruption. Previously unimaginable reserves of power were now available, either from single batteries of steam-engines or, even at this early stage, from motors installed in individual workshops, as in the zinc rolling mill in the Lipine factory in Upper Silesia (Turgan, 1870). Here, eight independently operated rolling processes worked in parallel with the eight 120-horse-power engines to which they were 'harnessed'. Operations could now be carried out on a new scale by 'Cyclopses of iron and brass, Vulcanian slaves with arms designed purely to strike and to twist, with teeth to bite and tear, and with the arms of giants' (Turgan, describing the Derosne et Cail factory in 1862). The Fives plant in Lille was equipped with machines capable of drilling the sideframes of several locomotives simultaneously (Turgan, 1885), and the 50-tonne drop-forge at Krupp took on a legendary status, whilst the cutting-machines at the Aciéries de Saint-Chaumon could handle and cut 15-square-metre sheets of steel. Increased numbers of tools could be set in motion: the La Foudre mill had 60,000 spindles. And operations could be carried out at a much higher speed, as at the Shumacher needle factory in Aix-la-Chapelle (Turgan, 1866). Here, the rhythm of production was set by a cutting-machine which supplied 300,000 lengths of metal wire a day; the wire was used to produce 600,000 needles.

Referring in the first *Cahier de l'Ecole Polytechnique* (1795) to the 'Course in mechanics' which he had recently inaugurated, Monge wrote:

Three distinct elements coexist in the forces of nature which are at man's disposal: mass, speed and direction of movement. It is rare for the forces of nature to so combine these elements as to give them the qualities required for our purposes, and the primary objective of machines is to convert available forces into other forces in which these elements are capable of producing the desired effect.

Machines which convert forces . . . something (a quantity of force) is transmitted through changing qualitative forms and effects. A machine combines a motor principle and an operational principle and it is, according to Bour (1865), 'an intermediary between a source of mechanical power and the work that is to be done'; and it is the peculiarities of its anatomy and the arrangement of its organs that allow it to perform the desired function of diverting power. In a report entitled *Traité des machines*, Carnot (1811) states that the various movements a motor imparts to a machine 'depend upon the link that is established between the respective bodies by the very form of the machine; these movements can be likened to purely geometric movements' (cited by Laboulaye, 1849, p. xiv).

The play of internal links . . . Machines, according to Laboulaye (p. xi), are 'bodies hampered by various links and guides'; they are systems of rigidly articulated organs, each of which receives an impetus from the previous organ and imparts it to the next. All machines, says Rankine (1872, p. 425), are based upon the same principle: 'A train of mechanisms consists of a series of moving pieces, each of which is follower to that which drives it.' Every organ is a condensation of the Machine itself; it receives energy from the part nearest to the motor and then acts as a motor which drives parts further down the system. The initial motive power is therefore transmitted, stage by stage, from simple non-specialist organs (shafts, pulleys and belts) to increasingly sophisticated organs and finally to the operational part of the machine.

All the organs belonging to the machine-system have one feature in common: they relate to higher organs as though they were free bodies moving within limits which are clearly defined by 'various links and guides'. This is the principle of the conservation of energy: energy is both transmitted through a series of organs, which are passive with respect to higher organs, and is given a form, as the passivity of those organs is strictly directional. And all objects of labour have one feature in common: they are alien to the machine-system, and they offer resistance. The art of the mechanical engineer is therefore the art of reducing resistance within the machine-system (internal work) so as to produce the maximum possible effect on the object, and so as to imprint upon it traces of operational motion. The motion itself is absorbed into the object:

> *The machine serves the needs of the arts by overcoming or destroying such forms of resistance as cohesion and weight. The work of the machine does not simply presuppose that resistance has been overcome once and for all; it presupposes that it is constantly being destroyed all along a trajectory which begins at the point where it is first manifested.* (Poncelet, 1839)

There are, then, two dimensions to the machine's 'intermediary role':

the transformation of motion and the transmission of energy. In terms of the history of technology, the former is the precondition for the latter. The machine's every working part is determined by these two dimensions, and it is that which gives it its apparent simplicity and the functional obviousness which so impressed scientists in particular: 'One has the feeling that the most complicated machines are simply combinations of individual devices, and that we should have a complete inventory of those devices' (Monge, 1792).[6]

An inventory of devices . . . Scientists did in fact often view all these inventions as though they were mere spectators. Sixty years after Monge, Bour (1865, p. 14) also addressed the Ecole Polytechnique and admitted that 'Science can do nothing to ensure the regular development of practice.' It was, for example, only in 1854 that a public laboratory for applied mechanics was opened at the Conservatoire des Arts et des Métiers.[7] But pioneering work was already being carried out by graduates from the Ecole Polytechnique (Arago, Savary and Chasles) and by their pupils, who became, as Gaudemar (1979, p. 178) puts it, 'commercial travellers in technology'. Poncelet instructed the workers of Metz in the science of mechanics between 1831 and 1837. Taffe (1835) travelled backwards and forwards across the south-west of France, observing, taking measurements, giving advice to factory-owners, and visiting a paper mill in Meyrargues, a saw-mill in Volonne, a water-powered mill in Siteron, a mill powered by a steam-engine in Aix, and a mill driven by a horse-gin in Marseilles.

Theoretical developments gradually came to terms with the following problems in applied mechanics:

1. The transformation of motion: the major development here was the emergence of kinematics, a hybrid science midway between spatial geometry and dynamics which Ampère describes as:

A compendium of all that there is to be said about every kind of motion, irrespective of the forces that produce it; it must concern itself with every possible consideration, as to the space within which motion occurs and as to the velocity of motion, by examining the various relations that exist between time and space. It must then study the various instruments which can be used to transform one form of motion into another. (1935, p. 50)

Kinematics is the science of motion, but it is also the science of the traces operational motion imprints on objects. In France, it is represented by Lantz and Bettancour's *Traité* of 1810, which was directly inspired by Monge's *Cours de géométrie descriptive*, and, much later, by Laboulaye's treatise on kinematics (1849). In England, it is represented by Willis's *Principles of Mechanism* (1841), an exhaustive study of organs for transforming motion and of the kinematic systems to which those transformations relate.

2. The transmission of energy: this is the object of energetics and dynamics, which make it possible to calculate how much useful work can be obtained at the operational level by using an external source of energy, and to calculate loss of energy by applying the principle of constancy in a variety of ways.

At this point, the natural sciences merged with the technologies used (with varying degrees of sophistication) to control first external sources of energy (water, wind, animals) and then internal sources (the steam-engines used before the discovery of electricity). Related technologies were used to regulate motors (fly-wheels, regulators, 'governors'), to reduce their size and to integrate them into autonomous machine-systems. The technology of transmission was all the more important in that energy sources were still external and the cost of the first machines made it necessary to centralize their source of energy; drives, belts and teledynamic cables sometimes transmitted the energy supplied by waterfalls for a distance of several kilometres, as in the mills of Alsace in the late nineteenth century. Finally, technology made it possible to control the productivity of machines. As a result, many industrial associations were set up following the example set by the Manchester Steam Users' Association in 1855 (see Bour, 1890).

Varying degrees of technological sophistication . . . In a short book which was awarded a prize by the Société Industrielle du Nord, an engineer called Leloutre describes how a new transmission system was installed in a large mill with 18,000 spindles. A number of accidents had occurred because the cast-iron fly-wheels on the machines were geared into pinions made of hornbeam. The teeth of the pinions were also badly designed:

and so, because the machines had to transmit a drive of between 450 and 500 horsepower, the pinions were literally shredded every eight

weeks . . . As they worked, the teeth became hot . . . The wood began to crack. The teeth became worn down by eight or ten millimetres and worked loose from their sockets. The vibrations that resulted from this state of affairs were so violent that one-metre-thick foundation stones split from side to side and great wheels weighing some 6,000 kilograms and turning at 120 revolutions per minute shattered into pieces.
(Leloutre, *1883, p. 201*)

The old transmission system had to be replaced by a belt. Closing the mill in order to dig a special ditch to house one large belt was, however, 'unthinkable'. A daring solution was therefore improvised. A smaller belt was used, but its thickness was doubled, tripled and then quadrupled. It held.

Shutting down the infernal machines for any length of time was unthinkable because they provided the drive for the whole mill and because everything depended upon the drive. The time of capital therefore appeared to merge with the time of technology. In his *Cours complet et pratique de filature de coton*, Drapier sets his reader a practical exercise in calculating output:

In order to produce one metre of No. 1 yarn, the spindles must revolve 760 times; in order to produce 1.50 metres of yarn, they must therefore revolve 1,140 times. The drive shaft, that is to say, must revolve 38 times. The drive shaft turns at a constant speed of 170 revolutions per minute. Given the time required for winding on, and a working week of 70 hours, we therefore obtain 22,050 metres of spun yarn per spindle per week. (1854, p. 37)

Human labour-time thus seems to be an extension of technological time. Human operational functions are seen as the weak link in the system as 'negligence contributes to the production of defective yarn even when reasonably good machines are available to spin it' (Drapier, p. 62).

In short, the productive moment in the cycle of capital appears to materialize in the consumption of raw materials at a rate set by a machine. Matter charged with energy frees energy; that energy is channelled by a machine which is brought into contact with passive raw materials; the machine works on the raw materials and produces value in the shape of cotton yarn. Steam-engines are value-engines or machines for producing economic signifiers; they are energetic metaphors for an economic process. Capital takes the form of both raw materials and finished

55

products; it seems that what is transferred between their respective values takes the material form of a transfer of chemical, thermal, kinetic or dynamic energy which obeys the principle of constancy. Thanks to the great industrial automaton, capital appears to have found a body of its own. Indeed, it appears to have found an ideal body which is divorced from social relations: a material support which is both natural and automatic. This representation is obviously a form of technological fetishism, as valorization *is* a social relationship. Living labour is still central to the realization of surplus value, but it is so enmeshed with the machine and so subordinated to the rhythms of the machine that it seems quite natural that, say, spinners should be paid on the basis of quantity of output (the quantity of labour supplied by the machine) rather than on the basis of the number of interventions they make.

In the age of manufacture, capital became productive and imposed its own rhythm and space on those of the world of labour. It imposed its own discipline and organization on the forms of that world. Mechanization meant organizing human labour around an automaton rather than bringing together large numbers of workers.[8] The machine system appeared to absorb human labour. The face of the new industrial order was that of a new and extensive rationality which initially seemed alien to working-class subjectivity and which had to be forced upon it:

> *Le Creusot is not simply a factory; it is a world of its own, a sort of iron empire which could well adopt the motto: 'All for iron, all through iron'.*
> *It stands in a highly productive coal and iron-ore basin. Day by day, it grows bigger, both on the surface and in the depths of the earth, digging tunnels and extending its railways in the search for coal and ore.*
> (Turgan, *1886)*[9]

The dominant image was one of a system which contained within it the principles of its own growth, its own dynamism and its own order: 20,000 workers at Le Creusot, and 1,500 at the Etablissement Cail's factory in Grenelle in 1862; 2,500 at the Fives factory in Lille in 1882; 2,000 in the rolling mills and blast furnaces belonging to the Société La Providence in Hautmont in 1884.

Productive space could be organized on the basis of an overall plan, as it was now a matter of bringing functions together within an enclosed area rather than of distributing them:

The two groups of buildings are connected by a tunnel . . . The buildings
to the north include storehouses for raw materials and workshops for
preliminary operations; those to the south house all the machine-tools
required by the turners, and the assembly shops are situated in a vast
shed with no internal partitions. The various trades are kept separate:
the only way the carpenters, foundrymen, grinders and blacksmiths can
communicate with the fitters and mechanics is via the tunnel through
which semi-finished goods are taken from one side of the factory to the
other for finishing. (Turgan, *description of the Etablissements Mercier,*
1865)

Two sheds at opposite ends of the main building (which measures 147
metres by 16) cover two wide stairways, one used by men and the other
by women . . . A system of mobile platforms runs the whole length of
the building; the cotton is taken up to the looms, and is brought down
again when it is ready to be packed and delivered to the customer.
(Turgan, *description of the La Foudre, 1863)*

Tunnels, mobile platforms, railways and the rationalization of transport
all structured industrial architecture, which ensured that the production
process was continuous. At the Saint-Gobain glassworks, casting took
place in a vast shed (70 metres by 25): 'Three furnaces stand along a
central line. One is working, the second is under construction, and the
third is drying out. It will take over from the first; after seven months of
firing, it will be burned out and it will be broken up' (Turgan, 1880). A
system of railway tracks radiating out from the shed where the raw
materials were mixed (sodium carbonate, sodium sulphate, carbonate of
lime and broken glass) meant that the oven could be refilled as soon as
the previous batch of molten glass had been removed. The glass was
transported by rail and then tipped out, still molten, on to the table where
it was laminated. The entire operation took five minutes.

Such schemes both separated and brought together men and their
functions; they performed them by means of an overall structuring of
time and space. The entire Godillot tannery in Saint-Ouen was designed
to break down an unvarying series of tasks:

One part of the establishment houses the main building in which the
hides are treated. It is divided up into parallel rows which house the
various shops through which the hides pass. When they arrive, the hides

are taken into the storeroom for raw hides on one side of the building, and they leave by the other side, having passed through each shop in turn. The building can be enlarged to any desired proportion by extending the width of the parallel rows of individual workshops; the arrangement, order and surface ratio of the various shops will remain unchanged.
(Turgan, *1880*)

The effects of this structuring of time and space were seen most clearly in the image of the flow of production, which no longer resulted from the integration of human activities, as it had in the age of manufacture; it was now imposed upon human activities. It no longer mirrored disciplined and synchronized movements, but a constant circulation of matter driven by the movement of machines:

The molten iron is hauled in small wagons pulled by little locomotives along a line leading to the entrance of the puddling sheds; it is then turned into pig-iron, and is taken out into the yard to be reworked and transformed into marketable products. During the process that leads from the arrival of the iron to the dispatch of the finished product, the raw material goes through a series of transformations, always moving in the same direction and always taking the shortest route. The admirable layout of the new forges at Le Creusot is seen to its best advantage when they are working at night. Everything – including the distance between the furnaces and the forges and presses they have to serve – is so finely calculated that no delays, mishaps or errors in handling the iron interrupt the operation or threaten the safety of the workers. The incandescent masses move with wonderful ease, and the relative darkness of those areas that do remain in shadow highlights the movements of the shining but dangerous loads, and makes it easier to see them. (Turgan, *1866*)

This obviously does not mean that the marketable products that left the forge were anything other than alloys or combinations of the work of inanimate forces and of human activity (the journalist [Turgan] notes that 'puddling is hard work'), but human labour was totally remoulded by this combination of forces.

Huge machines totally did away with the work of whole classes of workers. The productivity rate of the new paper-making machines, for example, was ten to twelve times higher than that achieved by the old vat-men. The machines used at the Papeterie d'Essonne (Turgan, 1860) could produce sheets of paper which were automatically cut to size and dried. The activities of the team of workers (a foreman, a machine-operator and a labourer to remove the finished paper) who bustled around the great bulk of 'Amédée' bore no resemblance to those of workers employed in earlier factories.[10]

In most cases, the machines were smaller than this and were either operated independently or worked in series (as in machine systems). But in all cases they replaced (or mechanized) human labour. At the Carrosserie Belvalette (Turgan, 1874), a series of mechanical operations reproduced the division of labour of the age of manufacture; spokes were cut out on a lathe and then polished mechanically ('the workman stands behind a protective guard' and passes each length of wood 'over a fairly slack belt on to which sand has been glued'; he could thus 'plane' 100 spokes in an hour). The mortice joints on the hub which housed the spokes were also made by an ingenious mechanical process.

In this case, we have therefore a series of machine-tools; but bigger factories relied both upon sets of successive machines and upon large numbers of identical machines. In the Trois Fontaines plant (Turgan, 1884), which produced watch glasses, motors driving a complex system of gears powered 264 small lathes (each pulley drove twenty-four lathes, and each workman minded eight or ten of them) and twenty-four grinding wheels housed in a special grinding shop.[11]

In all these cases, the nature of the tasks was completely transformed. There is a simple explanation for this: when the machine comes into direct contact with the object of labour, the traditional sequence of tasks breaks down and the nature of human intervention changes. Looked at very schematically, we now have two kinds of task: supervisory tasks and 'stop-gap' tasks. The former both make the worker central to the process and distance him from it. The mechanics' delegation to the 1867 Exposition Universelle, for instance, described the role of the engine-driver in a mine, after the introduction of new technology, as follows: 'The driver stands in the centre, facing the shaft bottom; he operates the starting lever, a gear lever and a powerful and ingenious steam-brake; his work does not interfere with that of the labourers.' Stop-gap tasks, on the other hand, bring the worker into contact with the object of labour but make him marginal to the process; the machine is in control and the worker becomes its appendage; he intervenes only in order to compensate for its mechanical failures. Examples included the women in Carmoy's nail factory, who delicately balanced a length of wire on a roundlet of brass 25,000 to 30,000 times a day, and the adolescents who fed the combing engine within linen tow at the Manufacture de lin Poullier: 'Young labourers are constantly busy pressing the tow between plates, loading it on to trolleys, unloading it and loosening screws. If they are to feed the combing engine steadily, these young workers have no time to lose . . . as each plate pushes the next one forward' (Turgan, 1884). In most cases, the distinction is not in fact so clear-cut. A worker operating an individual machine may both control it and perform stop-gap tasks, since tasks the machine cannot carry out (such as feeding the machine and removing the finished product) must be carried out by hand. This is how Turgan describes the hot-metal press used in the Mirmilliod cutlery works:

> *The process centres on a mould with two cylinders that revolve rapidly . . . In order to carry out the first operation, the workman waits until the cylinders are turning with their jaws open; the two jaws then come together, compress the metal, draw it and mould it. They continue to revolve and expel the blade. The worker quickly removes it with his pliers and checks to see that it is perfect. If it is not, he places it between the jaws of the mould again before the metal has had time to cool. The rapidity, ease and neatness with which the operation is performed is almost unbelievable. (1865)*

In more general terms, the dominance of the machine-system appeared initially to be an element in the standardization and crushing of individuals. It affected workmen, technicians and engineers alike. A member of the mechanics' delegation to the 1867 Exposition Universelle noted that 'At Le Creusot the authority of the masters makes itself felt everywhere . . . It is well known that workers do not want to be treated like soldiers or locked up in barracks', whilst the engineer, Lucien Moynot, stated in his memoirs that 'I did not like the factory at Le Creusot. I objected to being no more than a minor cog in a great machine which was beyond my control.' But this was not the only side to the dominance of the machine-system.[12]

These issues are increasingly topical, especially now that supervisory tasks are taking on a greater importance. We will return to this point. For the moment, we will take only one example: an ergonomic study of the operation of the 'Trio' machines used for packing cigarettes at SEITA (CNAM, 1972b). The Trio is in fact a series of machines which seem to function automatically, and the only functions the operator has to perform on any regular basis are of the stop-gap type: feeding it with silver paper, cellophane, wrappers and labels, etc. Such tasks take up only one quarter of the operators' time. The operators are responsible for the quantity of output, and breakdowns are frequent and varied. Some are frequent and predictable, as when the mechanism feeding the cigarettes into the hopper jams (observations revealed that, on average, this happened 135 times a day); others happen more rarely. The design of the machines takes into account the possibility of some breakdowns, but others are quite unpredictable, as when the mechanism sorting the cigarettes into packets of twenty fails. Some adjustments have to be made while the machine is still running (228 times per day); others mean that it has to be stopped (50 per day). All these interventions are emergency operations; they require 'the constant collation of visual, tactile and aural information'. CNAM's ergonomic study examines this collation of information in detail, and reveals that the machine-operator has considerable responsibilities: 'Under these conditions, it is clear that the operative's reactions to the information the machine gives him are not stereotypical or routine. They depend in part on his interpretation of the overall situation, and on the way he evaluates his own ability to respond to the situation. Different workers may react in different ways' (p. 16). 'Styles of operating' can therefore be identified, and the training period is all the longer in that training takes place 'on the job'. Finally, 'The workers say that they need a further year of working with a Trio after the training period before they feel at home with it.'

The division between the skilled tasks of machine-operators and the purely routine tasks of labourers is not, then, self-evident. It is because technology is not neutral that it appears to be part of a technical process.

In his discussion of the technical writings of Denis Poulot, who was the doyen of the metal-working industries of nineteenth-century Paris, Alain Cottereau explains what state-of-the-art technology meant at that time. Three criteria were used to define a good machine-tool: increased precision, greater speed, and the reduction of the worker's free will:

In the domain of machine-tools, a long series of complex and highly automated models failed to satisfy industrialists. Poulot analyses their primary shortcomings. The introduction of automated machines certainly made bolting and riveting simpler, but maintaining the machines was a delicate task which gave the operatives too much responsibility. In other words, these machines provided more scope for the workers involved in production to exercise their skills . . . Most of the prototypes therefore ended up on the scrap-heap. (in Poulot, *1980, pp. 47–8)*[13]

This sheds a new light on what was at stake in struggles over machines. The figure of *le sublime* had begun to emerge. Being a highly skilled worker, his employer could not do without him, and he could defy his employer by rejecting discipline and imposing his own standards without any fear of reprisals.[14] Being relatively well paid and capable of 'earning enough to keep himself for weeks in three and a half days', he was reluctant to stay with any one master, and even took a certain delight in defying his masters.[15] His lack of loyalty made him a target for the first profit-sharing schemes.

The master 'had only one workshop',[16] but *le sublime* had only one trade. Technological innovations were designed to do away with the need for skills which were the personal attribute of an individual worker.[17] Denis Poulot's tapping machines, for example, owed their success to the fact that only a narrow range of skills was required to operate them, and they were introduced in a world in which skilled craft workers were particularly common. They did not simply produce tap-makers; they also produced specialist workers who, in the eyes of the craftsmen, had every possible negative trait.[18]

It might, however, be more appropriate to examine the new aspects of working-class subjectivity which resulted from these forms of the socialization of labour in all their complexity. In some senses, the specialist worker of the age of manufacture was the forerunner of Ford's unskilled worker. The differences between them should, of course, be underlined:

In the factories and manufactories of the nineteenth century, the 'labourer' played only a peripheral role (maintenance, cleaning) or a secondary role (repetitively reproducing primary work carried out by a skilled worker); henceforth (from 1920 onwards), the reverse was true. The unskilled worker became the productive core, and other strata of the workforce were distributed around him and his work. (Gaudemar, *1979, p. 26*)

The accuracy of this typology is undeniable if we compare, for example, the labourer who removed the finished product from a paper-making machine and the unskilled worker on a car production line. The former was indeed peripheral to a process controlled by a machine-operator; the latter is at the centre of production, and it is the skilled workers (maintenance staff, for example) who are peripheral to the assembly line. But it is still true to say that the teams of workers who bustled around big machines (in paper-making or printing) had not undergone any fundamental structural change, and that, on the other hand, manufacture was a form of work organization in which unskilled workers were often *obviously* central to the production process, and that machines played only a minor role.[19] It is also true to say that large homogeneous workshops equipped with small machines (like the grinding shop at the Trois Fontaines watch factory) were dominated by the composite figure of a machine-operator who was, in many ways, the forerunner of the Fordist worker. He was central to the labour process, but he was also an appendage of a machine-system; he worked to the rhythm of machines, and his movements were calibrated and stereotypical; his time was subordinated to the needs of production (in the watch-glass shop the only decoration was the clock which dominated the room), as is that of the Fordist worker whose activities are dominated not only by external forces and by the assembly line in the true sense of the phrase, but also by the tools he uses (the mechanization of work stations and the introduction of the assembly line were complementary and decisive aspects of Fordist organization).

The transition from 'periphery' to 'centre' which Gaudemar identifies as the crucial moment in the emergence of the mass-worker (a term which he prefers to 'unskilled worker') in fact means the generalization and extension of the machine-system's dominance over living labour in the context of mass production. This does not necessarily mean that, as Gaudemar suggests, the mass-worker subjectively sees himself as being central to either the production process or the labour process, which is now dominated by the mechanized assembly line.

CHAPTER FOUR

MECHANICAL DISPLACEMENTS

The hogs move in front of this man; they are close
enough together for him to have just enough time to
pull his knife out of the throat of one hog and to plunge
it into that of the next . . . Whereas we would then see
a French butcher pick up a saw and wield it with all
his might, here a man simply moves among the sides
of pork that have to be cut up with an electrically-
powered mechanical saw which is connected to the
ceiling by a supple flex, like the flex on a housewife's
electric iron.

H. Dubreuil, *Standards*

L
ike the table of the age of manufacture, the mechanized assembly
line initially seems to be a means of production. It appears to be
one more machine in a world of machines, a table brought to life
by mechanical movement. It is neither – or so it would seem – the most
ingenious nor the most complex of industrial automata. In so far as it is
merely a mechanical handling device, it existed as early as the nineteenth
century: endless belts were in use at the Montchain tilery and at the
Davin mill (Turgan, 1862, 1866), and a mechanical goods lift was used
at the Menier chocolate factory (Turgan, 1870). These devices made it
possible to economize on the wages paid to children (or even to men,
when heavy loads were involved) and to transport materials requiring
specific atmospheric conditions in sealed containers. They were, then,
displacement-machines.[1]

From the outset, however, and despite the very different forms they
took,[2] they were very special machines; they were very strange machines
in that they did not act directly on the object of labour. A single object
moved between two points on a continuous segment of a line; the line

added nothing to it, and therefore had no particular operational function. Like the table in the age of manufacture, the line is a solution to the problem of continuity and a result of the fragmentation of the labour process. It is therefore initially no more than a means to extend the principle of the extreme fragmentation of tasks at little cost.[3]

But it does also introduce a new element. In the table system, the course followed by the object of labour was merely a linear reflection of the average speed at which the women workers carried out operations (a reflection which took the form of movement through space). The movement originated with them, and with them alone, even if they did obviously generate it under a certain disciplinary constraint. It was an expression of living labour.

With the mechanized assembly line, matters are very different. Its pace is set in advance, and it is external to the workers: it is an expression of a machine-system. From this point of view, the line is far from being an automated handling device; it is part of a homogeneous system, and a means of incorporating the activity of men into that of machines. It is obviously not the only means of doing so: machine-tools often 'gear' living labour to their own rhythms, as the saying goes.[4] But the line functions as an abstract machine, as a sort of general equivalent to the machine-system. It may have its technical usefulness, as when the objects of labour are heavy (cars), but this is not always the case (clothing, food . . .). In a sense, it brings about an inversion; whereas operational machines (such as large presses) had to be fed by hand and their finished products removed by hand, here it is human labour that is operational and the supply and removal of parts that are mechanized. The only property that the assembly line has in common with the operational machine is that it consumes labour power. From that point of view, the question of whether it is the machine or the worker who is central to the operation is less important than the fact that a wide variety of human activities are included within the uniform movements of a machine, and that the producers' subjective relationship with their work is based upon an obsessive cycle of 'tasks to be carried out' (an endless cycle of moments; the object of labour appears to be an empty matrix to be operated upon; when the task has been completed by traces of physical action, the task disappears and then immediately reappears).

'We have one and three-quarter minutes to fit the indicators, the bumpers and the gaskets. On top of that, we also have to change trolleys. You have to work fast, very fast. As fast as you can' (car assembly plant worker).

The first assembly lines were installed in the Ford factory in 1913, and they rapidly proved to be efficient.[5] Whereas the assembly of fly-wheel magnetos had been carried out previously by one workman and had taken twenty-five minutes, the task was now divided up among twenty-nine workmen and took only thirteen minutes. When the conveyor belt was set at the correct height, it took only seven or even five minutes: 'That line established the efficiency of the method and we now use it everywhere' (Ford, 1923, p. 81).[6] As Richard Edwards demonstrates, this was Ford's great innovation: 'While continuous-flow production appeared first in textiles, meat-packing, lamp production and elsewhere, it was the Ford assembly line that brought the technical direction of work to its fullest potential' (1979, p. 117).[7] Ultimately, 'In the Chicago plant, the greatest distance any material has to be trucked is twenty feet, this being the distance from the incoming freight-car to the first conveyor. After this it is mechanically handled during the entire process of assembling the units into a finished car' (Ford, 1926a, p. 113).

The assembly line was therefore the most significant element in a machine-system which gave the movement of capital a physical form:[8]

Our production cycle is about eighty-one hours from the mine to the finished machine in the freight-car . . . Let us say that one of our boats docks at Fordson at 8 a.m. on Monday. It has taken the boat forty-eight hours to come from Marquette to the docks. Ten minutes after the boat is docked, its cargo will be moving towards the High Line and become part of a charge for the blast furnace. By noon Tuesday, the ore has been reduced to iron, mixed with other iron in the factory cupolas, and cast. Thereupon follow fifty-eight operations which are performed in fifty-five minutes. By three o'clock in the afternoon, the motor has been finished and tested and started off in a freight-car to a branch for assembly into a finished car. Say that it reaches the branch plant so that it may be put into the assembly line at eight o'clock Wednesday morning. By noon the car will be on the road in the possession of its owner. If the motor, instead of being sent to a branch, goes into the assembly line for the Detroit district, then the completed car will be delivered before five o'clock Tuesday afternoon instead of noon on Wednesday. (Ford, *1926a, pp. 115–16*)

The La Foudre mill had already lent itself to this technological fetishism, to the concealment of social relations behind a technological façade. The only subject of production was the factory or the productive body of capital. It was a vast apparatus for moulding time, just like the clocks for which Henry Ford admits to having had an adolescent passion.[9]

The factory is a watch, but human labour is also regulated as though it were a watch; whereas Turgan saw mill-workers who could stand outside the process and who could take their ease while 'docile and organized' raw materials were being transformed into commodities under their own impetus, here human activity is absorbed into the overall cycle of the transfer of energy. The productive human body appears to be a source of energy or a raw material (and, from the point of view of the accumulation of capital, it is in fact the only 'raw' material). Just like the ore that is brought into the Fordson factory, it yields up the value it contains (social labour time) in accordance with a process which appears to be governed by the laws of physics: 'In our industries, we think of time as human energy' (Ford, 1926a, p. 110).

Machines have to be regulated, and the aim is to obtain an optimal quantity of useful effects; from this point of view, the assembly line makes it possible to control the quantity of effort required in a day by setting an average speed (one metre per second, to begin with). The line thus gives compulsory norms a technical form.[10] By making operations more specialized, it facilitates their mechanization: by 1936, 32 of the 160 work stations in the Ford V8 assembly plant were equipped with small machine-tools, many of them specially designed (Barclay, 1936).

Like a tool in a machine-system, the human body is turned into an instrument and appears to transmit energy and action; its effects on the object of labour are all the greater in that it is a passive element within the system to which it is geared:

The principal part of a chisel is the cutting edge. If there is a single principle on which our business rests, it is that. It makes no difference how finely made a chisel is or what splendid steel it has in it or how well it is forged – if it has no cutting edge it is not a chisel. It is just a piece of metal . . . The cutting edge of a factory is the man and the machine on the job. (Ford, *1923, pp. 18–19*)

Ford uses the initial object of Taylor's researches as a metaphor, but it may be more than a mere image. The chisel is a real mechanical model which both Taylor and Ford use to conceptualize the productive rationality of human labour. Its rationality is based upon the elimination of waste: 'For anyone to be required to use more force than is absolutely necessary for the job in hand is waste' (Ford, 1923, p. 19). Ford also argues that any technique which reduces the time needed to do a job by 10% increases productivity by 10%; in the absence of that technique, productivity falls by 10%. Thus, if 12,000 workers are spared the need to walk ten steps a day, the saving overall is equivalent to the strength and time needed to walk fifty miles a day.

The rational use of labour-power is also based upon a careful analysis of all costs, on savings in space, time and raw materials, on the reduction of stocks and on detailed stock-taking, on the use of standard and specialist tools, and on the rapid implementation of experimental results.[11]

Reducing the 'internal work' of the machine also means standardizing the human component. Discipline and specialization both play their part ('We expect our men to do what they are told. The organization is so highly specialized and one part is so dependent upon another that we could not for a moment consider allowing men to have their own way' (Ford, 1923, p. 11).[12] According to *Ford Factory Facts* (1917), every operative is a specialist, and specialization is the basic principle behind the entire Ford organization); so also does the simplification of social relations (workers who are taken on are asked only to state their identity and to list their skills; everyone in the factory is simply a Fordman; personal friendships were discouraged, and attempts were made to reduce the power of the foreman). Each workman and each foreman is important only to the extent that he occupies a specific position within a series of essential operations ('A big business is really too big to be human. It grows so large as to supplant the personality of the man' (Ford, 1923, p. 263)), although, as we shall see, external signs that they share the firm's moral objectives are also taken into account. The high-wage policy and the profit-sharing system introduced in 1914 guarantee the workers' loyalty, and prove that: 'There is nothing that a union membership could do for our people' (Ford, 1923, p. 262).

Two remarks are called for here:

1. As we have already noted, the assembly line gives the disciplinary order of the shop floor a technological appearance and that, combined with the enormous scale of the plant, makes it seem non-intentional and inevitable. As Edwards puts it:

The larger structure tends to legitimize the foreman's role. Exceptional circumstances aside, the foreman cannot be held personally responsible for the oppressiveness of the production process. If the legitimacy of the line is accepted, then the necessity for the foreman's job follows. The actual power to control work is thus vested in the line itself, rather than in the person of the foreman. Instead of control appearing to flow from boss to workers, control emerges from the much more impersonal 'technology'. (1979, p. 120)

2. Ford's scorn for union organizations leads him to paint a rosy picture. According to Beynon:

Detroit was a frontier city. Squalor, immigrant workers, shanty towns, corruption and violence. Open-shop factories with monotonous jobs paid on the piece (except at Ford . . .). Safety standards were appalling and fatal accidents a commonplace. An ideal breeding-ground for unionism and radicalism. The Industrial Workers of the World, 'The Wobblies', were making some progress in Detroit – as they were nationally. (1973, pp. 19–20)[13]

It is against this background that we have to understand both the high-wage policy (the $5 day) and the far-reaching programmes of the factory's Sociological Department which, under the leadership of John R. Lee, had a profound impact on social relations inside the company.

As a result of Lee's influence, great attention was given to the working environment: the factories were clean – a team of 700 cleaners, painters and window cleaners was constantly at work in the Detroit plant – well ventilated and whitewashed so as to leave no dark corners:

They claim that Ford is obsessed with cleanliness. And it is true that the shop floor is constantly being swept . . . The ceilings are constantly being whitewashed, and the walls are painted grey to shoulder-height. The toilets . . . In the United States, there are normally no doors to guarantee privacy, but at Ford there are no partitions at all, and when you enter these premises you see two rows of seats facing one another across a space of a few metres . . . But everything is very clean and is washed down several times a day. (Dubreuil, *1929, p. 323*)

At the same time, extensive welfare programmes were developed both for workers and for their families.[14]

River Rouge and Highland Park represented a new type of standardized factory adapted to the needs of mass production (as early as 1917, assembly was carried out in thirty branch factories scattered across the United States; each was built to the same model). When rationalization methods began to be introduced in 1911, the Ford plant in Detroit employed an industrial army of 42,000 workers who produced parts for 35,000 cars a year.[15] As in the rest of the United States, the labour force which was recruited into the motor industry often had little experience of industrial work, and was both cosmopolitan and highly mobile.[16] This workforce had to be supervised and controlled. Efforts were made to make workers settle in one city and to train them, whilst their welfare had to be taken care of both inside and outside the factory.

The factory was designed to produce a standardized object (the Model T, which came in only one version. It was cheap and came in 'any colour you like, so long as it is black'[17]), with standardized machinery and standardized methods. It was a coherent structure which could be reproduced, and in which human labour was standardized and regarded as an extension of a mechanical system:

A series of books entitled 'Ford Tool Standards' contains all the necessary data and give the complete story of our standard practice, down to the last detail. These books have saved thousands of dollars . . . but their real importance cannot be estimated, for they are primarily responsible for keeping the work uniform throughout the entire organization. (Ford, *1926a, p. 86*)

The technical equivalent of the 'economic' labour of capital was carried out in a uniform time-space which was shared by men and machines. This uniform space is an expression of the spectacular and regular movement of the great assembly line. Valorization results from the living labour which capital can invest because it owns money. But living activity represents a gap within the symbolic money system because money, being both a specific commodity and a general equivalent within the commodity system, can only represent traces of labour: dead labour. Capital cannot master the continuity of its cycle unless it is metamorphosed into a system of machines, into an active form of dead labour which can surround and infiltrate living labour.

'For us, the line is the boss' (car assembly-line worker). This is because the line is only the external face of the real yoke which remains invisible. Every worker internalizes the speed it sets by internalizing a sequence of mental actions which go hand in hand with the serial operations of the operational cycle. Standardizing this sequence in order to optimize the efficiency of the worker's movements means that the innermost workings of the human body have to be viewed as though they were the workings of a machine. In other words, a technology of the productive human body must be elaborated.

Chapter Five

The Body as Machine

The human organism, like any living creature, adapts relatively quickly to new environmental conditions. This is true. The senses – hearing, taste, smell and sight – have the ability to become more acute in order to adapt to different situations. Therefore they eventually become accustomed to new situations; reflexes can be conditioned. And why shouldn't their limits be extended?

En Direct, Peugeot house journal, June 1977

Me? Oh, I'm just a machine. When they talk about me they say 'Number 566', not 'Mademoiselle so and so'. That's the machine's number. So, me and the machine are one and the same.

'JQ', an unskilled worker in an electronics plant

In order to come to terms with the history of those sciences which, from Coulomb's memoirs, *Sur la force des hommes* of 1785, to modern ergonomics, developed under the general rubric of 'human work', we must first of all get away from traditional reconstructions which describe science as though it were a building erected stone by stone inside a perimeter traced by the far-sighted genius of a few founding fathers. Official histories, which are often based on the writings of the physiologists themselves, contain an element of corporate patriotism (cf. Valentin, 1972; Scherrer, 1967). But in the case of the sciences of work, this is not the only element involved. In an earlier article (Doray, 1978), I attempted to investigate why it is that most of those who are involved practically in these sciences are unable to state their objective clearly, and stressed that expressions such as 'the science of work' or 'the science of men at work' are both vague and ambiguous. There is, I believe, a definite advantage to be gained by using the expression 'the labour process' to define their object more clearly, as it implies a dialectical articulation with the other dimension of commodity production: the process of valorization.

What the mode of production presents as natural forms of labour are in fact forms which have already been subordinated to and moulded by valorization. The ability of certain scientists to ignore this consideration gives them something of the self-confidence of the empire-builder, but it is not without its serious theoretical drawbacks.

To mention only two difficulties:

1. From a theoretical point of view, it is difficult to see precisely what determines the object of these scientific practices. A theoretically based science elaborates and constructs its object by a process of breaking down the real. In the present case, labour appears to imply the notion of 'human strength'; wage relations turn it into a commodity which seems to be autonomous. It therefore appears to be a ready-made object for scientific investigation. Knowing what it consists of does nothing to elucidate the process which defines it, because it is a social product and because it is socially relative. The natural sciences are therefore dealing with an object whose coherence and unity are purely a product of social relations. This highly specific situation promotes novel, but potentially highly problematical, forms of co-operation between related disciplines, as we can see from the modern avatars of ergonomic multidisciplinarity. But it also promotes highly ambiguous displacements between the scientific appropriation of the object of knowledge and its practical exploitation in relations of production.

2. More specifically, it is difficult to take into account those dimensions of the labour process which do not correspond directly to the economic signifiers of the process of valorization. In his preface to Amar (1914), Le Chatelier expresses the employer's view of the sciences of labour as follows: 'For the industrialist, the only thing that counts is actual work, and the central problem is therefore the definition of the conditions which will produce the maximal quantity of actual work for a given level of fatigue.'

These questions are no longer posed in such crude terms, but they are still relevant and of major importance to the future of ergonomics. We will return to this point later.

It is paradoxical but significant that factories and manufactures were not the real birthplace of the physiology of labour (Perronet's studies are the exception to the rule). It was born of an encounter between the scientific imagination and forms of labour to be found in a military and penitentiary environment, where labour displayed a simplicity and a malleability unknown in industry. It was born in Bicêtre, where Hachette (1828) calculated the amount of work done in a day by the epileptics who were harnessed to the whim-gin which drew water from the well. It was born in the English workhouses and prisons where Baron Dupin observed the use of the treadmill.[1] It was born in the arsenal at Rochefort, where Hubert observed men working with different kinds of hammers, altered the parameters, repeated his experiments and established a productivity average. It was born in the construction sites at the Fort de Vincennes where Captain Coignet studied the productivity gained by using a system of human counterweights to raise loads, and in the square in Bayonne where Captain Niel erected machines similar to treadmills in order to drain water from the foundations and mix mortar. Soldiers were also used as guinea-pigs by Navier, who drew up comparative figures for the quantity of useful labour that could be performed in a day by men using different tools and engaged upon different tasks (the figures he obtained were widely used (see Poncelet, 1839, pp. 233 ff.)).

These were simple tasks carried out by docile human raw material. But there was more to the physiology of labour than a methodological exercise. It resulted in a search for a stripped-down object which could give the observer an unrestricted insight into the workings of its biological processes. Almost a hundred years after the original observations were made, Amar, according to Le Chatelier (preface to Amar, 1914), 'could not find in France experimental subjects who were prepared to tolerate the monotony of the experiments they were required to perform, and [he] had to go to North Africa to find individuals who had, presumably, the "physical and moral temperament of an ox", as Taylor puts it.' The overexploited porters of Algiers were both an ideal object for scientific experimentation and a model which could be transposed because 'in so far as they are motors, Arabs have no distinguishing characteristics'

74

(Amar, 1909). Whilst no one would dare to write that today (and in this particular case, Amar's own personality must also be taken into account; his career was cut short by it), the physiology of labour is still characterized by an area of ambiguity.

The ambiguity arises originally from the imaginary identification of the territory of the scientist with that of the industrialist. It was only by massaging its experimental results[2] that the physiology of labour could construct an abstract man in the form of a porter who simply sold his labour-power.[3] 'Scientific' management found its equivalent to Amar's porter in the productive body of the industrial worker. The porter had a lot in common with Taylor's pig-iron handler.[4] Amar's porter was the forerunner of the unskilled labourer of large-scale Taylorist industry.

All these ambiguities, which still leave many important questions unanswered, should not, however, conceal the fact that these scientific practices resulted in a considerable accumulation of knowledge. We can already detect an embryonic move towards scientific abstraction in these analytic, simplified and classified descriptions of human labour, and in Navier's quantitative studies, which were later to be used by Poncelet. The tasks studied were everyday activities ('climbing a staircase', 'raising a weight with the help of a rope and then retrieving the rope'), but their very simplicity and repetitive nature ('uniform tasks carried out over a long period of time' (Poncelet, 1839, p. 230)) meant that they had already taken on an abstract form. They were in effect classified molecules of human labour. The unit chosen to evaluate the quantity of useful work involved in each task was, in one sense, still very empirical (work measured in foot-pounds per day); the system allowed human tasks to be compared, but it did not allow them to be inscribed within a general system of equivalents. It was not a unit of work, as it involved the criterion of time, nor was it a unity of power which could be generalized: the notion of a 'day' is a concrete unit which cannot be applied outside a particular system of human work. The use of the expression 'day' should be seen, rather, as an attempt on the part of these technological propagandists to make the move from the abstract to the concrete in terms that anyone could understand, by basing their intermediate calculations on general units of power.

It is difficult now to appreciate just how far physiological thought distanced itself from empiricism in only a few decades.[5]

The movement away from empiricism presupposed at least two kinds of developments:

1. A detailed *bio-energetic study* of the productivity of the human body. The principles for such a study were established as early as 1786 when, a year after the publication of Coulomb's memoirs, Lazare Carnot wrote, using the imagery of the day: 'An animal is like an assemblage of corpuscles separated by springs which are compressed to a greater or lesser degree and which therefore contain a certain quantity of living force. When the springs are released, they convert latent force into real, living forces' (cited by Amar, 1914).

The notion of converting latent living force into real living force was crucial, as it implied the entire concept of the optimal utilization of the 'goodness' of animated motors. As Poncelet puts it:

> *Animated motors may in themselves be regarded as reservoirs of labour or of actions which may be exhausted with greater or lesser rapidity, and which must therefore be maintained or replenished frequently. Now the degree of fatigue experienced by these motors . . . is, in a word, one of the essential elements in the cost of a day's work in any given country. We can therefore see that, for the industrialist or factory-owner, it is less a question of making men and animals yield the greatest possible quantity of absolute labour each day at risk of compromising their health than of using, in the most advantageous way possible, all the available internal action provided by food and rest. (1839, pp. 229–30)*

Similar preoccupations were to lead Taylor to look for a general and natural law which would allow a foreman to know in advance how much a workman suited to his task could be expected to produce in a day.

A connection had also been established between the workings of the human body and the notion of energetics which had gradually developed on the basis of Coriolis's (1826) work on mechanical productivity, and on the basis of various theoretical expressions of the notion of constancy. Work could now be seen as the conversion of energy within a system. Basically, the human body was seen as obeying the same laws as an engine in a mill: the traces of labour that were inscribed on the object of labour were the result of the transfer of energy that had taken place. The productive consumption of labour-power could therefore take on a technological form.

a. A transfer of energy: something is consumed internally and accumulated externally. Lavoisier had made it possible to measure and compare the cost of the internal combustion required to produce 'different applications of force'.[6] He had realized that all activities have something in common:

> This kind of observation leads us to compare different applications of force which would appear to be unrelated . . . It is not without a certain accuracy that the French language uses the term 'work' [travail] to refer to the efforts made both by the mind and by the body, to the work of the cabinet and to the work of the mercenary. (Lavoisier, cited by Amar, 1914, p. 688)

It was not, however, until the notion of the conservation of energy emerged in the nineteenth century that a real connection could be established between biochemical phenomena and the mechanical work which transferred energy to the outside of the body. The significant discoveries were those made by Julius R. Mayer in 1845, who calculated the calorific cost of a day's work, by Liebig in 1842, whose research on the calorific value of different foodstuffs showed that the 'cause' of the phenomena of life was to be found in the nutritional value of food, and by Loule in 1849, who established the mechanical equivalent of the calorie. The statistical studies made by Helmholtz, Hirn, Bert and Chauveau also had a contribution to make.

b. The 'optimal utilization' of muscular force became a practical notion: 'Monsieur Chauveau established, on the basis of a detailed analysis and delicate experiments, that if a given task is to be carried out, it costs less, for example, to double the speed than to double the load' (Amar, 1914, p. 25). In 1903, Chauveau's pupil Laulagnié defined the 'economic optimum', or the optimal ratio between speed of movement and weight of load. As Amar (1914, p. 27) puts it, 'If we want a motor to operate in accordance with the law of minimal expenditure, load and weight must be combined in appropriate proportions.' But these experiments lasted for only five minutes, and were obviously carried out in conditions that were far removed from normal working conditions.

The great experiments carried out by Atwater and Benedict in Washington between 1900 and 1902 (at roughly the same time, Taylor was trying to discover a 'general law of fatigue') were designed to study the expenditure of energy on a long-term basis and in conditions approximating normal working conditions: the subjects were placed in hermetically sealed chambers replicating energy systems, and all exchanges with the external environment were monitored and quantified.

Energetics made it possible to quantify transfers of energy between the body of an animal or a human being and the environment, and to describe initial and final states. It made it possible to reject vitalist preconceptions and to approach human work with the theoretical tools of the physical sciences. But it did not lead to any greater understanding of forms of human work or of the anatomy of the productive body. That was to be the object of the analysis of movement.

2. The *analysis of movement* was basically to bio-energetics what kinematics was to energetics. Its function was to break down the fleeting and complex movements, and to measure and analyse their component elements. Marey (1894) explains clearly that, until the invention of chronophotography, physiologists had only two techniques at their disposal:

a. Equipment for recording movement over a period of time. These were often analogical devices, and they developed considerably from the mid-nineteenth century onwards as a result of experiments on the physiology of the muscles,[7] and on neurophysiology, which required the recording of rapid movements.[8]

b. Photography, which was as yet little used except as a practical means of recording, say, experimental conditions. It was, however, a practical method for obtaining an instantaneous, automatic and faithful representation of space, and it made it possible to observe experiments from a distance without interfering with experimental phenomena. As early as 1865, Onimus and Martin had the idea of superimposing photographic images of the systolic and diastolic phases of a frog's heartbeat; their photographs of the same organ at two different moments provided a purely spatial image of its movements. Photographs taken against a dark background also made it possible to produce visual images of the movements of solid bodies, and to assemble synthetic photographs of their trajectories. Spatial geometry became a series of visual images.

Chronophotography was a synthesis of photography and techniques for recording space. Images were superimposed or arranged at carefully defined intervals to produce images capturing a whole range of spatial and temporal data. Jansen (the inventor of an 'astronomic revolver') and then the American Muybridge designed similar devices for capturing movement.[9] These were primarily of interest to artists.

Like Muybridge, Marey invented a photographic gun in 1881. The interest of his work lies both in its scientific rigour and in the means he had at his disposal. He succeeded in interesting the authorities in his studies of human locomotion, and especially in their potential military applications; two sections of his work (Marey, 1873) are entitled, respectively, 'A study of the utility of military drill' and 'Determining how much a soldier can carry'. As a result, exceptional experimental facilities were made available to him: the Station Physiologique at the Parc des Princes, which was equipped with a 500-metre circular running track, mobile platforms for photographers and large black backdrops. Marey was well aware of the fact that his method could be applied in a variety of areas, including mechanics (the study of falling bodies, of ballistics, of the resistance of the air, hydrodynamics, and the study of vibrations) and that it could be used to improve the technology of the human body:

> The images taken must be of the strongest and most agile subjects, such as champion gymnasts. These élite subjects will thus reveal the secrets of the skills they have acquired unconsciously . . . The same method lends itself equally well to the teaching of the movements that have to be performed in carrying out skilled tasks. It can be applied to all manual activities and to all kinds of sports. (p. 135)

Chronophotography also made it possible to record the inner workings of the body:

> Until now, students of mechanics have only been able to evaluate human work in specific circumstances . . . A man walking along an inclined plane raises or lowers his own weight by a certain distance. If the weight of his body is multiplied by the difference in height, the work he performs can be calculated in foot-pounds. But according to this criterion, walking across a flat surface involves no apparent work, and yet it does involve muscular actions which cause fatigue. (Marey, pp. 152–3)

Simple calculations (the weight of the body and of the limbs, the moment of inertia) allowed Marey's images to be interpreted in terms of the work required to raise or lower the centre of gravity, and in terms of the angle and velocity of the limbs as they moved. All this resulted in recommendations as to the optimal use of muscular strength while walking or running.[10]

The walking and jumping men, the seagulls and the dancers whose movements through the air were captured by chronophotography were, of course, free bodies. Industrial labour gears the body to forces which are much more heterogeneous than gravity, and calculations based upon images cannot replace dynametric studies. Even so, these photographic methods prepared the way for the calibration and standardization of movement. They were later to be adopted by Taylor's associates, and they are still used today in some work-study departments.

Animated motors and animal-machines are spaces which allow the technology of machines to be transposed to the human body: 'The modern genius has created machines which can legitimately be likened to animated motors. In exchange for the little fuel they consume, they release sufficient force to animate a series of organs and to make them execute the most varied tasks' (Marey, 1873). The functional anatomy of organisms and that of machines obey the same laws:

> All the machines used in industry must have organs which act as intermediaries between an available supply of force and the resistances to which it is to be applied. The word 'organ' is the very word that anatomists use to designate the parts that make up the animal-machine. The laws of mechanics are as applicable to animated motors as they are to other machines. (Marey, pp. 61–2)

And the machine re-creates the functions of organs:

> Take an apparatus which, acting under the influence of a crank and a connecting rod, causes a flexible rod to move rapidly backwards and forwards through a vertical plane. If we adapt a membrane similar to that of an insect's wing to the rod, it will act as a vein. (Marey, p. xi)

But these mechanical replicas of biological bodies are also ideal replicas, as the functional anatomy of mechanics does not depend upon such contingent factors as the need for self-preservation or the unicity of an organism. A machine's organs are divided and kept apart, both by the concentration of power and by the resistance of metal:

> *In our machines, we normally find a great number of parts which are quite distinct from one another, and which touch only at certain points; in an animal, on the other hand, all the parts adhere to one another; any two points on the body are connected by tissues. This results from the nutritional function to which all living organisms are subject. We therefore see that it is absolutely impossible to obtain a continuous rotary movement which passes from one part to the next whilst preserving the continuity between those two parts.* (Foucault, *cited by* Marey, pp. 69–70)

Connecting rods, propellers and pistons: the organs of machines are a perfect expression of physical laws which are imperfectly expressed in the functional anatomy of the biological animal. 'There is therefore a profound difference between the mechanisms employed by nature and those created by man: the former are subject to special demands which do not apply to the latter' (Marey, p. 70). For physiologists influenced by the thought of Claude Bernard, the organism is primarily a vesicle, an internal environment which adapts to the determinism of an external environment. The related organs of the living being are not so much a positive manifestation of a life-force as a conditioned response to external constraints which nothing can escape. Even the skeleton, that hard kernel of the organization of the anatomy, is no more than a piece of soft wax moulded under external pressure. 'Pressure can distort it . . . We might say that it takes the form which the soft parts that surround it allow it to take' (p. 91). Aneurism of the aorta perforates the sternum, and varicose veins become encrusted in the tibia. More generally, 'No element of form results from chance.' The pyramidal hierarchy of functions corresponds to a series of constraints which work inwards: the bones are shaped by the muscles; the muscles are shaped by the nervous system; the nervous system obeys the will, and the will obeys necessity; and necessity is the price that has to be paid for the phenomenon of life, which a certain metaphysical tradition within physiology and medicine was only too happy to regard as a gradual subversion of the inorganic kingdom.[11] The organization of living things is inward-looking, and governed by the need for self-preservation.

With the machine, a displacement occurs. It too is an assemblage of organs: a ram, a crane or a sawhorse. Language and the imagination identify it as a body. Turgan describes Derosne et Cail's engine works:

> Here we have our locomotive with its boiler in place, and with its wheels fitted to their axles . . . The animal is taking shape; we now have to connect the viscera to the limbs, and cover it with a protective shell. The part which connects the viscera to the limbs is simply a connecting rod.

But in substance, the machine belongs to the inorganic kingdom. It is a body without a conscious mind and without subjectivity, a 'marvellous slave' (Turgan) or a mercenary instrument which lends its own movements to an alien intentionality. It infiltrates the space-time of living labour, reifies it, and incorporates it into its own system.

Taylorist man is a slave to the movements of a machine, and he cannot control it either technically or socially. Above all, he suffers from the divorce between that part of his body which has been instrumentalized and calibrated and the remainder of his living personality.

In 1972, workers at the Mendes factory complained that: 'We are not machines; we are human beings, and we deserve respect.' Workers at a Playtex factory complained in 1977 that: 'Performing the same repetitive actions day in, day out, year in, year out, makes you feel that you never create anything. Working piece-rate makes you lose all pride in your work. You're a robot, so you work and work and keep quiet.'

'Machines' rather than human beings; robots rather than thinking beings . . . it is quite true that the Taylorist model of man excludes speech, desire, identity, sexuality and a number of other dimensions of the human personality. We have already mentioned the divorce that occurs between that part of the personality which takes on a positive meaning in the economic signifiers of production that mechanical models can embody so well, and the 'remainder' of the personality. It is this divorce which structures the theoretical field of 'scientific management'. It is, for example, only on this basis that we can understand the dominant role given to the natural sciences in existing theories of human labour (the reduction of the producers to the role of immediate agents of the labour process) and the role of biologically inspired models in the field of industrial psychology (naturalistic representations which imply no theory of the subject of relations of production). In order to address the biological body and to elaborate a behavioural engineering, it is necessary to objectify the human subject, to reduce its complexity and to regard it not as something which speaks to another subjectivity, but as a concrete and desubjectivized manifestation of laws revealed by natural abstractions. Data has to be collected and stripped of its affective and personalized value. In scientific management, every element of the work of every worker becomes the object of accurate, detailed and scientific investigations, and knowledge replaces opinions.

This is the style of approach Taylor recommends. The knowledge of the workers must be retrieved, but as management does not always have any direct understanding of the details of the labour process, this means systematically gathering together 'all the traditional knowledge which in the past has been possessed by the workmen, and then classifying, tabulating and reducing this knowledge to rules, laws and formulae' (Taylor, 1914, p. 36). Taken as a whole, the knowledge of the workmen is a faithful reflection of reality, but they have no clear understanding of their own skills because they are so bound up with individual habits, so surrounded by secrecy and so closely linked to the labour process itself that they cannot be divorced from the concrete. It is only when it is transcribed into abstract technological or physiological terms that their knowledge can acquire a general meaning. When it takes on this abstract form and is restored to him in the form of orders and norms, the worker's knowledge is as alien to him as a language whose vocabulary and grammar mean nothing to him:

> Now one of the first requirements for a man who is fit to handle pig-iron as a regular occupation is that he shall be so stupid and so phlegmatic that he more nearly resembles in his mental make-up the ox than any other type . . . He is so stupid that the word 'percentage' has no meaning to him, and he must consequently be trained by a man more intelligent than himself into the habit of working in accordance with the laws of this science before he can be successful. (Taylor, 1914, p. 59)

But there is more to Taylorism than this. Distinguished scientists regard it as a perversion of the scientific approach because it bears the scars of the social violence that characterized the society which gave birth to it.[12] Aspects of reification which the scientist would regard as normal in an experimental context become unbearably offensive when they are blatant indications of a certain style of social life. It is well known that Taylor liked to use animal metaphors to describe his instrumentalized workers, and his metaphors did more for his reputation than 'the science of shovelling' or 'the science of bricklaying'. The classic example is the pig-iron handler who is guided by his *mahout*, but the language of the scientist soon becomes that of the horse trader: 'There is as much difference between labourers as there is between horses' (Taylor, 1914, p. 157) and 'There are big powerful men suited to heavy work just as dray horses are suited to the coal wagon' (p. 173). One man may be 'an intelligent gorilla' (p. 40); another is as phlegmatic and stupid as an ox.

This is a crude reflection of the industrial mobilization that took place in the United States in the early years of the century. Much the same tone was adopted in economic journals and in lectures given at Philadelphia's Academy of Political and Moral Sciences. Workers were naturally lazy, irresponsible and depraved; they did not belong to the same race as their economic masters. In an article on competition between races, the *Journal of Commerce and Commercial Bulletin* (New York, 1898) argued that those races which have displayed the greatest aptitude for production and trade have taken the lead because, having taken a grip on the material elements of civilization, they have become the most powerful; in the past century, the Anglo-Saxon and German races had developed these attitudes to such a degree that they enjoyed the most favourable position.

At the other end of the scale, the black community was stereotyped in negative terms, as were unskilled labourers in general. According to this literature, the 'Southern Negro' shared the pig-iron handler's total and natural inability to think, if not his phlegm. According to one Dawson, a Negro dressed in European clothes was as totally irresponsible as his 'naturally dressed' African cousin. That the Negro could obviously not reason was a natural rather than an accidental state of affairs. Negro children proved very good at tasks which required only an ability to observe and to remember . . . although they could not reason, they were gifted with remarkable memories.

None of this is anecdotal, nor is it a mere context from which a kernel of pure rationality can be extracted without difficulty. Taylorism is imbued with a utilitarian and instrumental vision of human labour which denies the existence of the worker's subjectivity. It is because the system has an exceptionally robust constitution that it is still on the agenda some eighty years after its invention. But it is also true to say that for a long time its internal coherence corresponded to the coherence of the mode of production. It is no paradox to suggest that, if Taylorism does have a solid kernel, it is to be found in the way in which it displaces social violence into the technical field rather than in any of Taylor's supposedly 'scientific' discoveries.[13] In that sense, we can explain the vitality of Taylorism by looking at what it conceals as well as what it helps to reveal. Certain of Taylor's errors are highly significant in that, predictably enough, the complexity of reality undermined the utilitarian results he hoped to obtain.

For a long time, for example, Taylor tried to discover a law of physical fatigue which would allow a foreman to know in advance how much of any kind of heavy labouring a man who was well suited to his job ought to do in a day. No such law existed in the scientific literature of the time. Numerous experiments were carried out over a period of years, but they did not help him to formulate the law he wanted. When, many years later, Taylor reflected upon his failure, he explained it in thought-provoking terms:

> When a labourer is carrying a piece of pig-iron weighing 92 pounds in his hands, it tires him about as much to stand still under the load as it does to walk with it . . . A man, however, who stands still under a load is exerting no horsepower whatever, and this accounts for the fact that no constant relation could be traced in various kinds of heavy labouring work between the foot-pounds of energy exerted and the tiring effect of the work on the man. (1914, p. 58)

Taylor simply ignores the evidence of the facts (carrying 92 pounds of pig-iron without 'exerting' so many foot-pounds is tiring, too) because he is solely concerned with discovering the law that governs the quantity of 'external work' that is exerted (and this, according to Le Chatelier, is the only form of work which concerns industrialists). It is as though providence should have established a law for the industrial use of labour-power, as though capitalist norms for the utilization of human capacities should have been inscribed on the productive body.

Obviously I am not suggesting that Taylor's thought is reducible to his errors, heartening though they may be. I am suggesting that we have to see its limitations. It is important to do so because the influence of Taylorism on a whole range of contemporary scientific practices takes the form of a reduction of the field of knowledge.

CHAPTER SIX

NORMS, PRODUCTIVITY AND WAGES

'Sir', said Kovalyov, with a sense of his dignity, 'I don't
know how to understand your words. The matter
appears to me to be perfectly obvious . . . either you
wish . . . Why, you are my own nose!'
The nose looked at the major and his eyebrows
slightly quivered.
'You are mistaken, sir, I am an independent individual. Moreover, there can be no sort of close relations
between us. I see, sir, from the buttons of your uniform,
you must be serving in a different department.' Saying
this, the nose turned away.
Gogol, 'The nose'

References to the utilitarianism and normative violence implicit
in Taylorist management will be no more than empty formulae
unless we can clarify the issues involved.

Everything revolves around a few simple propositions. Because of the
existence of wage-relations, labour-power becomes circulating capital; it
does not cease to be a concrete and living manifestation of the individuality
of the wage-earner, but it does become something else too. It becomes
abstract labour-power, and abstract labour-power is a form of capital.
The consumption of labour-power is part of the concrete existence of the
wage-earner who makes over his labour-power in exchange for means of
subsistence. At the same time, it is also a moment in the cycle of capital;
it is the moment when productive capital (that share of capital which has
been transformed into brain and brawn) is realized in the form of
commodities. If labour-power is to exist simultaneously in both these
forms, the concrete activity of labour must acquire a meaning in terms
of the abstract world of the valorization of capital.

The practical involvement of individuals within the space of their sociality occurs against the background of this relationship between the concrete and the abstract. We will begin by examining that relationship.

Marx deals with this question in very basic and general terms in the opening pages of *Capital* (1976, Chapter 1: 'The commodity'), where he discusses *forms*. He does not refer specifically to the particular commodity known as labour-power, but discusses the circulation of objects in commodity exchange in quite general terms.

To say that an object is worth something means evaluating it in terms of a system of equivalents, which may or may not be monetary. The simplest non-monetary form of equivalence can be expressed by the equation: 'Twenty yards of linen are worth one coat'. Indeed, 'The whole mystery of the form of value lies hidden in this simple form' (Marx, 1976, p. 139) because once we formulate this equation, we immediately draw a 'contrast' betwen two expressions of the same thing. In so far as it is a real concrete object that exists before our eyes, the linen has a particular texture and can be put to a specific use. In so far as it is involved in an economic exchange, it takes on a very different dimension: twenty yards of linen can be represented by (or exchanged for) one coat.

This requires some explanation. What does exchange *mean* in terms of the circulation of commodities? It is in reality *human activities* which have left material traces on objects that are being exchanged. And in that sense, the question of the commodity *form* is complex because that which gives the object a value is present (contained) within it, and because the object itself cannot express its value.[1] The value of the object is 'made up of' the material traces of the labour that is crystallized inside it, and it is in the nature of commodity exchange to cause living labour (human activity) to circulate in the form of objects containing traces of labour. If, for example, we say that twenty yards of linen 'contains' x hours of labour, we are saying both that the labour is dead and no longer exists as an activity, and that its material trace remains and is inscribed in a piece of linen. It is only by taking on the form of a material trace that human labour can endure through time, that it can circulate as an object. But the immediate and concrete form of that trace, or the inscription of living labour in the object of labour, is not in itself enough to express the commodity value of the labour which produced it. If it is to become meaningful, to take on a significance and allow a commodity exchange to take place, it must be evaluated in terms of a system of equivalents which allow it to be compared with other products of human labour. It must therefore be abstracted from its immediate form, and must make the *transition* from concrete to abstract.

The element which gives the commodity its meaning (in the value sense) is therefore both *contained* within it (a material trace of living labour) and *external* to it (the trace can take on a meaning only if it changes its form and can be re-presented within a conventional system which allows commodities to be compared; the nature of the system may vary from pure equivalence, in the case of barter, to a monetary form).

Thus, we come to the symbolic dimension of economic exchange:

The measure of the expenditure of human labour-power by its duration takes on the form of the magnitude of the value of the products of labour; and finally the relationships between the producers, within which the social characteristics of their labours are manifested, take on the form of a social relation between the products of labour . . . Through this substitution, the products of labour become commodities, sensuous things which are at the same time suprasensible or social. (Marx, 1976, pp. 164–5)

These 'social' things are at once 'sensuous' and 'suprasensible' because they convey a meaning. Just like the words of a language, they are at once signifiers and things signified. They are things signified because there is a material link between them and the particular living labour of which they are traces; they are signifiers because there is a link between them and the external representation of their value.[2]

Human labour is an activity which belongs to the past and which has vanished, but it continues to exist in the form of a trace. The value of that labour cannot, however, be signified unless the trace is represented within a system of symbolic equivalents which may or may not be monetary. Although labour continues to exist as a trace, it has no economic meaning in itself. If it is to have a symbolic value, it must be represented in the form of a market valuation of the object, and a link must be established betwen the object and a conventional representation of its value. Commodities appear to be 'fetishes' (Marx) because the invisible social relations they articulate and make meaningful (the exchange of the labour contained in twenty yards of linen for the labour contained in the coat) no longer seem to exist as such: 'The definite social relation between men themselves . . . assumes here, for them, the fantastic form of a relation between things' (Marx, p. 165). It is as though things began to 'speak' in the place of human beings. This is the basic characteristic of the commodity imaginary.

Marx approaches the problem with the intellectual tools of his day. Taking the example of the linen and the coats (and adopting the curious fictional convention whereby the value of things is expressed in terms of coats rather than, say, money), he terms the linen the *relative form* whose value is to be expressed, and the coats the *equivalent form* whose intervention allows the value of the linen to be expressed. Within this system, the coats therefore represent the value of the linen;[3] they are its economic signifier, the commodity which expresses its value in the material terms of equivalence. In the following account, it is the coats which *have* a symbolic value:

> *For instance, forty yards of linen are 'worth' – what? Two coats. Because the commodity coat here plays the part of equivalent, because the use-value coat counts as the embodiment of value* vis-à-vis *the linen, a definite number of coats is sufficient to express a definite quantity of value in the linen. Two coats can therefore express the magnitude of value of forty yards of linen, but they can never express the magnitude of their own value. (Marx, 1976, pp. 147–8)*

The equivalent (commodity B), which has no value of its own, represents the linen (commodity A) and becomes 'a mirror' (p. 144) for its value: 'By means of the value-relation, therefore, the natural form of commodity B becomes the value-form of commodity A, in other words the physical body of commodity B becomes a mirror for the value of commodity A' (p. 144). Basically, the unity between A and its reflection (which appears in the quantitative form of units of value: two coats) constitutes an economic sign (signifier + signified). In a sense, the arithmetical sign '+' marks the unity of the economic sign, whilst the A/B opposition marks the 'contrast' between signifier and signified.

But the equivalent is not simply a neutral reflection of object A; it represents that object by using determinate signs belonging to a particular system and transcribes it in terms of quantities of value, which are expressed here as coats. The coat in question thus becomes what might be termed a civilized form of linen; it is invested with the entire symbolic system which it represents. In the eyes of A, it becomes the representative of the symbolic order itself:

> *the coat cannot represent value towards the linen unless value, for the latter, simultaneously assumes the form of a coat. An individual, A, for instance, cannot be 'your majesty' to another individual, B, unless majesty in B's eyes assumes the physical shape of A, and, moreover, changes facial features, hair and many other things, with every new 'father of his people'. (p. 143)*

When the coat is invested with the role of equivalent, it is:

> *a thing in which value is manifested, or which represents value in its tangible natural form. Yet the coat itself, the physical aspect of the coat-commodity, is purely a use-value. A coat as such no more expresses value than does the first piece of linen we come across. This proves only that, within its value-relation to the linen, the coat signifies more than it does outside it, just as some men count for more when inside a gold-braided uniform than they do otherwise. (pp. 142–3)*[4]

It is because it can, when abstracted from its natural form, enter into relations not only with the linen but with every other object belonging to the same conventional system of equivalents, that it is like an important figure wearing a gold-braided uniform. Marx develops this point when he moves from the simple form of value to its total form and shows that a single signifier (20 yards of linen for example) can correspond to a range of interchangeable things signified: one coat, ten pounds of tea and forty pounds of coffee are all equivalent to twenty yards of linen. It is then possible to move on to monetary forms of equivalence.

We have approached the question of the socialization of human labour by looking at the sphere in which its products circulate, because the equivalence of products is both obvious and general in that sphere and because this is the traditional approach to the question of the commodity. But we must now pick up the thread of our earlier discussion and look at the exchanges that take place within production itself. In terms of the subject we are dealing with, this means taking up the question of the elaboration of norms for the utilization of labour-power; this is a more complex question because monetary equivalents to dead labour cannot represent living labour in any direct way.

Although we did not go into the issue in any great detail, we have already seen that the history of the earliest practical structures of production reveals successive forms of the socialization of labour and of the imposition of norms.

The table system synchronized tasks on a small scale and made individual tasks equivalent to others. It can be seen as a mechanism for inscribing productive functions within the time of the process of the valorization of capital. Each task was identified and isolated; it had to be performed as part of an externally imposed sequence which expressed the rhythm of collective labour. The link between each specific task and the time allotted for it (and the time allotted for each task was the same because operations were carried out synchronically) gave living labour an abstract meaning. The mechanized assembly line introduced a whole new dimension to the equivalence of tasks, primarily because it allowed the flow of production to be controlled from the outside; the flow of production became an expression of the machine-system and norms were established by forces beyond the collective worker's control. The most common and most socialized structures do not, however, involve the mechanical imposition of oppressive norms. They tend, on the contrary, to individualize each task and to describe it in detail.

What does the implementation of the norm mean at the level of the individual work station? The range of standards used in a clothing factory making brassières provides one answer. The job-description sheet (*Pratiques et folies*) relates to a reputedly simple task: assembling pre-sewn bras. The woman worker is given a job-description sheet so that she can evaluate the extent to which her output matches the norm (100%). The method used to establish the norm is the most common of all: MTM [Methods Time Measurement]. The time unit is short and abstract (1/100,000 hours, or 1/27 second). The whole task is broken down into seventeen operations, each of which is clearly identified:

1. Take batch of 48 bras from box and place on table; 2. Open box, untie knot; 3. Arrange work; 4. Take left cup and place under presser-foot; 5. Take right cup and overlap slightly; 6. Position whole garment; 7. Sew cups together; 8. Remove from presser-foot; 9. Pick up scissors; 10. Cut threads, one bra at a time; 11. Stack batch of 48 bras; 12. Cut tag from ticket and stick on work sheet; 13. Write works' number on tag in box matching ticket (in case of faulty work); 14. Take elastic band;

15. Fit elastic band; 16. Tie up batch of 48 bras; 17. Lay aside. (1981, pp. 98–9)

Each operation is given a time-value, and the sum of the seventeen time-values gives the basic time needed to produce one article (306/100,000 hour). This is the basic time for the operation. Extra time is allowed for variable factors such as changing cotton or spools, mechanical breakdowns, breaks (twenty-five minutes a day), going to the toilet, and minor errors in handling. The basic time is thus increased by 23%. The norm is set at 370 time-units per bra, or 1,776 time-units per batch of forty-eight. The norm is therefore 50.67 batches (2,432 articles) per nine-hour day.

The job description may seem lengthy, but it is in fact very brief if we recall that, officially, it 'contains' a woman's entire working day. Everything centres on the relationship between activities which, even though they take a stereotypical form, are instantaneous, specific and concrete, and quota-times measured in units which are abstract, universal and extremely small.

Just like the 'contrast' between the relative and equivalent forms of the commodity, the establishment of a term-for-term correspondence between elements of concrete tasks and abstract time-quotas presupposes the refinement and generalization of the principles of identification and equivalence which, as we have seen, were already implicit in the table system of the age of manufacture:

 A principle of identification: the entire labour process is broken down into a series of technically articulated operations, such as pre-sewing bra cups. Operations are then broken down into a series of tasks (seventeen, in this case), and each task is reduced to a series of simple movements ('arm extended, hand in prone position'). The analysis moves from the general to the particular, and an abstract model of the operation can therefore be built up by adding together the normal time-quotas for the work station.

 A principle of equivalence: when fragmented and broken down into molecules of elementary activities, concrete labour has no physiognomy of its own. The abstract model that is built up represents human labour in general, and the MTM system can therefore establish universal equivalents which are applicable to all branches of industry.

A principle of identification and a principle of equivalence: these methods of establishing norms are in fact no more than a generalized form of the technical mechanisms which were once used to synchronize collective labour on a small scale (the table system and the mechanized line) by establishing a rigid flow of production between work stations. But in this case, the normative principle is not based upon a technical mechanism: the norm appears to be universal, 'scientific' and natural. It is in reality no more than a particular combination of elements providing a basic vocabulary that allows concrete movements to be translated into units of intensity of labour (intensity of labour is the common element in all these elementary calculations, and it is therefore also common to all the practical applications to which quota-systems can be put). Thanks to that vocabulary, the labour process can be incorporated into the abstract movement of the valorization of capital at every level. The translation of actions which are instantaneous (inscribed in time), unique and personalized (and therefore concrete) into quantitative units of abstract time which imply a system of equivalence applicable to all individuals and all activities is obviously a decisive moment in calculating how value can be realized in the form of concrete labour. The subtle inclusion of concrete labour within the time of capital and value is an essential precondition for its further normalization.

And 'subtle' is the appropriate word, as this is primarily a matter of cunning and patience. In 1932, Thomas W. Mitchell admitted that the attitude of the personnel in a given factory or industry might make it necessary to delay research into the determination and application of operating standards until after the introduction of other elements of the system. To support his argument, he cited the experience of Carl C. Barth, who spent four years organizing the Pullman Company without making a single time-study. Even when conditions were right, no attempt should be made to introduce standards into all departments at the same time; they should be introduced in only one sector, preferably one where tasks had already been mechanized, and they should apply to only a small number of workers.[5] It was in the employer's interests to train workers to the point where standard conditions became normal conditions, to the point where the workers were convinced that standards were a good thing and were convinced of management's honesty.

It was in 1880 that Taylor introduced time-study methods at the

Midvale Steel Company. The principle was simple: a small number of skilled workers were studied and the time they took to perform various operations was measured and analysed. Not many stop-watch operations were required; indeed, according to Babcock (1928, p. 160), the longer the operation, the fewer observations needed to be made. An operation taking five minutes required ten observations; an operation taking two minutes required fifteen observations, and one taking one minute, thirty observations. Operations which took half a minute or less required at least sixty studies.

The purpose of timing short operations is obvious; it meant that tasks could be broken down and that every component element could be studied. The study of motion represented a further step towards the analytic evaluation of work, especially when the cinematographic methods developed by Gilbreth from 1910 onwards became available. A synthetic picture of the operations carried out by different individuals meant that it was possible to establish an optimal form for every motion. Obviously, the purpose of all these studies was not to arrive at a description of the movements of a skilled worker, but to establish norms and forms. According to Taylor, the most important element in scientific management was the idea of the task: each worker's task was set at least a day in advance and, in most cases, the worker was given a full set of instructions describing his task in detail and indicating how he should set about it. The implementation of this goal ('the third principle of "Scientific Management" ') was the mission of the planning department, its prototype being the bureaucratic apparatus dreamed up at the Bethlehem Steel Company to plan down to the last detail the activities of 600 ore-shovellers.[6] Supervising and controlling the workforce at a distance (in both spatial and temporal terms) obviously meant that data had to be collected and collated by a planning office, a 'general organization' office (which also had the task of ensuring that shop-floor activities were 'balanced') and by 'production records' departments using Gantt charts or the methods pioneered by the Thomson and Lichter Company to produce chart progress.

Time-study was then, as Mitchell implies, merely a 'cog' in a much more complex machine. Time-studies themselves were carried out at two levels. At a 'distal' level, teams of observers armed with stop-watches were sent into the workshop along with 'instructors' who trained the operatives. At a 'proximal' level, time-study officers recorded and collated the data so as to give the factory a memory. Norms for tasks could thus be established on the basis of elementary time-studies.[7] Most of the 'methods' used to predetermine time-quotas derive from similar practices: the MTA method, the Work Factor method developed by J. H. Quick and his colleagues and marketed by the Work Factor Company, and the method used and sold by General Electric. The best known, however, is Methods Time Measurement (MTM), which was developed by Maygnard, Stegmerten and Schwab.[8]

The practical and psychological advantage of predetermining time-quotas ('time-study without a stop-watch') is obvious. In the most favourable cases, it was possible to establish operating standards which could even predict and quantify deviations from the norm; it was also possible to arrive at 'laws' (Taylor) or even 'algebraic formulae' (Babcock) which provided for every possible situation which might arise given variable working conditions, as when working with machines. Standards could be most easily established in cases where human labour was geared to machines which were not highly automated. According to Babcock, human nature was such that – given a certain number of averagely skilled workers, identical standard conditions and an identical sequence of elementary operations – every worker would inevitably perform the same actions and would complete his work within a standard period of time. Machines therefore seemed to be the ideal instrument for the establishment of standards, and interest inevitably shifted to the possibilities they opened up rather than manual operations themselves. As early as 1919, D. W. Merrick, who took his inspiration from Taylor, began to suggest that it was possible to establish both unit-times and absolute times for any operation carried out by a machine, and to argue that any manufacturer of standard material should be able to provide his customers with a table of standard times similar to a table of interest rates. He might have added that such a table would also have been very similar to the table of the consumption of labour-power.

The relationship between machines and standardized tasks has one further effect: machines encourage the use of stereotypical movements, but they also emphasize differences between individuals by giving them an immediately visible and quantitative form. The calibration of individuals goes hand in hand with the normalization of movement.

Taylorism has always been deeply imbued with an adaptational approach. It can be seen, in crude form, in the 'historic' interventions from which Taylor's doctrines emerged, in his profile of the 'stupid and phlegmatic' pig-iron handler, and in the tests he used to select the women he employed to check ball-bearings for bicycles (Taylor, 1914, pp. 89–90).[9]

Psychotechnical methods and individual psychology obviously contributed greatly to the development of forms of selection and methods of identifying useful capabilities. In 1920, Ford assigned individuals to the tasks to which they were thought to be best suited on the basis of 7,800 individual job-profile sheets. Propaganda issued by the Ford Motor Company emphasized the social benefits of the utilitarian identification of even limited skills (everyone stood the same chance; 9,500 'sub-standard men' who were handicapped in some way were able to become or remain Fordmen).[10] As one might imagine, this kind of investigation can give rise to very hostile reactions, as at the Renault plant in Flins:

> They dissect you 'scientifically', label you, calibrate you, gauge you . . .
> It starts with a home visit, and then there's the 'medical' . . . You
> become so many points . . . Good biceps: 20 points; average intelligence:
> 11 points; you know a lot: 26 points. All the points are added up, and
> they use them to select men, to decide which class or category to put them
> in, and to decide which job they can do most productively. Yes, the
> machines get points too! When a man has been duly calibrated, he has
> to adapt perfectly to a machine which dominates him with all its modern
> might. (La Vie ouvrière, 1955)

The worker's identity tends to be absorbed into the machine-system. Two points should, however, be stressed here.

      1. The widespread view to the contrary notwithstanding, the founders of 'Scientific Management' did not overlook the importance of the 'human factor'. Many publications bear witness to their attempts to control attitudes, feelings and modes of behaviour and to adapt them to the task in hand. In an article published under the auspices of the Taylor Society, Orway Tead, for example, recommends that newly recruited workers should be given 'personal interviews' and should undergo 'general intelligence tests' and 'special ability tests'; they should also be tested for 'personality, character and temperament'.[11] The techniques used to determine the psycho-affective disposition of future operatives were discussed during a meeting of the Taylor Society in New York in

December 1928.[12] They relate to the broader psycho-sociological element in Scientific Management (and similar techniques), a point to which we shall return later.

2. The psychotechnical methods used for the Taylorist selection of men were primarily a means of ensuring the preventive and 'gentle' elimination of the weak. When competition was fierce, as when Taylorism was suddenly introduced at Renault in 1908, 'natural selection' operated in a much less progressive manner.[13]

The establishment of norms for tasks and the calibration of men were essential elements in the wage-system recommended by Taylor. Under the differential piece-rate system, standard times for individual tasks were established by a special department responsible for setting basic wage rates, and they were used to define 'a fair day's work'. The introduction of individual standards allowed management to establish a scale of positive and negative sanctions which related to 'individual efficiency' and which were not directly proportional to the quantity of work performed (as had been the case with simpler forms of the piece-rate system and in wage-bargaining systems). This has to be understood against the background of what Cottereau (in Poulot, 1980, p. 73) describes as 'a permanent battle between the bosses, who wanted to stimulate productivity, and the workers, whose counter-offensives took the form of soldiering'.[14] That was the real issue.

First of all, this system differs from worker–shareholder systems (worker–shareholder schemes, profit-sharing or Christmas boxes which are paid when the company is successful) and from systems which pay bonuses purely for regular attendance at work (as at Westinghouse). It is not designed to win the workers' collective loyalty.

Nor are norms established by a bargaining procedure (as they were under the guild system, and as they were under most of the productivity schemes that were introduced on a more or less contractual basis in traditional factories managed on the 'initiative and incentive' system).

Taylor sums up the principles behind his method and the results it can be expected to produce by claiming that wages should be paid on an individual basis, and not on the basis of functions; wage rates should be based upon hard facts, not assumptions, and that presupposes acurate information (to be obtained by a central office). Wages paid on the basis of hard facts improve the quality of the workforce, allow workers to earn high wages, and do away with the need for petty discipline. Finally, he claims that his system will convince workers and management that their interests are the same, and will promote co-operation between them.

Inevitably, one begins to wonder whether the high wages recommended by Taylor were an effect of the introduction of Standard Times or, as Heron (1975, p. 227) suggests, an essential precondition for their implementation and a means of 'buying social peace' by perfecting 'a system of paying wages that were significantly higher than those paid elsewhere and of directly linking individual productivity to the super-wages paid at the employer's discretion'.[15]

The practice of paying high individual wages was implemented in Ford factories from 1913 onwards.[16] In combination with the stultifying effects of the technical structures, it produced the consenting workforce which allowed Henry Ford to display a haughty contempt for union organizations:

> *The experience of the Ford industries with the working man has been entirely satisfactory, both in the United States and abroad. We have no antagonism to unions, but we participate in no arrangements with either employee or employer organizations. The wages paid are always higher than any reasonable union could think of demanding and the hours of work are always shorter . . . Of course radical agitators have tried to stir up trouble now and again, but the men mostly regarded them as human oddities and their interest in them has been the same sort of interest they would have in a four-legged man.* (Ford, 1923, p. 262)

The text is interesting in more than one respect, and it underlines the fact that the issue of 'social peace' was central to the structures of Taylorism and Fordism. Taylor never stopped insisting that this was so and, until a few years before his death, this remained the central kernel of his doctrine: 'In its essence, scientific management involves a complete mental revolution on the part of the working man . . . This is the essence of scientific management, this great mental revolution' (Taylor, 1911, p. 27). In a sense, Hyacinthe Dubreuil grasps this point when he extols the 'extraordinary mental freedom' that results from the passive acceptance of constraints. This is how he describes one worker at Ford:

> *After working for twelve seconds at a job which probably involved all he knew, the Negro held up the part he was working on in his pliers,*

showing his white teeth in a broad grin . . . standing there between the
furnace and the presses, he was like a king in his own little realm, and
he experienced more joy than one would have thought it possible to find
beneath his black skin. (1929, p. 189)

Dubreuil, whom one might not have expected to display such insights,
has grasped the truth that the Ford worker is, in a sense, a king in a
miniature kingdom shaped by the constraints that are imposed upon
him.[17] Within this narrow and apparently non-intentional framework,
he can express his personality by inventing minor strategies to economize
on movement and to control both his productive body and his thoughts:

The disadvantage is that this is a tied work station: the rhythm of my
movements is strictly determined by the movement of the overhead hooks.
When I was on a bonus, I had my own little tactics to make the time
pass; I'd speed up the work when I started, slow down before and after
mealtimes, to give myself time to digest, and set myself peak rates to
break the monotony. Even though it was hard working on chairs, I'd
got used to the fact that a worker is relatively independent of his work-
bench . . . 'Right, another two, then I'll have a cigarette and a minute's
break'. That's not possible here; the speed of the line makes no
concessions. But then it becomes mechanical, like a habit, and you
rediscover a certain freedom . . . I let my mind wander, with just part
of my brain watching for faults in the paintwork. (Linhart, 1978,
p. 49)

Assembly-line work, bonuses, productivity bonuses . . . We are now
in a position to summarize the most significant structures we have
mentioned:

      With the table system of the age of manufacture, a norm was
set for each woman by the rhythm of a small collective, which was itself
subject to disciplinary constraints; the norm was set by outside forces.

      With the mechanized assembly line, the norm is directly
imposed by a mechanism which 'makes no concessions'. Once again, it
is imposed by outside forces. Each worker initially relates to the norm
on the basis of his or her relationship with the flow of production; the
norm appears to be technical and impersonal, and its internalization takes
the form of a learning process which is at once mechanical, instrumental
and desubjectivized.

With bonus schemes or productivity-based systems, the implementation of norms does not necessarily take the physical form of the collectivization of tasks. It is mediated by a general system of equivalents to which the operative does not have the key. But he does have a certain amount of room for manoeuvre, and he is 'his own boss', if only in that he has room to manoeuvre at the level of his own efficiency, at the level of a personal attitude which is not predetermined, as in assembly-line work; the operative therefore lives his relationship with the norm on a permanent basis. This has two implications. On the one hand, he is no longer a mere instrument of a structure; on the other, he is, in subjective terms, more strictly subordinate to it than ever, as he is the necessary agent of the practical implementation of norms for his task. This goes beyond the work station itself, and it is not surprising that the most orthodox forms of Taylorism should have rapidly given rise to innovations which were simultaneously discovered by currents which claimed to be breaking with the Taylorist instrumentalization of human beings.[18] When constraints are both rigid and accepted, it is obviously in management's interests to convince the workers that they too should take a utilitarian view of their own bodies and make efforts to economize on living labour. Taylor insisted that the workforce should co-operate in all possible ways, and would tolerate no opposition:

> There is hardly a single act or piece of work done by any workman in the shop which is not preceded and followed by some act on the part of one of the men in the management . . . and under this intimate, close personal co-operation it becomes practically impossible to have a serious quarrel . . . So I think that scientific management can be justly and truthfully characterized as management in which harmony is the rule rather than discord. (1914, pp. 44–5)

In that sense, Taylorism is at once a precursor of the human relations movement and an heir to the entire 'sharing' tradition which had begun to take shape fifty years earlier in Europe.

CHAPTER SEVEN

SHARING?

There was a fire here in the factory. I could see the
flames spreading, and I went to collect my belongings;
they were in my drawer up there on the first floor . . .
my overall, my personal things . . . There were flames
everywhere in the entrance . . . People were saying,
'She must be mad', but I thought to myself, 'I know
my way around the factory; perhaps I'll manage to get
out!' I could see the flames . . . Another time, I went
into the entrance lobby, and there were lots of people
I didn't know. I went from one person to the next,
saying, 'Let me in! I work for Chaix!' No one would
listen to me, and people were giving me funny looks.
There were more and more people, and finally I woke
up.
Denise, 1979 (For four years, she was involved in the
occupation of the print works founded by Alban Chaix.
The occupation was an attempt to prevent its closure.
Chaix was a founder member and secretary of the
Société pour la Participation du Personnel aux
Bénéfices, the organization set up to promote employee
share-owning schemes in 1879.)

The idea of reducing manifestations of a basic conflict by partly
linking wage increases to profits is certainly not new. In France,
it has a long history. It has its roots in the imagination of a few
employers who were initially inspired by the idea of a social utopia, and
then by a realization as to where their real interests lay. In 1859, Godin
Lemaire, a manufacturer of heating equipment, founded the Familistère
de Guise, which the *Bulletin de Participation* (1879, No. 1, p. 87)

described as 'a palace for the families of between 350 and 450 workers'. The Familistère was based upon the principle of mutual exchange between the community and its members;[1] profit-sharing, which was introduced in 1877, was a logical extension of that principle. As early as 1842, Leclaire, the owner of a paint factory who was to become mayor of Herblay under the Second Empire,[2] established a form of employer–employee association, and the example he set was soon followed by Etablissements Laroche Joubert in 1843; the Société des Chemins de Fer d'Orléans, 1844; Sociétés Steinheil, 1847; Thünen, 1847; de Berny, 1848; and the Compagnie Générale d'Assurances in 1850. Profit-sharing was also a working-class dream which gave rise to the many Worker–Producer Associations established in various trades. Whilst these experiments enjoyed a certain official support (Leclaire succeeded in passing his scheme off as 'the finest flowering of social Napoleonism'), it was really during the intensely political period leading up to the Commune that they became a subject for debate. In the years that followed the Commune, such major figures as Levasseur, Michel Chevalier and Courcelle Seneuil began to lend their support. By 1873, employers who were in favour of profit-sharing had begun to gather round the printer Alban Chaix; in 1879 they formed an association headed by Charles Robert, a Conseilleur d'Etat and the director of the Union insurance company. They published a bulletin and founded what was to become the Musée Social. The original members represented a variety of industries, most of them employing a core of craft-workers (five printers, one musical-instrument maker) or clerical workers (four insurance companies, one bookshop and one department store).

As we have already noted, the primary and explicit aim of 'profit-sharing' was to ensure that wage-earners remained loyal to the company. It was also designed to overcome resistance and to do away with apathy.[3] As Robert Charles (*Bulletin de Participation*, 1915, p. 115) remarked, there was something about the system which moulded workers' mentalities without any apparent constraints and which turned them into something resembling peasant small-holders: 'Instead of saving himself time and effort, the participant worker is prepared to give his all, to give "maximal utility", as they say in industry.' In more general terms, profit-sharing had a moralizing effect and encouraged the habit of saving. The *Bulletin de Participation* for 1880 contains a report on a study of the use made of the sums of money redistributed by the Maison Redoubly (formerly Leclaire). Fifty-eight of the 140 workers interviewed said that they had invested the money, and twenty-two said that they had used it to help needy relatives. The author concludes (p. 99): 'I trust that these examples will make it clear that workmen are far from being as perverted and ignorant as certain people would like to believe.' Examples of participant workers who denounced lazy comrades or drunkards and who refused to have anything to do with them were also cited. The third and final objective was the most obvious of all: preventing strikes. Leclaire himself (*Bulletin de Participation*, 1880, p. 99) could claim to have achieved 'marvellous' results at this level: 'The workers were so diligent that there was simply no more absenteeism on Mondays; it is said that they even worked on 24 February 1848, and even during the June days they did not stop work until the shooting began.' In 1870, Duval, the editor of *L'Economiste français*, proposed the establishment of a society to study ways of preventing strikes; profit-sharing was one of its main recommendations. It is therefore not surprising to find that most profit-sharing schemes had rules stipulating that workers who absented themselves from work without good cause would lose all benefits owed to them. The system was not ineffective.[4]

The most lively debates around these experiments concerned, on the one hand, the restrictions to be placed on the power of the workers (and here the proponents of profit-sharing went to great lengths to assert the rights of the employer; in a lecture given at the Sorbonne in 1869, Charles Robert insisted that 'The maintenance of order, I would even say the dictatorship of the employer, is a basic principle of profit-sharing; the involvement of workers in management would spell anarchy and ruin') and, on the other, the limitations of profit-sharing itself. Doubts were expressed as to the possibility of extending it to large factories with a high level of capital investment. It is a fact that, with the exception of the Compagnie Fives in Lille, profit-sharing in France was restricted to modest companies where the 'family atmosphere' had more to do with personal relations with the employer than with any feeling of belonging to a firm.

In Great Britain,[5] the mine-owners Henry and Archibald Briggs found themselves in difficulty because of the miners' organizational ability (sixty-eight weeks of strikes over a period of ten years) and because of the climate of class hatred that had developed in the Whitwood area of the West Riding of Yorkshire.[6] They were bold enough to introduce the scheme described in the Company Prospectus for 1864:

> *Whenever the divisible profits accruing from the business shall (after the usual reservation for redemption of capital and other legitimate allowances) exceed ten per cent on the capital embarked, all those employed by the Company, whether as managers or agents at fixed salaries, shall receive one half of such excess profit as a bonus, to be distributed amongst them.* (cited by S. Taylor, 1884, p. 118)

The scheme immediately had the desired results. The miners worked harder, and 'stoppages of work for frivolous reasons' ceased. The workforce handled equipment more carefully, and a former leading figure in the 1858 strike told a commission of inquiry held ten years later that 'It was a very common expression when picking up a large nail to say, "This is so much bonus saved".' A second supporter of the scheme said, 'I believe that in this system we have found a remedy for strikes and lockouts. The feeling is quite altered.' The dismissal of miners who 'drank their bonuses' was greeted with general approval. Torft, a miner who became a martyr to the cause by defending profit-sharing – alone – during a union meeting in which he was hit by a clod of earth ('It did not hurt me, only my feelings were hurt'), summed up the situation: 'The system has done a vast amount of good; it has destroyed a vast amount of ill-feeling, and I have not the slightest doubt that by perseverance and so forth it will have the effect of bringing the whole of the men round to our side' (cited by S. Taylor, pp. 137–8).

But the clod of earth which hurt Torft's feelings so badly was merely a harbinger of setbacks to come. After a period of super-profits due to the intensification of labour, the price of coal fell in 1874. A long and hard-fought strike put an end to nine years of social peace when the management tried to cut bonuses so as to avoid having to pay too great a wage increase. As we know from the correspondence between Henry and Archibald Briggs and the Association for the Social Sciences and from the Royal Commission of Inquiry into Trades Unions, the Whitwood experiment aroused a great deal of interest and discussion. It was no accident that it should have taken place in the mining industry, in other words in a large-scale industry which was scarcely mechanized. Capital was virtually dependent upon traditional working-class organizations, and it was only by using the 'carrot-and-stick' method that labour could be intensified.

The fairer distribution of wealth and the integration of working-class organizations into the political system were in fact crucial issues at a time when the unions, which had for a long time been reduced to clandestine activities, were beginning to form powerful 'amalgamated' unions modelled on the Amalgamated Society of Engineers (founded in 1852) and when the revolutionary current was beginning to attract a far from negligible audience.[7]

Developments were in fact contradictory. On the one hand, the power of the unions grew as their membership increased (450,000 unionists were represented by the 1877 Leicester Conference), as they came to control more and more associations (friendly societies, cooperatives, etc.) and as a minority revolutionary current emerged. On the other hand, the unions became increasingly integrated into the system at an ideological level as a stricter delegate system strengthened the hand of the union bureaucracy and as unions gained institutional representation in the House of Commons from 1875 onwards.

Whilst men like Stirling were still fighting a rearguard battle to defend social conservatism, the Leicester Conference of 1877 revealed the extent to which the unions had been integrated.[8] It opened with a report from the Parliamentary Commission (which stressed that the nation's industries were in a healthy state, that workers were displaying a marked tendency to use peaceful methods, and ended by calling for a fairer distribution of wealth) and with Merrick's inaugural address. Merrick took up the same themes, and insisted on the need for government arbitration in industrial disputes. A Member of Parliament then described a series of forthcoming Bills. After a debate and a vote, Brassey, a Member of Parliament and a major industrialist, congratulated the unions on their attitude and their healthy tendencies, and stated that unionism answered one of English society's needs. The Conference voted for direct union representation in Parliament. *The Times* (12 April 1877) commented that the tone of the discussions was always moderate, that no bitterness against the employers was expressed and that no invective against society was heard.

The introduction of profit-sharing and of worker–shareowner schemes in Great Britain during the last quarter of the nineteenth century has to be seen against this background. At the beginning of the twentieth century, these schemes were in use in little more than a hundred companies, but they were all large concerns (ship-building, textiles, chemicals).[9] The most widespread system involved the issue of shares to workers.

In Germany at the turn of the century, profit-sharing schemes were similarly concentrated on a few large companies. The most famous example was the Carl Zeiss Foundation, which then employed between 4,000 and 4,500 workers at its factory-city in Jena. The company, which employed a large, concentrated and well-qualified workforce, had for decades been in the forefront of social paternalism. As early as 1875 (nine years before the relevant legislation was introduced), its workers enjoyed a health insurance scheme, and in 1888 invalidity and old age pensions were introduced. The factory had its own savings bank, a building society and a free medical service. When Auerbach (1906) visited Jena in 1903, he found that the 'House of the People' ('the pearl of Jena') had a reading room, a library (which lent out 100,000 books a year), a trade school, a concert hall, lecture rooms, a room for art exhibitions and a science museum. The foundation subsidized a children's home, a society for providing health care in the home, and a university. It was in short an immense structure which was designed to produce and control social life, just as the factory produced its own electricity and machinery.[10]

In 1896, Abbe, who owned the factory, turned it into the Carl Zeiss Foundation, which was administered by the Grand Duchy. The Duchy appointed a management committee selected from the supervisory staff, it organized the redistribution of profits between owners and workers, enforced the application of the law, and ensured that the workers carried out their duties properly. High wages were paid, usually on a piece-rate basis. In this context, profit-sharing 'has a very important function. It is a barometer which shows whether or not piece-rates have been correctly set . . . and indicates the need to alter them when they are too high' (Auerbach, 1906, p. 87). These measures were in fact part of a much broader plan (which in a sense anticipates the rationalization movement of the period 1920–30), including an eight-hour day, the organization of rest periods and attempts to organize recreation. From that point of view, Abbe's social ideas were similar to those of Henry Ford, at least in so far as they were an expression of a rationalization project which affected life both inside and outside the factory.[11]

The profit-sharing scheme introduced by Ford in Detroit in 1913 was not in itself innovatory, as similar practices were already widespread in the United States, especially in big firms where they took the form of either a share distribution or a direct redistribution of profits. In 1909, the United Steel Corporation issued over 30,000 shares to its employees (together with a very complex set of rules defining the status of worker–shareholders); and in 1916 Kodak redistributed profits of over $1 million. Information on these schemes is not difficult to come by in that in 1917 the Department of Labor published an enormous study of what had long been seen as a major industrial and social question.[12]

The novel feature about the Ford scheme was that it represented a large rise in income; in theory, it was possible for workers to double their wages. It also involved the extensive use of individual criteria for eligibility. According to the *Bulletin de Participation*:

Once members have been selected for the scheme, they become the Company's first-class workers. Then there are two lower classes of workers who cannot be admitted to the scheme until more favourable information has been received about them. Any worker at Ford who has not been included in the first class knows that, once he has put his life in satisfactory order, he too will have a share in the Company's profits.
(1917, p. 161)

Release from purgatory implied acceptance of company interference in one's private life, and conformity to criteria laid down by the company. Such is the meaning of the circular issued to the personnel when the system was introduced: the company allocated workers a share of its profits to allow them to take care of their future needs and those of their families. Workers were expected to improve their living conditions, to keep their houses clean and comfortable and to ensure that they lived in a healthy, well-ventilated and well-lit environment.

In practice, about one hundred investigators were responsible for collecting information about the morality, respectability, habits and opinions of applicants over a period of several years.[13] In other words, a Fordman was eligible for membership of the profit-sharing scheme when, rather than passively accepting the constraints imposed on him, he became a split personality who exercised strict control over his way of life, his relations with others and even over his own thoughts, and who did everything to ensure that his social individuality corresponded to what the company expected it to be. Being a mere instrument of a machine-system, he was, according to Merrheim (1913), 'an automaton with no will-power, unable to think or to take any initiative . . . producing goods with the regularity of a steel automaton'. By making it obvious that he had internalized the constraints imposed upon him, and by adopting the childlike tactic of identifying his own objectives with those of the company, he could in fact elude some of the constraints, win the management's trust and even negotiate a certain margin of autonomy.

The affective mechanism behind this method of training, which is fairly universal, had already been identified by Taylor, who stressed that a 'stupid' worker and his mentor form a sort of dyad; being unable to internalize knowledge and rules, the worker is bound to his trainer by a profound affective bond which results in 'friendship' and 'cordiality'; it is as though his desire to identify with his trainer, and perhaps even to share in his enjoyment of power (at the expense of his own productive body), provided a basis for the extension of managerial functions, for the worker's consent to the system and for the development of a 'company spirit'.

These preoccupations explain the series of reports published under the auspices of the Taylor Society during the war-production years (Wolf, 1915; Valentine, 1915, 1916; Person, 1917; and Cooke, 1917).[14] They are all concerned with the moral basis of 'consent', and they all recommend that management strategies should systematically take subjective conditions into account. Valentine, for example, argues that before a decision is actually taken, consent for its implementation must be obtained on the grounds that the age of coercion and non-consenting obedience is over.

From the late 1920s onwards, a new current began to imbue the field of psychology with the preoccupations of 'Scientific Management'. As Bingham (1928, p. 87) points out, certain psychologists began to participate in the activities of the Taylor Society and the American Management Association, and articles on industrial psychology began to appear in the publications of the American Psychological Association.[15] The most important development was the establishment of the Personnel

Research Federation, which encouraged management, universities and union organizations to collaborate on research. The initiative came from major companies such as Kodak, General Electric and Western Electric, and it received support from the Engineering Foundation, which encouraged a psychological approach to industrial problems, and especially from the National Research Council and the Social Science Research Council. It published a journal (*The Personnel Journal*) and financed a laboratory at the Carnegie Institute of Technology. The first congress of the International Association for Industrial Relations was held in 1928.

The Personnel Research Federation also became a focus for collaboration between employers' associations and the biggest labour union: the American Federation of Labor (AFL). This development in Taylorism, which tended to encompass the subjective element, was in fact directly related to developments in working-class organizations. This period saw the rise of a form of mass unionism dominated by a powerful and often corrupt bureaucracy which has gone down in history as Gomperism. For a long time the AFL had adopted a defensive and aristocratic position, but in 1912–13 membership was opened up to unskilled workers. Given these conditions, it is not surprising that the neutralization or even the utilization of working-class organizations should have been seen as a *sine qua non* for the development of Taylorism. 'Like Valentine, Cooke stresses the point that profit-sharing is not effective if it is restricted to individuals. He regards it as a collective function' (Bruere, in Société Taylor, 1932, p. 590).[16]

These efforts were not in vain, for although the AFL had denounced Taylorism as 'an inhuman, hideous system' which 'reduces human beings to the status of mere machines' (cited by Friedmann, 1946, p. 260), AFL secretary Gompers agreed to attend a meeting of the Taylor Society in 1925; and, two years later, a union conference in Philadelphia discussed ways to ensure that 'collaboration between employers and workers' would lead to an improvement in production methods. The so-called 'human relations' current developed out of this Taylorist revisionism and related discussions from 1915 onwards.

Oscar Ortsman (1978a, p. 23) rightly notes that, basically, this current did not develop in opposition to Taylorism, and that it was designed to 'give it certain advantages, and to provide the conditions which would allow it to become fully effective'. These conditions related both to the climate inside the factory and to the quality of inter-personal and inter-group relations. The human relations current was, notes Friedmann, a theoretical recognition of the 'moral' dimension to the lived experience of work, and of its practical importance. 'In general terms, no modification of the physical and financial conditions of work will have any predictable or calculable effect if it is not related to the moral and social attitude of the worker' (Friedmann, 1946, p. 128). Hence the distinction between the formal and informal organization of the firm:

> These different forms of organization have their own systems of ideas and beliefs, and a logic of their own. Formal organization is governed by the logic of cost and efficiency. Informal organization obeys the logic of feelings, in other words the system of ideas and beliefs which expresses values specific to human relations between different groups inside the factory. (Mottez, 1966, p. 23)

The early research carried out by Elton Mayo and his team at Western Electric's Hawthorne factory in Chicago in 1927–32 is famous, if not well known (see Roethlisberger and Dikson, 1939). It will be recalled that the research was carried out in an electrical assembly plant, that the women workers involved were volunteers and that it led to two discoveries.[17]

1. Granting significant material benefits (shorter working hours, longer rest periods, the right to talk, free lunches . . .) did not lead to a fall in output. In some cases it actually led to increased output. This observation was not in itself totally original.[18]

2. The second conclusion was more unexpected. The gradual removal of these benefits did not result in a return to the earlier situation. On the contrary, in many cases output continued to rise. The women's reactions to the manipulation of their environment were at once so consistent and so paradoxical that the researchers became intrigued. For example, *any* variation in lighting, good or bad, produced a positive response. The conclusion was inescapable. While the women were producing radios, and while their environment was being manipulated, they were also producing something else; and that 'something else' helped them to produce radios. What had changed was the 'psychological climate' within the group (friendly relations at work and outside the factory) and relations between the group and the hierarchy (the group found itself at the centre of attention and had established contact with the research workers, who presumably had good intentions). The

importance of 'good horizontal and vertical relations' was confirmed some years later when Mayo and his colleagues studied absenteeism in the Californian aircraft industry.

In terms of the practical objectives of the research project, this was an important discovery; at a theoretical level, the notion of good horizontal and vertical relations is obviously somewhat hollow, and if it does have a content, it consists, as Miles (1965) shows, of unspoken assumptions about human nature (cf. Orstman, 1978a, pp. 26–7). Broadly speaking, the assumptions involved are those of the managerial class: individuals have a natural need to belong; they want to be loved and recognized for their true worth; they want to be useful, and if their need to belong is satisfied, they will support the company's objectives. The hierarchy must therefore help each worker to recognize that he or she has a place in the social life of the factory, give him a margin of autonomy and define his conditions of autonomy, and provide material incentives.

These assumptions did in fact provide an adequate basis for interventions into the social life of the factory, or even for attempts to create a social life (transforming a pack of lone wolves into a social group, as Mayo put it). Attempts were made to create 'integrationist' or 'centripetal' currents (Friedmann, 1946, p. 314) and to inspire an *esprit de corps* or a 'company patriotism' capable of checking uncontrolled forms of solidarity. Clubs, leisure associations and sports contests were organized to defuse serious – or potentially serious – forms of conflict.

The reason why conflicts could be defused so harmlessly is because it was assumed that, far from expressing radical contradictions which give rise to other phenomena (including the feeling of belonging to a group or class), relations between groups and classes are based upon conventional rules for social games.[19] And this implies a complete representation of society. Poitou (1972, p. 61) analyses it by looking at the notion of the group, which is central to developments in US psychology: 'Ultimately, there is only one notion behind the various definitions of the group: that of voluntary and co-operative association.' This formulation helps to explain how psychology has been ideologically rooted in the American social formation where 'the myth that the independent small producer is the basis of all social life is still very much alive (Bruno, Pêcheux, Plon and Poitou, 1973). It also allows us to identify the element of mystification – deliberate or otherwise – in these theoretical models. On the one hand,

'It is capital which organizes cooperation, and not the workers themselves. It is capital which brings them together, which organizes their labours; it is the authority of capital which establishes the unit for their collective formation and which subordinates their activities to goals' (Poitou, 1972, p. 106). On the other, 'Workers and the capital which employs them have no interests in common' (Poitou, p. 107).[20]

There is indeed an element of mystification involved, as the intentionality of capital seems to have vanished, leaving behind only the illusion of a collective expression of the personal objectives of the workers. Socialization apparently results from the will of individuals and it can, it would seem, be represented by an economic model in which commodities and services are exchanged by autonomous and utilitarian subjects.[21] The group therefore functions as a co-operative and non-contradictory system which is open to its environment, but it defines itself primarily in relation to itself and to the individual strategies of its members.

The group involved in production, and in capital which is the invisible subject of production, merges in an ambiguous identification with the company, and individuals become almost a miniaturized representation of that company; the utilitarian and autonomous subject of this psycho-sociology is an atom of free enterprise, the Robinson Crusoe of the industrial world and one of the many offspring of *Homo economicus*, the actor-subject of production whom we find in all classical and neoclassical theories. It is this individual whom Taylor addressed in his attempts to persuade the 'average worker' that his conviction – that it was in his best interests to restrict his output – was a mere 'prejudice' and that he should work at an optimal speed in exchange for a 'liberal' increase in wages (Ortsman, 1978a, p. 17). Taylor's average worker has a utilitarian relationship with his own body, a relationship which mirrors capital's expectations. He has every intention of maximizing his income by using the factory as an instrument to mediate his personal goals.

The human relations movement began to take the complexity of his motivations into account. This is the man addressed by Maslow (1954) and by subsequent writers like Johada, Allport and Herzberg (Herzberg, 1971). It is assumed that he has a coherent battery of adaptational needs which can be hierarchically classified and categorized; it would not be difficult to demonstrate that these needs are primarily a reflection of what the factory expects of its workers.[22]

Here we see the contradiction within the corpus of industrial psychology: according to the behaviourist and neobehaviourist tradition which is its primary point of reference (neobehaviourism, for instance, owes a great deal to the work of Skinner), the human psyche is a black box whose workings can be explained only in terms of in-puts and outputs. Skinner, for example, cannot find words harsh enough to condemn psychoanalysis and, more generally, what he calls mentalism; whilst the needs defined by Maslow have nothing to do with speaking subjects.

At the same time, psycho-sociology did infiltrate psychoanalysis and thus gave birth to the ego-psychological model of a subject divided between a rational, active ego which is alloplastic and extroverted, and the remainder of subjectivity, which is more regressive, moulded by the environment or passively adapted to it, which is introverted or autoplastic, and which is motivated by a need to maintain the equilibrium and unicity of its inner world.

The contradiction is in fact no more than apparent, as the 'conflict-free ego sphere' which is grafted on to the Freudian subject and which remodels its entire dynamics is nothing more than a projection on to the individual of the adaptive structuration which these psycho-sociological currents have already attributed to the group.

Poitou demonstrates that a Janus image emerges from the various models proposed for the analysis of groups: the group is structured by a tension between an external system which is extroverted and obedient to the reality principle, and an internal system which tends in regressive fashion to deny the existence of the external system.

We have, then, two pairs of opposites:

1. An external system: production, control over the environment and material goods, hierarchical diversification of status, equitable distribution, action groups and work groups;

2. An internal system: maintenance, affective relations, cohesion, equality of rights, egalitarian distribution, world group (Poitou, 1972, p. 102).

An ideological representation of social life is projected on to a group ideology, which is then projected on to the subject . . . the point is that this adaptational model of the dynamics of the two systems is the dominant model, and it is supported by both social practices and cultural models (a representation of labour, but also one of family roles, for example). In one sense, all significant management doctrines are determined by this model, as we can see from Ortsman's classification of technocratic doctrines (Taylorism, human relations, work enhancement, the 'last technocratic avatar' of Taylorism) and of liberal responses (self-training groups, techniques for organizational development). Ortsman then outlines the various socio-technical currents which attempt to articulate the two essential terms (social and technical) in a coherent fashion. We shall return to this point.

EGO-PSYCHOLOGY: A DISTORTION OF PSYCHOANALYSIS

Bruno, Pêcheux, Plon and Poitou (1973) describe the distortions of psychoanalysis which result from the development of psycho-sociology as follows: 'A system of profound needs is constructed without further elaboration; early repression or frustration then produces a whole range of reinforcement mechanisms' (p. 103). Ego-psychology has a special place here: its influence stems from the fact that, from the outset, it gave rise to an ambitious doctrinal elaboration on the part of its founders (Kris, Loewenstein and especially Hartmann). Their aim was quite simply to revise psycho-analysis and to transform it into 'one of the basic sciences of sociology' (Hartmann, 1958, p. 20), sociology itself being bio-logically based. The revision of psychoanalysis takes the form of introducing a new term into the classic structural 'topography' (Id, Ego and Superego): a 'conflict-free sphere', or a central agency which gradually asserts its power and autonomy as the individual psyche develops in the same way that races develop.[23]

This theoretical construct is supported by a philosophy of consciousness and action, in which the object of psychoanalysis becomes lost in a grand psycho-socio-biological synthesis centred on the idea of adaptation. Desire and fantasies are relegated to the status of the regressive working of the psyche; the dynamic of the subject is destined to transcend or dominate those aspects of the psyche. Ego-psychology tends to ignore anything which might be

(continued over page)

---

able to shed light on social facts (the dialectic between the subject's present position and his individual history; the dialectic between that individual history and social history; the dialectic between the imaginary and the actions of the subject, etc.). The ego is put 'in the first rank', to use Althusser's (1972, p. 316) expression, and sociality (environment, 'conditioning') is placed in the second rank. Ego-psychology in fact relies upon a normative vision of adaptation in which 'instinctual drive-processes' are gradually dominated by 'will-processes' (Hartmann, p. 74) and in which acceptance of a 'social value hierarchy' (p. 75) is a criterion for mental health.

It is interesting to note, as does Clément, that Jacques Lacan's approach to psychoanalysis stems from a radical critique of this deviation:

Jacques Lacan's position derives from a combination of factors which made possible a major reworking of Freud's theories. The starting point can be found in a radical critique of 'American-style' psychoanalysis and of its theory of adaptation. Lacan was one of the first to state in very clear terms that there is a close link between ego-psychology and the 'American way of life'. (Clément, 1973, p. 117)

Lacan (1966, p. 335) attacks ego-psychology on the grounds that it is the 'theology of free enterprise', and Clément rightly stresses that in practice ego-psychology tends to be 'a way of re-educating the subject so as to strengthen the ego's defences against the influence of the drives' (p. 75). One has only to glance at the work of early-twentieth-century American psychologists such as Paton (1922) to see how the normative, productivist and utilitarian aims of ego-psychology can be nourished by a moral puritanism: 'undirected or wishful thinking' is likened to 'autistic thought' and is contrasted with the 'aggressive, directed logical thinking' of the rational subject' (pp. 123–4).

CHAPTER EIGHT

ON ALIENATED LABOUR

'This is your first visit? Well then, it's nothing to be
surprised at. The sun beats on the roof here and the
hot roof-beams make the air dull and heavy.'
Kafka, *The Trial*

This 'conflict-free' subject whose desires and scale of values
correspond so closely to what the company and society need from
him poses no problems. But this subject who is alienated in a
pragmatic reality where desire is reduced to need and where the imaginary
is reduced to being a blind spot in rational thought, and whose relationship
with society is based upon mutual exploitation is of course no more than
a rather sinister fiction. This subject is in fact what remains of the
subjectivity of the producers in representations which bring the individual
and groups to the fore, but in which the productive work of society is
identified with the work of capital.

And in terms of economic thought, this subject has a long history. By
expressing – *grosso modo* – the point of view of merchants and financiers,
the mercantilists elaborated a vision of society in which the world of
artisans and peasants appeared to be alien to the sphere of wealth creation.
The only real subject of the economy was the merchant who made his
fortune outside (or in opposition to) the sphere of production, and whose
capital – 'money which begets money' – increased in trade with distant
countries, in the circuits of the unproductive exchange of value: 'Mercan-

tilist thought is dominated by the principle of compensation, which is merely an economic transposition of the mechanical principle of the conservation of motion' (Bertrand, 1978, p. 10). As Marx notes, the formation of value plays no part in mercantilist thought.[1]

The physiocrats broke with this doctrine. Quesnay (1888, p. 537) states quite clearly that 'trading does not mean producing'. Wealth does not belong exclusively to merchants; it belongs to the kingdom, even if it is identified with the private possessions of the prince and the privileged.[2] Considered in absolute terms, wealth does not originate in the skill of traders or even in the enlightened thought of the despot; its origins lie in nature, as shaped by providence, and men's ability to exploit nature is already inscribed in the properties of the land.[3] For Quesnay:

The principle behind all expenditure and all wealth is the fertility of the land. The land gives the cultivator an advance; he fertilizes the land in order to make it produce more. The only contribution the artisan can make is to shape the few instruments needed to turn the soil, and if there were no artisans, the cultivator could make them himself. Precisely who cultivates the land does not matter; the land must already have produced what he consumes in order to live, and it is not labour which produces his means of subsistence. (p. 533)

The real subject of production is providential nature, and providence requires rich landowners. We have, then, a bipolar vision of society. At one extreme, we have the sterile classes, or the despots and farmers who have been entrusted with 'primary funds',[4] who jointly own the land and govern it with varying degrees of wisdom.[5] Farmers are the real agents of economic functions. It is they who distribute the net product, who return wealth to the land,[6] and who thus ensure that the process of accumulation continues. The *Tableau économique* of 1758 provides an initial account of the process of accumulation by using the mechanical imagery of the day.

At the other extreme, we have the labourers and landless agricultural workers who express and exploit nature's productive properties. As Marx (1969a, p. 51), citing Turgot, notes, the labourer's ability to produce surplus value ('To produce more than he needs to consume in order to continue to exist') is regarded as a 'gift of nature'. Economically and politically (that is, in terms of 'economic government'), the labourer is a non-subject.[7]

On the one hand there are the sterile classes, who are the subjects of an economy governed by natural and universal laws,[8] and who are the true inhabitants (citizens) of the country; on the other there are the productive classes, who are the desubjectivized agents of the production of wealth. Although the mode of thought is feudal, it is obvious that this doctrine expresses capital's view of labour.

The nineteenth century certainly also produced a very different representation of nature. According to this representation, nature is not fertile and sovereign, but at once submissive and dangerous; it is this representation which leads to the constant use made of the Robinson Crusoe myth in the economic literature of the period of the industrial revolution.[9] Political economy had of course known since the time of Adam Smith that only human labour can produce commodity-values. But despite all the great conceptual reworkings of bourgeois economic thought, a distinction was made between the subjects of valorization and the agents of the labour process. That distinction was an intellectual reflection of the complete divorce that separates the world of capital from the world of labour.[10]

> *Political economy proceeds from the fact of private property. It does not explain it. It grasps the* material *process of private property, the process through which it actually passes, in general and abstract formulae, which it then takes as* laws. *It does not comprehend these laws, that is, it does not show how they arise from the nature of private property. Political economy fails to explain the reason for the division between labour and capital, between capital and land.* (Marx, *1975, p. 322*)

The above lines are from the beginning of Marx's comments on 'estranged labour' in the first of the 'Economic and philosophical manuscripts' of 1844. Marx often makes similar critical comments in the works of his maturity. In breaking with the economic thought of his day, Marx was trying to get away from the mercantilist view of the object of economics (for mercantilism, the valorization of capital is a 'fact' which poses no problems other than those of the particular laws that govern it) and to investigate social relations between different economic subjects and different classes. He expresses this ambition in his earliest theoretical writings: 'Up to now we have considered the relationship only from the side of the worker. Later on we shall consider it from the side of the non-worker . . . Let us now consider the relation between this man, who is *alien* to labour and to the workers, and the worker, labour, and the object of labour' (1975, pp. 331, 334). At this point the manuscript that has come down to us breaks off, but we can at least reconstruct the thread of the argument. Marx initially describes the relation with work as a practical relationship between the subjectivity of 'the worker' and that of an 'other' who is alien to labour. It is a practical relationship because 'In the practical, real world, self-estrangement can manifest itself only in the practical, real relationship to other men. The medium through which estrangement progresses is itself a practical one' (1975, p. 331). And Marx's work will be dominated by the analysis of these 'practical media': the relationship between the cycle of capital and the cycle of labour-power; the relationship between the theoretical subjectivities (the capitalist and the wage-earner) whose sociality is expressed in a set of determinate economic conditions.[11]

Alienation is central to the economic relationship; the alienation of labour does not simply mean that some element of the worker's inner world is lost ('the worker places his life in the object' (Marx, 1975, p. 324)) and is appropriated by the owner of the means of production. Activity itself becomes alienated because, if labour is to take on a social meaning,[12] the 'meaning' of its representation must, so to speak, be inverted; rather than being a means of expression for the producer, activity is the moment in which the system in which his work is inscribed becomes a technical and regulatory mechanism that imposes itself on him:

> *The relationship of labour to the* act of production *within* labour . . .
> *is the relationship of the worker to his own activity as something which
> is alien and does not belong to him, activity as passivity, power as
> impotence, procreation as emasculation, the worker's own physical and
> mental energy, his personal life . . . as an activity directed against
> himself, which is independent of him and does not belong to him.* (Marx,
> *1975, p. 327)*

Alienated labour is, then, a socialized activity, a relationship with the 'other', but it is a desubjectivized form of socialization. The actors cannot subjectively come to terms with the social relations implicit in their activities as they have no means of understanding them. We will later attempt to describe this phenomenon more clearly by using the term 'Taylorist dissociation' to refer to the way in which a high degree of objective socialization of labour coexists with the exclusion of the worker's subjectivity from practical socialization.

Marx was well aware of the fact that there is a persecutory and desubjectivizing element in this relationship with the other. He writes:

An immediate consequence of man's estrangement from the product of his labour, his species-being, is the estrangement of man from man. *When man confronts himself, he also confronts* other men. *What is true of man's relationship to his labour, to the product of his labour and to himself, is also true of his relationship to other men, and to the labour and the object of the labour of other men. (1975, pp. 329–30)*[13]

The quotations may appear somewhat long, but we have to respect the letter of the text. And let there be no misunderstanding of the fact that, even though Marx's language is still permeated by Hegelian philosophy, this text represents a new vision of political economy. Marx introduces a 'viewpoint' which had until then been denied any role: that of the subjectivity of the worker.

We know that Marx arrived in Paris in October 1843 to work on the *Franco-German Yearbooks* with Arnold Ruge. In March 1844, he began to move in democratic circles and attended meetings organized by immigrant workers (there was a large German colony in Paris; many of the immigrants were craftsmen who worked as cabinet-makers and carpenters in the Saint-Antoine area[14]). In other words, Marx encountered a politicized proletariat that was becoming conscious of its identity. That Marx assimilated the subjective viewpoint of the workers in whose circles he was moving and that he used it to elaborate a dialectical representation of social relations (alienation of the product; alienation of activity; alienation of the subject as alienation from other men) emerges quite clearly from a comparison between his writings on 'estranged labour' and the statements made by delegates to the Exposition Universelle twenty years later (*Rapport des délégations*, 1867). The object of handicraft labour is marked by 'its true author', who brings it into the world (monumental masons); it 'emerges' from the hands and brain of the worker (roofers and artificial-flower makers); it perpetuates a trace of his 'imagination', of the 'free movement of the creative chisel' (cabinet-makers); it transmits and objectifies some singular and recognizable feature of the 'soul' of the artisan who conceived it (furniture designers).

Production/reproduction: we see here a lasting cultural trait. In metal-working industries, parts which have been badly made are still 'killed', just as they were in the days of Poulot's *sublimes*, and machine-tools are still brought into the world:

Seeing the machine start up is interesting, because everything you have made comes to life . . . What is a machine? An inert heap of metal. It becomes interesting when you can press buttons and see that mass of metal begin to move . . . How can you put it? It's very impressive. (electrician in a machine-tool assembly shop)

This vital relationship obviously tends to be lost in the new industrial order, which makes impersonal physical forces central to the production of life. The creativity of labour takes on the unrecognizable form of a play of mechanical forces:

In Paris you can see factories where everything is finished on the factory floor; everything is driven by steam. There you can see foundries, rolling-mills, stamping machines, engravers, burnishers, silver-platers, gold-platers . . . solderers. (button-makers)

According to the mechanics, 'The steam-engine is the soul of all industry, since it is the steam-engine which gives birth to the motion and force required to drive the countless machines that fill our greatest factories.' Its 'soul' is a reifying machine: 'They are trying to turn man himself into a sort of machine' (shoemakers). The brush-makers spoke of 'living machines' existing in a closed universe where 'exhausting work' made men old at twenty (leather-workers), where the body was worn out and destroyed (nail-makers and masons), and where it was eaten away by toxic substances (wallpaper-printers). What had been destroyed was part of the worker's identity and part of his relationship with the world. Whereas an article made by an artisan was something 'unique', 'beautiful', 'irreplaceable', 'like a mirror' or 'ideal', the triviality and anonymity of 'junk' devalued both the meaning of labour and the identity of its maker. As the leather-workers' delegation put it:

Some of you may have seen the feverish activity which reigns in specialist shops where the worker is no more than an automaton working ten, eleven or twelve hours a day and has no idea of the value of the product he holds in his hands, where he is incapable of remedying the mistakes made by earlier operatives, carries out his skilled task as best he can, and then passes on a product which goes through the hands of ten or

twelve men in a day before it is finished. Anyone who has seen that must,
we say, wonder what effects such a system will have on the future of the
workers. By sacrificing men to products, this system destroys the worker's
spirit of initiative and enterprise; it stupefies him by stunting his physical
development, destroying his mind and, in a word, turning him into a
machine.

The loss of a social element in alienated labour was central to the idea of
reform, or at least to such reformist ideas as could be expressed in the
very restricted context of these statements.[15] 'What is the motive which
forces men into this terrible duel between capital and labour, into a duel
which takes all society's strength?' asked the leather-workers' delegation.
The nail-makers claimed that:

If we go back to 1842, 1844, 1846 or even 1848, we find that masters
and men understood one another and got on well together. That state of
affairs has given way to suspicion and hostility, and it has therefore been
said that masters and men are irreconcilable enemies because today's
masters want to have in a few years what it took our old masters most of
their lives to accumulate.

The precision-instrument makers expressed the view that: 'A co-operative society would do so much to resolve the problem: then, it would be
possible to be both master and man.'

'Being both master and man . . .' We have already had occasion to
mention the many producer-cooperatives that were set up in the 1850s
by workers from many different trades. We have also mentioned their
failure: the experiments ended in bankruptcy or in the creation of new
industrial prisons. At what is perhaps a more fundamental level, attempts
to create a 'worker capitalism' failed because of the power relations
implicit in the capitalist mode of production. If the master or the capitalist
is to own something (labour-power) to which the worker relates and
which he registers in his being (because it concerns both his existence
and his body), society must necessarily be divided into a category of
'masters' and a category of 'men', and classes must be guaranteed to be
naturally watertight. There must be a division into those who relate to
labour-power in the register of *having* (a symbolic register) and those
who relate to it in the register of *being* (a dimension of identity which can
be neither totally symbolized nor totally socialized).

The split in society is mirrored by a split within the very individuality of the wage-earner. There is a division into that part of his individuality which is economically alienated in production and which is directly inscribed in the alien cycle of capital, and that part of his individuality which is not directly inspired in production. Taylorism discovered the 'science' of this division. There is a major contradiction in the process of socialization which it sets in motion: the very thing which acquires a meaning in the cycle of capital loses its meaning for the worker who has no access to the economic signifiers which control his labour (he experiences only constraints which are imposed upon him and which create the general context for his working life).

From the capitalist's point of view, labour results from the appropriation of the human capacity for production, and the existence of wages relations facilitates its appropriation. The productive consumption of labour-power transfers the potential value 'contained in' labour-power (which has now become productive capital) to marketable commodities. The whole point is to effect that transfer in optimal conditions.

From the worker's point of view, labour does not seem initially to be abstract, as it is both a manifestation of his individuality and a means of providing a living for him and his family. The decisive moment is the moment of activity, and it takes the form, not of a *transfer*, but that of the *production* of movements and activities which are inscribed on the objects of labour, and which are a manifestation of his personal abilities. At this level, he cannot perceive himself as an abstraction (or as a form of capital's existence), for his identity cannot be split, and he experiences only the continuity of his existence.

'Being both master and man . . .' The age-old aspiration of the producers is still thwarted by the duality of 'viewpoints' instituted by capitalist relations. For the producers, the stakes are high: they concern the conditions for the subjective investment of a decisive part of their social being.

As we have already said, the distinguishing feature of human societies is the ability to make labour (and therefore activity) circulate in the form of objects, and to turn traces of individual activity into a social product which can be exchanged, and perhaps even accumulated as a social patrimony. From this point of view, the objects of productive labour are necessarily cultural goods; they are significant objects which acquire their meaning from elsewhere, from the symbolic structures of society. The very activity of labour itself signifies the identity and social position of its agents, and it implies a representation of the social order.

From this point of view, the greatest transformation brought about by capitalism is without any doubt the process whereby the symbolic dimension of labour becomes monopolized by the criteria of the valorization of capital. As Godelier (1971, p. 93) stresses, 'In most precapitalist societies . . . labour is inevitably a multiple act which is at once economic, political and religious . . . labour does not exist as a purely economic activity.'[16] But in the light of what was said earlier, we now have to ask: from what 'point of view' can labour be said to be a 'purely economic activity' in a highly developed capitalist society such as ours? It is certainly not so from the point of view of the producers; as we have already said, the existing productive structures are designed to introduce a division between the prerogatives of management and 'the rest', the latter being a question of working-class subjectivity. All technocratic doctrines refer to 'the rest' and 'the social', as opposed to the economic and the technological registers, which have a coherence of their own.

Yet the social is increasingly part of the technical or economic realm, as qualitatively new demands for the involvement of workers in the organization of production emerge. This is a considerable historical development, and it will be discussed below. For the moment, we shall simply note that the emergence of this tendency makes it more obvious than ever that the social meaning of labour is being monopolized by the criteria of the valorization of capital. But a price has to be paid, and other cultural dimensions and other systems of values must be constantly repressed (it was in this context that Poulantzas referred to the 'significant' void surrounding the law of capital).

These dimensions and systems are constantly repressed, but they cannot be destroyed, as counter-tendencies are always at work. Moynot (1975) suggests that this great psychological and social space, which is rooted in the subjective experience of the worker, should be described in terms of 'psychological appropriation'. It enables the producers to negate the fact that their tools, the objects of their labour and even the meaning of their activities have been expropriated in economic, juridical and cultural terms. Although its existence is denied by wages relations, by the organization of labour and by the dominant discourses, psychological appropriation still finds expression in language ('I pick up my what's-it; I stuff my circuit into my cassette') and in the imaginary. It becomes a social force in struggles which look forward to different social relations. If intuition is not enough to indicate its existence, medical studies of the stigma of losing one's job are in themselves an eloquent indication of the symbolic effectiveness of this appropriation of productive space; to say that those who lose their jobs after years of inscribing their activities in labour lose something of their identity and of their human relations with others is an understatement (see Combe *et al.*, 1980; *Prévenir*, 1980; and Comegno *et al.*, 1980).

The mode of production gradually detaches from living labour an aspect of concrete human beings, and inscribes it both symbolically and practically in the system of capital. We then see the emergence of the coherent figure of the productive body, and the desubjectivized or willing worker of Taylorism is its ultimate incarnation. He is an unreal figure because his existence is founded upon the negation of 'the rest', of that part of the real producers which cannot be inscribed in economic signifiers. But he is also a creature of the productive order, and therefore a very real image of its ambitions.

Taylor, who was a methodical man, finally met this figure in the flesh: Schmidt. It was not easy to find him. Schmidt was chosen from a group of seventy-five pig-iron handlers. He was a strong Pennsylvania Dutchman who was so suggestible that 'a penny looked about the size of a cart-wheel to him' and who had a reputation for placing a high value on a dollar. The dialogue between Schmidt and Taylor merits reproduction:

> *The task before us, then, narrowed itself down to getting Schmidt to handle 48 tons of pig-iron a day and making him glad to do it. This was done as follows. Schmidt was called out from amongst the gang of pig-handlers and talked to somewhat in this way:*
>
> *'Schmidt, are you a high-priced man?'*
>
> *'Vell, I don't know vat you mean.'*
>
> *'Oh yes you do. What I want to know is whether you are a high-priced man or not.'*
>
> *'Vell, I don't know what you mean.'*
>
> *'Oh, come now, answer my question. What I want to find out is*

whether you are a high-priced man or one of those cheap fellows over there. What I want to find out is whether you want to earn $1.85 a day or whether you are satisfied with $1.15, just the same as those cheap fellows are getting.'

'Did I want $1.85 a day? Vas dot a high-priced man? Vell, yes, I vas a high-priced man.'

'Oh, you're aggravating me. Of course you want $1.85 a day – everyone wants it! You know perfectly well that has very little to do with your being a high-priced man. For goodness' sake, answer my questions, and don't waste any more of my time. Now come over here. You see that pile of pig-iron?' (Taylor, *1914, pp. 44–5)*

This goes on until Schmidt finally 'sees' and, deluded by his desire to be well thought of, agrees to accept a fool's bargain which will allow him to make $1.85 by handling 48 tons of pig-iron a day rather than making $1.15 by handling thirty tons. There is something masterly about this. Were it not for the context, we might be dealing with a stage hypnotist or a circus act. In reality, the work of ideology is obviously much more complex than this, and not all individuals are so credulous, greedy and phlegmatic. We shall return to this point.

CHAPTER NINE

TAYLORIST REALISM AND THE REALITY OF TAYLORISM

We need to know what we mean by human relations at work; and then we can ask, 'What work is there in a film?' . . . Over the last few years, I've been filming postcards, and that has made me think again about frames [*cadres*]. Why should frames have become square or roughly rectangular, rather than round? And why do you have to fit a lens which tends to be round in order to film a frame? . . . You have to know where you're going before you can decide anything. If we know that, we can get some idea of what a frame can be and what we can do with it. And then you remember that in France we talk about *le cadre de la vie* [living conditions]; some people are *encadrés* [supervised], and the people who run things are usually called *cadres* [supervisors].

J.-L. Godard, *Introduction à une véritable histoire du cinéma*

Schmidt the pig-iron handler existed only in Taylor's imagination. No one could mistake that mechanized body, which is fragmented and organized by part-functions, for a real man. Yet either Schmidt or his double did handle mountains of pig-iron every day. What is the basis of Taylorist realism? Why is it so effective?

Is it, for example, an exceptionally good method for analysing the labour process? In that respect, the criticisms put forward by certain currents within modern ergonomics are of particular interest. In a paper originally read to a conference on 'The Internationalization of Capital and the Labour Process' held in Mexico in March 1980, Durrafourg (1980) radically challenges the notion of 'work load', which is central to the Taylorist approach. He stresses that the basic assumptions (the existence of an average, invariable man, and of stable tasks which are reproduced from one cycle to the next) do not stand up to an analysis of the facts, and suggests that the whole concept has to be revised: 'The underlying question behind any evaluation of the work load is or must be, "For whom?"'. If we ask that question, the concept of a work load allows us to think about the relationship between the characteristics of the population and the characteristics of the tasks that have to be performed. It then acquires a scientific status.'

If we pursue this line of argument, the following points emerge:

1. There is an obvious discrepancy between the Taylorist representation of the task (a series of standardized operations carried out on a standardized object with standardized tools; the whole task is a repetitive cycle which can be transposed into other areas) and real work. The main differences between the two relate to:

The stability of tasks: as we have seen, technical job-descriptions are calculated with an improbable precision (1/100,000 second), whereas conditions vary considerably; raw materials vary, and tools become worn.[1]

The distinction between the execution of tasks (seen, in accordance with a mechanical model, as a series of stable tasks to be carried out one after the other) and 'the rest' of the job. The 'rest' of the job includes checking machines for faults. And faults are rarely aberrations within what is otherwise a constantly smooth process; they rarely occur during only one cycle or affect only one article. Anomalies are an inevitable feature of working with difficult materials, and ensuring that they do not exceed a certain threshold is a constant feature of the 'operative's' work.[2]

2. There is also a major discrepancy between modern analyses of the movements involved in production and the mechanical model used by Taylorism. To take just one simple example: unlike a machine-tool on a stand, the human body obviously does not remain motionless. The Taylorist analyst usually ignores the dynamics of posture, which has no direct output (or, at best, sees it as an inevitable effect of the imperfections of the human machine).

3. Whilst the mechanical-serial model can claim to be a

relatively accurate image of the movements involved in production to the extent that it is quite true that the number of implements a man can use simultaneously is limited by the number of his bodily members, which are his natural instruments of production (as the inventors of a treadle spinning-wheel with two spindles in the eighteenth century discovered, 'adepts in spinning who could spin two threads at once were almost as scarce as two-headed men' (Marx, 1976, p. 495)), the same cannot be said of the mental activities involved. Those activities cannot be channelled into a single direction at a given moment.

I am not denying the urgent need for scientific research into the purely quantitative dimension of the mental work involved in industrial situations. But I would argue that the notion of a work load (defined as the 'activity rate' of the productive body, or as the ratio between real time and productive time) is problematic even at the level of physical activity: how can a serial model account for both operational movements and postural activity? And it is surely quite impossible to arrive at a Taylorist definition of a 'mental work load'.

It is clear, then, that an analysis of the labour process reveals the limitations of the assumptions of Scientific Management. The latter presupposes a rigidity which is simply not found in real tasks, in the movements involved in production or in the associated mental processes. How, then, can we explain the mechanical regularity which is so characteristic of Taylorized shops and which appears to be so perfect that it seems to be a natural feature of certain forms of industrial work?

A detailed analysis of a specific work station again represents a challenge to received ideas. A woman is employed as a solderer on an assembly line in an electronics factory. In 1 minute 38 seconds, she has to carry out two very different operations: she must first place a wire under a terminal spade tag, and then solder it. Observation reveals that she habitually performs the tasks within an almost constant space of time. But she does so because she uses a compensation strategy. The time taken to perform the first 'all or nothing' operation varies; if the wire will not fit under the tag, she has to try again. The second 'variable' operation takes up the rest of the available time; the soldering-iron is not always in contact with the wire for the same length of time.

What conclusions are we to draw from this? We can only assume that the effectiveness of the Taylorist model is not an expression of the supposed 'science' of work. It is an expression of something else.

1. Given a number of unstable tasks to be carried out by different individuals who act in different ways at different times, a coherent system of standard-time evaluation relates the concrete to the abstract and facilitates the practical calibration of living labour. At a micro level, it affects the way in which individuals manage the time allotted for their tasks, and the way in which they internalize the norm. The 'realism' of the norm is therefore less important than its existence. Norms divide up time in such a way that the worker can take the initiative in only two ways: by departing considerably from the theoretical job-description sheet,[3] or by developing a truly astonishing virtuosity.[4]

2. Taylorist descriptions of tasks, which reduce them to a pure sequence of useful gestures to be carried out in a calibrated period of time, cannot account for the total amount of work that is carried out. Analyses based upon a study of the work actually done (and upon the corresponding definition of work) reveal a whole range of skills, initiatives and responsibilities, and it has been suggested that they represent a 'fragmented involvement' on the part of the operative. It is not simply a matter of reacting to unexpected events, anticipating accidents and checking the quality of products (Durrafourg, 1980). In short, the notion of an abstract operative and of an abstract quantity of activities to be carried out in order to meet a norm is a fiction which has nothing to do with the real socialization of labour. The socialization of labour means that operatives do become involved in controlling machines, and that there is a degree of co-operation between members of the collective.[5] Durrafourg describes a typical example:

> The official setter is the only one who is allowed to set the machines, but he cannot do the job by himself. He sets the machine, and makes one part . . . Then an unskilled woman worker comes along and checks the part to make sure that the machine has been set correctly . . . No one can set a machine without help from the operatives.

From this point of view, it is not, as Taylor claims, because initiative and knowledge have *really* been taken away from the shop floor that 'Scientific Management' is so effective. It is because it establishes a division of responsibility which ensures that the coherent system of norms forced upon the producers becomes an essential mediating factor in every aspect of the organization, collectivization and socialization of their work.

3. In other words, Taylorism (and Fordism) introduces a dissociation between, on the one hand, the vigorous objective socialization of labour (all tasks are, in principle, equivalent to all other tasks, and collective labour is planned) and, on the other, the practical expropriation (and this is also an ideological, cultural and political expropriation) which divorces the producers from the *means* of that socialization. And this dissociation establishes and legitimizes the existence of managerial power as an instrument for the subordination of the labour process to the process of the valorization of capital.

Taylorism's effect upon industrial life extends far beyond its immediate and explicit applications. In order to take stock of this dimension we will look in Appendix I (p. 137) at four sets of house journals published by French motor companies: *Citroën* (July 1937–November 1938). *Notre Usine*, Peugeot (March 1948–March 1949), *Berliet Informations* (July/August 1952–October 1954) and *SIMCA Informations* (July/August 1952–April 1955). All these documents concern the same branch of industry. Naturally enough, they are not homogeneous, either in historical terms or in terms of style of management (Citroën pioneered Fordism in France, Peugeot practised a repressive paternalism, whereas SIMCA stressed the importance of 'human relations', but at the same time tried to repress unionism). The detailed reasons for this diversity need not concern us here, since this is not a study of house journals as such (on that topic, see CCEES, 1977c) but an illustration of the 'ideological labour' involved in the Taylorization of the factories concerned. The particularly explicit nature of the texts clearly reveals what is at stake: promoting acceptance of working conditions and an atmosphere of 'cordiality' or social peace, a feeling of belonging to the company, and the value-criteria specific to the commodity mentality.

The organization of consent, cultural expropriation, the legitimization of managerial power, and the subordination of the labour process to the process of valorization . . . The issues raised by 'Taylorism' are political issues, and they have to be understood in terms of the history of social facts. That dimension will merely be mentioned in passing here, and we shall limit discussion to a few questions relating to the 1920s. A rapid survey of the hundreds of journals produced by Parti Communiste Français [PCF] cells in 1924, 1927 and 1931 (Appendix II, p. 146) will serve as an introduction.

An article by Lequin (1979) sheds some interesting light on the question of rationalization in French industry during this period. His main argument is easily summarized. This period saw a very sharp increase in material investment (which rose by an average of 28% per year between 1927 and 1930) and an annual increase of 6% in investment per worker. Lequin stresses that the rise in productivity produced by retooling and technical concentration does not necessarily mean that labour was reorganized to any great extent, and that it was based primarily on a reduction of the workforce. In fact, 'It seems impossible to describe rationalization as the dominant tendency within French capitalism in the 1920s' (p. 128). It may not have been the dominant trend, but there is no shortage of examples of rationalization: the motor industry is the obvious example, but rubber, electricity, railways and mines were all affected, as were, to a lesser extent, textiles and the glass industry (cf. Desbrousses, 1975). This was also a period of intense ideological struggle. The crisis of 1926, echoes of the Russian Revolution, and the austerity measures adopted by the Poincaré government on the basis of recommendations from experts appointed by the Cartel des Gauches are all indications that major ideological issues were being raised: the social purpose of production, and the rationality of capitalist objectives in relation to the general interest.

In October 1926 Léon Jouhaux's Confédération Générale du Travail [CGT] took the initiative of launching a sustained campaign on the theme of 'economic reorganization'; it was not until six months later that the employers' organization (Confédération Générale du Patronat Français) expressed its views on rationalization by stressing the themes of the depoliticization of the factory and of class collaboration.

This is the background to the newsletters produced by the PCF and the articles published by L'Humanité during this period.[6] We also have to take into account the hard-line positions adopted by the Comintern during its frequently confused discussions of rationalization (capitalist rationalization – especially in America and Germany – was seen as a refinement of exploitation, whereas Soviet rationalization was regarded as serving the general interest). A more detailed reading of these documents leads to one inescapable conclusion: the analysis has less to do with new aspects of rationalization or with Taylorism and Fordism than with underlying constants and relations of production; it is concerned with the most general aspects of the logic of capitalist profits rather than with specifics. In cell publications, the word 'rationalization' is used to refer to almost every aspect of work organization, which is seen in absolute terms,[7] rather than in terms of its negative effects on the workforce (dishonest use of piece-rates, speed-ups, loss of freedom, fatigue, lack of hygiene, and so on). A phrase used by Raveau in *L'Humanité* (3 February 1927) sums up all this: 'rationalization, normalization, Taylorization, standardization, Fordization and other scientific applications of . . . the exploitation of the proletariat'.

One may well wonder why the revolutionary element within the labour movement avoided making any detailed study of the question of work organization, whilst Jouhaux's CGT and the reformist wing of the SFIO [Section Française de l'Internationale Ouvrière] took such an interest in it. It is as though the dilemma facing the labour movement forced it to choose between simply abandoning the issue and lapsing into class collaboration. This is a major question, and one which is not without its contemporary relevance, but in the present context we can do no more than indicate possible explanations.

A two-part article by Monmousseau (1922) is worthy of note in that it expressed the view taken of factory councils by the Communist leadership of the CGTU. He initially declares that: 'As well as directing destructive actions against the bosses, trade unionism must be capable of penetrating the cogs of economic organization', but he immediately limits the application of this principle. The idea of union control and of factory councils must be popularized, but it would be a mistake to put it into practice in a period when the revolutionary forces are in retreat because, 'Union control is an offensive action . . . It is the means whereby the workers will collectively learn how to win their economic liberation. One day it will be forced upon the bosses, but they will never accept it.' In more specific terms, he warns against the danger of introducing 'a parliamentary spirit on the shop floor' and against the possibility that shop stewards might become the 'bosses' auxiliaries'.

This contrasts not only with the reformist CGT's policy of establishing a union 'presence' in economic decision-making, but also with the resolutions adopted two years earlier by Comintern on 'workers' control' of production.[8] It is obviously a realistic position, as the French labour movement had been weakened by the split between its two main currents. There were also problems at an international level. After the defeat of the German and Hungarian revolutions, the Soviet Union, surrounded by serious difficulties, had taken the line of 'socialism in one country'. In Italy, the council strategy which seemed to have succeeded with the remarkable factory occupation movement in Turin (the very movement which had inspired Comintern to adopt the positions mentioned above) had failed for lack of a political outlet.[9]

THE TURIN FACTORY OCCUPATION MOVEMENT

The immediate origins of the movement go back to the first 'internal commissions' set up in the Turin metal-working industry in the period before the First World War. 'The first legal recognition granted to an internal commission in Italy dates back to the collective labour contract signed by the FIOM – the metal-workers' union – and the "Itala" car factory in Turin on 27 October 1906' (Corrado, 1955, p. 13). The commissions were consultative bodies designed to defuse disputes in the workplace. The worker-delegates were trade unionists. The commissions took on a more markedly defensive character during the war when, together with 'committees for industrial mobilization', they organized life in the requisitioned factories. In 1919, Gramsci's paper *Ordine Nuovo*, which, significantly enough, described itself as a review of 'socialist culture' and which regularly published writings by workers and studies of factories (see Platone, 1951), called for delegates to the commissions to be elected directly by all workers, whether unionized or not. The elections, which took place in August 1919, detonated a powerful movement which led to the occupation of factories and landed estates (especially in the Po valley) in 1919–20. This insurrectional situation raised in new terms the question of the working class's ability to organize production in the factories; almost all the technicians had fled. It also allowed the working class to extend its

(continued over page)

---

practical appropriation of a vital sector of social life, and thus raised the issue of the seizure of state power. Raw materials were requisitioned, stock-piled and distributed. Factories sold their products to the public; retail co-operatives were founded, and a broad solidarity movement developed. Disobeying management orders, the railwaymen of Livorno resolved to deliver raw materials to the factories; the postal workers devised a system to get round the boycott that had been imposed on mail addressed to the occupied factories. Within the space of a few months the working class had learned what was meant by the seizure of power in social life and taking control of productive space. Gramsci immediately grasped the importance of what was happening:

> *In order to establish the Council, every worker has had to become conscious of his position in the economic domain. He felt initially that he was part of a basic unit, the shop-floor work crew, and he felt that the introduction of technical innovation to the mechanical equipment changed his relations with the technicians: the worker is now less dependent than formerly on the technician, the master craftsman, hence he has acquired greater autonomy and can exercise discipline himself. (1977, p. 164)*

His apparently paradoxical claim that mechanization gives the worker a greater autonomy is supported by an analysis which dialectically relates the evolution of the material base of production to the evolution of mentalities, and the struggle for new relations at work to the struggle for the conquest of political power.

To say that the position of the PCF was 'realistic' does not exhaust the question. The position of the PCF and the CGTU, as opposed to the all-purpose demagogy of the reformist leadership of the CGT,[10] was tantamount to a denial that constant working-class interventions over the question of work organization could have any beneficial effects. Both positions reflect the expropriation of the working class, at the level both of the socialization of the forces of production and of coherent political and technical structures.

The profound transformations that took place in trade union movements in the major capitalist countries in the 1920s have to be understood against the background of this expropriation, and Taylorism is obviously no more than one particularly significant element within it. The decision of the AFL and the ADGB to participate in the rationalization of industry in America and Germany respectively was also significant (in France, the CGT took a similar position). These organizations, which were linked both through the International Federation of Trade Unions and the ILO, saw their own objectives as part of a seemingly inevitable transformation.[11] And as revolutionary unionists fell back on general political themes, the question of work organization became depoliticized;[12] as a result of this, Saint-Germain (1976) claims that there was no basic difference between the component elements of the labour movement, and Gaudemar (1979, pp. 211–13) speaks of the 'mystification' of the unions. The position adopted by the Fédération Unitaire de la Métallurgie, for example, cannot be ignored; it indicates that it seriously underestimated the social relations implied by the assembly line and, more generally, by the technical mechanisms of the rationalization of industry. The problem is all the more obvious in that it had lasting effects (not the least of which was, as Saint-Germain points out, the CGTU's subsequent increased support for rationalization, which it saw primarily as a means of obtaining higher wages[13]). This line must also be related to the simultaneous development of 'Soviet Taylorism'.[14]

A more serious analysis would have to ask just how much room French working-class organizations had for manoeuvre, and would have to relate the possibility of interventions on the part of the labour movement to the question of the preconditions for intervention (the material base of production, the balance of power in civil society, the possibility of adapting state structures, the international context). Whilst it is quite true to say that the position adopted by a minority which was close to La Révolution prolétarienne and which argued against all assembly-line work – and thus went against the line taken by the leadership of the Fédération de la Métallurgie – has a modern ring about it, it may simply have resulted from an overestimation of the working class's ability to intervene at that level, particularly at a time when the technical structures of the mode of production had begun to acquire a high degree of cohesion, with all the economic objectives and social relations that implies. It so happens that cohesive structures, like utopias, negate the existence of real human beings.

HOUSE JOURNALS IN THE MOTOR INDUSTRY

In many areas, industrialists have organized brass
bands for their employees . . . This is a good idea . . .
Music produces a feeling of togetherness and cordiality
. . . It drives away ill-feeling . . . Cares vanish . . . The
imagination forgets about narrow ideas and mean, petty
thoughts.

J. Lefort, *Intempérance et misère*

It is a well-known fact that a good rhythm sets the feet tapping.
'Allons, enfants de la SIMCA', writes *SIMCA Informations (SI)* in
February, playing on the first words of the *Marseillaise*. 'Entrez dans
l'Aronde', says *SI* (February 1953) [the pun is on *la ronde* and *Aronde*, a
dance and a SIMCA model respectively; 'Put on a Mini' might be a later
equivalent]. Just see how they dance: 'The music sets the steel dancing
to its rhythms. With every beat, a machine begins to pulsate, a line starts
up hundreds of yards away. The factory is a living organism, and its heart
beats at a rhythm of twenty-seven cars an hour' (*SI*, October 1954). A
hearty good humour is the order of the day: 'I'll sleep on it,' an
unskilled woman in the upholstery shop jokes to a reporter from *SIMCA
Informations*. And of course there is no point in keeping a good joke to
yourself:

Have you ever told a joke – or what you thought was a joke – to a small
group of friends? If you have, you will know how the presence of a man
with a long face can put you off. Even the best jokes fall flat because of
the man with the long face and the grim expression, even if the other
listeners are what you might call a good audience . . . The ones who
give you sidelong glances, the moaners, the bad-tempered ones who take

offence at the least little thing, those who don't give a damn, the ones who are embittered, sarcastic, plaintive, jealous or bitter, the ones who always seem to be miles away or to have got out of bed on the wrong side . . . they're all poisoners; they poison the atmosphere, and destroy the team spirit which makes work more pleasant, easier and lighter. (SI editorial, *December 1952*)

Not 'being miles away', getting into the swim of things, feeling good in company overalls, and doing it to please others: 'You are prettier than any powdered woman . . . provided you smile. A woman who is grim, hard-faced and haughty looks ugly, and no one will forgive her for that' (*Notre Usine* – *NU* – March 1948; 'Beauty tips'). This is an elementary rule of group life, and if you do not feel on sufficiently good terms with the outside world, we have a cure for you: 'I suggest that you obey the motto "With a smile" whenever you can, and that you play the happiness game. This is a very special game, and you can play it alone at any time. It consists of remembering that things could be a lot worse' (*NU*, August 1948; Antoine Peugeot speaking to apprentices on prize day). And to help the process of autosuggestion, the next issue includes a report on a man whose 'work is hard' . . . a miner.

The point is to make the factory look like a dynamic and pragmatic community. House journals constantly sing the joys of work:

The car body shop is an extraordinary dressmaker's workshop. This is where we make clothes for the Aronde with stamped sheet steel from the presses. It takes more than 700 stitches to hem this metal dress . . . But this kind of needlework has nothing to do with what goes on in the rue de la Paix, with what you read in Mademoiselle de Paris, *or with the apprentice dressmakers who are so good at melting the hearts of romantic journalists and worthy old gentlemen. Here, the little seamstresses are tough men; the big lads in the body shop are not exactly shrinking violets.* (SI, *June 1953*)

The virile fraternity of brain and brawn, and a spirit of mutual assistance 'make for good teams', efficiency and generosity. (In an astounding article entitled 'A truly democratic people: the bees', *NU* for March 1949 claims that 'True democracy means devotion and sacrifices, not benefits', and extols the totalitarian discipline of the hive and the absolute devotion the worker bees show towards their larval queen.) The same model appears in the sports pages, with their reports of the exploits of company teams: football (SIMCA), rowing, canoeing, cycling and swimming (Citroën), and rugby, handball, judo (Berliet). The product itself (a car) easily becomes a symbol of the dynamic expression of the group. *Notre Usine* reports in December 1948 on a 2,000-kilometre trip by moped; *Berliet Informations* (*BI*) covers the performance of the firm's trucks on the Linas Montléry test track or on long trips across Africa. Similar reports also appear in *SIMCA Informations*.

As on the terraces, creating a 'good spirit' is primarily a matter of creating an atmosphere. Despite all the efforts, however, there are times when no one has the heart for it. The players cannot always see the point of it all, and sometimes they are not even sure which side they are on. As Taylor found out, most workers are convinced that working harder does them no good. And it is in fact difficult to persuade them that they are wrong. Workers therefore have to be made to feel that they belong to the factory, and that feeling must outweigh their awareness of their own individual interests. The firm becomes a sort of global referent which is at once impersonal and ubiquitous. 'What does Berliet do? . . . I would like you to know more about the many cogs that go to make up this immense machine; that will give you a better idea of how the car-model you are working on depends on you for its success, and how its success guarantees you a better future' (*BI*, July/August 1952; editorial by E. Parfait, Chairman and Managing Director). *Berliet Informations* regularly published reports on different sections of the factory. The identity and functions of individuals, complete with photographs (twenty-five people in the foundry were identified in this way) and the links between the different departments were clearly described. SIMCA used the same technique: the 'Looking around the factory' column described a different department in each issue. In the case of SIMCA, the hierarchy was introduced in detail: an article on the engineering department is illustrated with portraits of the head of production and the chief engineer, surrounded by five section leaders, nineteen foremen and forty-nine team leaders. The portraits make up a jigsaw showing the anonymous shape of the production machinery. The overall structure is the dominant image, as in the Christmas present *SIMCA Informations* gave its readers in 1952: a large aerial photograph of the factory to pin up in the kitchen. *Notre Usine* published similar articles, but they were remarkable mainly for their banal captions: 'It is interesting to see the assembly line at work; it is even more interesting to watch the final assembly stage' (July 1948).

Metaphors are used to make the productive order appear natural; the factory is like a hive 'whose buzzing cohorts teach us that, if we are to live together in society, we have to conform to well-established principles . . . no one can reject them without compromising the whole structure' (*NU*, March 1949). The general interest determines everyone's role and position: 'Every man has his place . . . Our job is to define the needs of every work station and to decide where individuals should work on the basis of their abilities' (report on the 'psychotechnical department'; *SI*, March 1955). Only a megalomaniac with no sense of reality could reject the idea that everyone's activities have to be inscribed in the same overall grid: 'Be modest; avoid the temptation to have too high an opinion of your own importance' (speech at a prize-giving ceremony in the apprentice school; *BI*, August 1954). A degree of selflessness or self-abnegation is obviously desirable:

> *Whenever you drill a hole, you should remember that it was SIMCA who provided, developed and adjusted the machine that drills it. It is SIMCA who provides the parts, checks them, takes them away, counts them and pays for them. And who assembles them on the next line? The anonymous workers who devote their efforts to SIMCA. (SI, July 1952)*

To illustrate how little individual identity matters in this vast, anonymous structure, a 'Martin–SIMCA contest' was held [Martin is reputedly the most common surname in France]. Thirty workers called Martin were identified; those whose birthdays fell during the month of the contest had the privilege of seeing their photographs and life-stories in the paper (*SI*, February 1955).

This loss of identity is not without its advantages. In this context, three sets of themes can be outlined:

      1. The firm is powerful: Berliet is 'a town with a population of 30,000 people'; the SIMCA group is 'a community of 20,000 people'; if all the trucks Berliet produces in a month were lined up nose to tail, the line would stretch for four kilometres – 'in other words, the first would be at the gates of the Montplaisir factory as the last was leaving the Vénissieux factory' (*BI*, December 1954). And the firm is well known: Vincent Auriol visits the Berliet stand at the Motor Show.

2. The firm is interested in you and in every aspect of your life. SIMCA is touched by the postcards some people are kind enough to send when they go on holiday. The firm also cares about your children. Thousands of SIMCA children are given model Arondes at Christmas. Rather less generously, Berliet gives daddy the plans to make a model GLR8 truck.

3. The firm is benevolent and protects those who obey its laws. It can even confer unexpected distinctions. You can trust it:

> The management always makes sure that you have the most up-to-date tools and the best possible working conditions because it wants to help you to increase productivity. That is why the management introduced productivity bonuses. The management has not deceived us. It has given us material benefits, and we must repay it by working harder. The management trusts us; we must trust the management. (SI, October 1952)

The firm has a presence, a personality, and plans for everyone. Nothing escapes its notice: the firm *is* the factory. This truism is the basis for all the transactions – real or imaginary – involved in the construction of a 'company patriotism'. And here we find a remarkable change. The earliest house journals attempt to reconcile the interests of the workforce and the general interest by promoting a vaguely social discourse which emphasizes the usefulness of the product. Who could fail to be moved by the story of the tripe-butcher from Charleville-Mezières; now that he drives a Citroën, he can supply his customers with fresh tripe from the abattoir in Douai. Other articles deal with changes in mass-consumption patterns.

Between 1952 and 1955, SIMCA's discourse no longer centres on the national interest, but on the economic war the company is waging. It describes its victories (SIMCA factories throughout the world), its alliances ('The Ford–SIMCA merger means that there are now 20,000 of us in Nanterre, Poissy, Puteaux, Saint-Denis and Argenteuil. 20,000 people have been brought together in a real community of interests' (*SI*, March 1955)), its enemies, and its leaders, who write for the paper as circumstances demand.

Everyone is urged to pursue his personal interests as best he can in this economic battle by supporting the company in its aims, by, for example, trying to win customers from within the groups who visit the factory. SIMCA went even further by launching an astonishing campaign to encourage every worker to become a salesman. It appealed to the wives of SIMCA workers to 'talk about SIMCA in the market, at the hairdresser's, and in the shops', because 'propaganda gets around and eventually reaches the ear of the customer, and it is the customer who gives us a living' (*SI*, August 1952). The result was a monthly column in *SIMCA Informations*. Making the workforce 'swallow' the interests of profit means promoting the values on which the commodity mentality is based. And SIMCA rewarded its supporters: 'A word to the wise: win a customer, and win a bonus' (*SI*, November 1952).

But the front line in the struggle to win the assent of the workforce is the battle for productivity. This battle is fought by those who are behind the lines, but it must be won if the company is to be victorious on the commercial front. And here, capitalism tries to make further savings on living labour by adopting specific strategies designed to save time. As we have already seen, in the context of the rigid structures of a Taylorized factory, it is only by perfecting their manual skills that operatives can spare themselves physical effort. They are thus forced to support the firm's objectives in a very practical sense.

The house journals make great efforts to further this tendency by promoting certain attitudes, and especially discipline and self-discipline.

Physical self-discipline: 'To do your job quickly and well you have to have the discipline of an athlete' (*SI*, June 1953, on the body shop) because, 'You must be a part-maker, not a shavings-maker. Make as few shavings as possible, with as few movements as possible' (*BI*, August 1952). They also recommend a certain asceticism: 'We all want to make good use of our free time so as to get back to work afterwards' (*BI*, July/August 1952). Workers should not be afraid to think of their bodies as machines, explains a SIMCA doctor (*SI*, September 1953), as he describes a technique for 're-oxygenating' workers in the paint shop; they spend twenty minutes a day in an oxygen tent, 'for the sake of their health'.

Mental self-discipline: being efficient means being careful: 'Don't let yourself be distracted by your personal preoccupations or by your surroundings; and do not distract other people' (*NU*, May 1948).

Concentrate, but pay attention of technical details: 'Your mind is like a parachute; if you want it to work, it has to be open (*NU*, December 1948). And here we see the central contradiction in Taylorist management: how can the collective knowledge of the workers be appropriated without a subsequent wastage of useful abilities?

SIMCA tried to find a solution by making extensive use of suggestion boxes. Anyone could try his luck in the bonus stakes, and he could do so anonymously if he so wished (a code known only to the worker concerned and to the management allowed the author of a useful suggestion to be identified – and rewarded).

Winners were praised for their methodical thinking: 'This man has realized that having good ideas is a matter of methodical thinking; you have to look at things in a new light, break down the operation and ask yourself if it really serves the desired purpose. This method is called analysis' (*SI*, July 1953). 'This is the way to rise above your work and to display more human dignity' (*SI*, January 1954; Chairman and Managing Director Pigozzi writes to those who have put forward suggestions).

Rising above things, but not above the natural order of things. The image of the hive is pressed into service again: every worker bee knows his or her place in the hive, and 'What if we looked at how bees organize their work rather than asking who is in charge?' (*NU*, March 1949). It is difficult to be careful, to think analytically, and at the same time to see out of the corner of your eye. Hence the practical tips on photography given in *Berliet Informations* (July/August 1952): 'First of all, do not try to "kill two birds with one stone" by photographing both the child and the background at the same time. You have to concentrate on the child.'

'Concentrate on the child', and don't pay too much attention to the background – *Notre Usine* (May 1948) gives the same good advice:

Attention requires mental concentration, and the harder you concentrate, the narrower your focus of attention. The more you concentrate on one object, the less you concentrate on others. When you need to be meticulously careful, it is impossible to concentrate on two things at once.

The advice given by *Notre Usine* in January 1948 comprises a real 'philosophy' of assent: concentrate on your own sphere of activity, without indulging in ideological, interpretative thoughts, and without trying to change the world:

You sometimes hear of wonderful countries across the Atlantic where the buildings are 100 storeys high; people tell you that paradise has been built in the Siberian steppes, in the Ural mountains, or on the banks of rivers that are ice-bound for six months of the year . . . Allow me to describe a paradise they often deliberately forget to tell you about: France, your own country. It is there in front of your very eyes, there for the taking. Do you understand? Don't you realize that you have to look for it here, and not on the benches of the Assemblée Nationale, or in political gatherings . . . Don't dream too much about universal happiness . . . remember the sound traditions of France . . . Work, and the quality of your work, will be your reward for all your efforts . . . Enjoy what you have. You are rich. You have the inexhaustible wealth of the beauties of your own country.

Here is another piece of sound advice from 'Emile', who purports to be a Peugeot worker:

It does you good to collect your thoughts from time to time and to look deep into your own soul. When you do so, you quite naturally close your eyes; the sun may be shining, but it is dark inside. And then you begin to see things for what they really are. Dangerous illusions are dispelled one by one. Try to find a quiet, lonely spot, close your eyes, and just examine your conscience:

'Am I being as careful as I should be at work?'

'Am I a good workmate?'

'Perhaps I should be kinder to my workmates, the people next door, and my wife. Perhaps I should pay more attention.'

Will you try it, my friends? Both men and women can try. Surely you can find a quiet spot from time to time. Just close your eyes, be honest with yourself, and make good resolutions.

An appeal to a 'sense of morality', imaginary transactions with the law, selflessness, meditations in 'quiet spots' and a religious attitude to work, 'an inexhaustible source of joy and happiness' (*BI*, August 1945) are constant themes in this literature. It would not be difficult to find more modern examples of propaganda urging workers to 'share' the company's aims. 'Moral feelings' are mobilized in an imaginary transaction with the law, and those who deserve them are given their symbolic rewards:

We have decided to introduce a special badge which will make the members of our great family easily recognizable whenever and wherever

they take part in Berliet activities. It is a reproduction of our logo: a small locomotive in gold heightened with brilliants – one for thirty years' service, three for forty years – and we are giving it to you as a souvenir. You will also be given a parchment certificate to prove that you have the right to wear the badge. (BI, *February 1953*)
Amen.

PCF CELL LITERATURE:
1924, 1927, 1931 . . .

They say that French workers are socialists. We have
not noticed anything of the kind in our factories.
Henry Ford, *Today and Tomorrow*

The newspapers discussed here were published on a more or less regular basis, and the best of them relied on information supplied by a handful of worker-correspondents (*rabcors*). They were either distributed clandestinely inside the factories or were sold at the factory gate by outside militants, and they were in themselves a spectacular form of subversion. The titles speak for themselves: *Le Bagnard rouge* [*The Red Convict*] (Marseilles docks, 1924), *Le Forçat de chez Peugeot* [*Peugeot's Prisoner*] (1931), *Le Bagne Arbel* [*Arbel Prison*] (1931), *Le Cri des dégraissés* [*The Cry of the Hungry*] (Querval, 1931), *L'Encaserné de chez Damoy* [*Prisoner at Damoy's*] (1931), *Le Cri des exploités* [*The Cry of the Exploited*] (Le Bourget, 1924), *Les Exploités* [*The Exploited*] (Usine Rotschild, 1924), *L'Exploité des chantiers de la Loire* (1931), . . . *des ferroneries* (1931), . . . *de Penhoët* (1931), . . . *de chez Renault* [*The Exploited in the Loire shipyards,* . . . *in the ironworks,* . . . *at Penhoët,* . . . *at Renault*], *L'Exploité réfractaire* [*The Exploited Rebel*] (Lafage, 1931).

'Prison', 'exploitation', 'barracks' . . . these are the words which so annoyed Denis Poulot, the radical employer, fifty years earlier. The titles are not calculated simply to annoy; they indicate a desire to take a confrontational stance by assuming, often in an ostentatious or ironic mode, an identification with the 'bad object' of the dominant repressive discourse: *L'Antidémocrate* [*The Antidemocrat*] (Unic, 1924), *Le Couthon entre les dents* [*Knife between the Teeth/Couthon between the teeth*] (Couthon,

1924), *Le Râleur* [*The Moaner*] (Usine O-Renault, 1924; Adhemar, 1924; Boubon, 1931), *L'Autre du Louvre* [*The Other at the Louvre*], *Du Fil à retordre* [*Making Life Difficult*] (Wallart, 1931), and even *Le Tartare rouge* [*The Red Tartar*] (Marseilles, 1931). It is often a case of the persecuted turned persecutor: *Les Rayons rouges* (BRC, 1931), *L'Oeil bolchevik* [*Bolshevik Eye*] (Hauser, 1924), *L'Oeil rouge* [*Red Eye*] (Delage, 1924; Union d'Electricité, 1924), *L'Oeil du diable* [*The Eye of the Devil*] (Prado railwaymen, 1931), *L'Oeil Rouge du combat* [*Red Eye at War*] (Thomson, 1931) and *L'Oeil rouge des quatre routes* (1931).

'Seeing red' can represent a political reappropriation of the factory, and many titles play on distorted signifiers: *Le Coin rouge* (CEM, 1924), *L'Eglantine* (municipal gardeners, 1924), *Pathé Journal* (Pathé, 1924), *Le Point de mire* [*The Target*] (Hotchkiss, 1931), *Le Rail bolchevik* (Narbonne railway station, 1931), *La Rame rouge* [*Red Métro*] (Choisy métro depot, 1931), *La Cisaille* [*The Shears*] (PO Tours, railwaymen, 1931) and *Le Jouet vengeur* [*The Toy's Revenge*] (toymakers, Paris, 1931). Other titles use a simpler form of the same device by adding the colour of struggle to a symbol of the factory: *L'Avion rouge* (Potez, 1924), *La Banque rouge* (Société Générale, 1924), *le Mètre rouge* (United Shoe, 1924), *Le Cubillot rouge* (Cie Franco-Belge), *Le Câble rouge* (Geoffroy Delose, 1931), *Le Citron rouge* (Citroën, 1931) and *Le Lion rouge* – the PCF's answer to Peugeot's *Notre Usine*.

Many titles address the reader directly, and invite identification: *Le Jeune Bolchevik* [*Young Bolshevik*] (Cail, 1924), *Le Jeune Léniniste* (Combe et Poirier, 1924), *Le Bolchevik* (Voison, 1924), *Le Bolchevik de la SMC* (1924), *Le Communiste de chez Zig-Zag* (1924), *Le Communiste de chez Salmon* (1924), and so on. The newspaper becomes a banner, a symbol of the subjectivity of a working class which is self-conscious and active: *L'Action bolchevique* (Rouget, 1924), *La Lutte* [*Struggle*] (SNPC, 1931), *L'Emancipateur* (Skene/Devallée), *L'Emancipé* (Hispano Suiza, 1927; Compteurs de Montrouge, 1931), *Le Libérateur* (Dreguet, 1924), *En Avant!* [*Forward!*] (Douai railwaymen, 1931), *Le Réveil* [*The Alarm*] (Central Championet, 1924; Chausson, 1924; Lemoine, 1924; Rosengart, 1931), *Groupons-nous* [*Unite*] (Imprimerie Nationale, 1924), *Le Phare communiste* [*The Communist Lighthouse*] (Citroën, 1924), *La Vigie* [*The Look-Out*] (Post Office revenue office, 1927), *L'Etincelle de chez Thomson* [*Thomson's Spark*] and *Notre Voix* [*Our Voice*] (1924).

1924, 1927 and 1931 . . . at these points in its history, the discourse and the vision of the PCF begin to take shape as it oscillates between an anarcho-syndicalist defence of working-class territory and the beginnings of a general offensive against the whole of society. In papers from this period, we see in very clear – and no doubt exaggerated – terms how the main arena of conflict is displaced from the struggle against 'the foreman' to a struggle against the somewhat less intentional logic of a system as 'capitalist rationalization' becomes a central issue.[15]

1924: THE FIGHT AGAINST THE FOREMAN

Hey, you there! You, the one that rings the bell, the boss's toothless watchdog! Try not to bite us too hard, and try not to threaten the comrades who go fly-posting; it's none of your business that it might cost them dearly if they get caught. We can always tell the boss about your past, about what you were before you got your hut . . . (municipal gardeners, *1924*)

That pig in the white overall, the one they call 'The Grocer', the one who envies the fascists their regalia. He's his boss's toady all right! He ingratiates himself with the boss, but he can be hard on workers who are too weak to fight back. The other day, he hit one of our poor comrades. The lad's workmates have no cause to be proud of themselves; they should have given that brute of a grocer the treatment he deserves: a good hiding. But it won't do any harm to make the toady wait. (Le Bolchevik de chez Renault, *1924*)

Such verbal violence is not unusual. It reflects the violence of the factory, and it is rooted in a traditional defiance of authority and a rejection of discipline on the part of the workers. Not surprisingly, the lower levels of the hierarchy (foremen and charge hands) are a favourite target. In the worker's representation of the factory, the power of the boss himself is much less obvious than that of former workers who have 'gone over to the other side'. 'Fraternization' with them is a serious offence in the eyes of the working-class community. The use of violent stereotypes, which are probably quite widely accepted, reduces the possibility of fraternization.

Foremen are puppets and figures of fun. They are 'useless' (Cail, Skene, Chemin de fer de Montrouge, Peugeot), 'parasites' (municipal gardeners), and 'babes in arms' (Combes et Poirier, Le Bourget). They are 'good for nothing' (Peugeot, Schneider) because 'they get fat on the sweat of slaves' (Renault). They 'twiddle their thumbs from morning to night' (Ducros), 'their clothes are as filthy on Monday as they are on Saturday' (railwaymen, Hellemes), but 'They spend all their time doing their nails' (Schneider). Unlike the old master craftsmen, whose authority was respected, they are greenhorns who 'know nothing' (Lorraine Dietrich, Post Office, Renault, Piganeau, Stromberg). They are puppets, dandies, creeps, imbeciles and nonentities.

Now that these men are in charge, the workers want to make it quite clear that they are the *real* bosses. Their language often displays a schoolmasterish sadism (a foreman at Schneider is a 'cretin', one in a shipyard is 'a little ignoramus'; another at Paris-Nord is a 'charming character'). The model of the classroom is often invoked to put foremen in their place: one 'should have his ears pulled' (Schneider); another gets 'a thrashing' (Delage); one needs to be 'taught the error of his ways', and one had to be 'educated' because he was 'more dead than alive' when he arrived (municipal gardeners). 'The workers are willing to take orders, but only from people who are as intelligent as they are' (Peugeot).

Having none of the attributes of an authority figure who can be respected and who deserves respect, foremen are viewed simply as agents of repression. They are 'slave-drivers', 'watchdogs', human 'cattle-drivers' and 'pigs' (Electrolyse française). They ingratiate themselves with the upper levels of the hierarchy ('crawlers', 'boot-lickers', 'flunkeys', 'zealous servants' and 'toadies'), and they enjoy their power. They are nicknamed 'Napoleon', 'The Kaiser' or 'Mussolini'. They are sadistic dictators: 'brutes', 'disgusting characters', 'slave-drivers' and even 'vultures'. They use their unrestricted power to satisfy their perverted needs, like the 'big fat head slave-driver with the temperament of a drunk who sweats alcohol from every pore' (Citroën). Some 'think they have the right to use factory girls to satisfy their bestial needs' (Salmon). They behave like satyrs, and they are obscene figures of authority.

The individuals at the lower end of the factory hierarchy are instruments of the boss's power and, by using them appropriately, management can infiltrate working-class territory. They are obviously a source of information: 'police spies', 'cops' and 'informers'; 'The spy service here could tell the official swine at the Quai des Orfèvres a thing or two' (Lorraine Dietrich, 1924).[16] They are behind attempts at intimidation, but they also try to win people over and to cause splits in the workers' ranks. They have to be 'unmasked' as 'false friends', 'hypocrites' and 'traitors'.

This defiance of authority and refusal to fraternize with the hierarchy can take the form of mass movements, as when Citroën came out on strike over the introduction of the Taylor system in February 1924. But it can also take the form of the implementation by working-class organizations of a code of collective and individual conduct.

Attempts at intimidation are firmly resisted. Accounts of harassment are published to warn other comrades. Counter-threats are also used: 'He ought to take care; the Seine isn't far away from his office' (Citroën).

Struggles are organized against minor attempts to create an industrial barracks: against the closure of a gate which stops men going to wash their hands in the Seine, against the use of whistles to order people about, against clocking-in systems which record who arrived late for work, against the pointless ritual of clocking out.

'Boot-lickers' are denounced, and comrades are warned about being too naïve and falling for false displays of gratitude (at Zig-Zag all workers are given a Christmas present – of four packets of cigarette papers). Such gestures cost the bosses nothing. Bosses and workers live in different worlds, and it would be comical if the 'honourable manager' of Peugeot came to eat in the canteen, or if Mme Kellner and her daughter undressed in the factory's unisex changing-room after their game of tennis. The state of changing-rooms, toilets, wash-basins, safety levels and fumes are common themes which are used to show what the bosses really think of their workforce.

Forms of counter-discipline are applied. 'If the fitters in 67 understood their duties, they would not have to put up with all this bother from the foremen' (Renault). A worker who, for an extra two sous an hour, agreed to operate two machines instead of one is denounced at Peugeot, as are the men at Delage who 'worked like animals' by putting in 200 hours a week.

The cohesion of the working-class community is not, however, based on internal discipline alone, essential though that discipline may be. It implies a constant effort to integrate and understand old men, youngsters, invalids and foreign workers, and a constant struggle against segregation:

The Moroccans and Algerians (who are not men at all, according to our bourgeoisie) who work in the foundries need a good shower at the end of a hard day's work. They have often said how embarrassing they find it . . . a few buckets installed at random are all they have for wash-basins. They have to strip naked to get a proper wash. So that's what they do. Oh, the gentlemen from management were shocked and outraged at such behaviour; but they alone are responsible. We are not saying that we agree with this form of protest, and we are not saying that men should behave like this in front of horrified women. Far from it. But we are saying that the workers have to get organized. (Cie Franco-Belge, *1931*)

1927–31: THE SYSTEM AND ITS 'RATIONALITY'

The newspapers published in 1924 speak the same language as the *sublimes* of the nineteenth century, and denounce working conditions by comparing them to other places of incarceration (the army, prison camps, jails) and to archaic systems of oppression (serfdom, slavery). The order imposed by the bosses is not seen as a productive order, but as an aberration which has been grafted on to the world of work: 'Antediluvian' tools, sheds 'dating back to Roman times', an 'imbecilic' entry-card system (Citroën). In Tours, railwaymen denounced the 'competent' (*sic*) authorities who invented cement railbeds with no drainage; their comrades in Helleme denounced the Bedeaux system on the grounds that it 'made things go from bad to worse'.[17] The introduction of Fordism was greeted with violent sarcasm from Renault workers:

The top man on the moving pavement in shops 43 and 18 (M. Verdure) has coined the slogan 'Everything in its place, and a place for everything.'[18] His set-up looks like an incredible jumble . . . The great M. Verdure would make a good officer in the Engineers, if he isn't one already, that is. How his head must hurt! . . . Poor man!

This haughty tone is somewhat surprising, coming from a factory which had been faced with the introduction of elements of Taylorism as early as 1908, and which had been through one of France's three 'time-study' strikes in 1912–13. But by 1927, *Le Bolchevik de chez Renault* no longer saw rationalization as an engineer's whim. Fordization was now beginning to affect the factory on a huge scale, and changes in work organization had even led to a renewal of union action in the militant 'O' factory in 1926 (there were no strikes at Renault between 1918 and 1926). The broader context described earlier also helped to make rationalization a major ideological theme.

Assembly-line work and 'Americanization' began to be denounced:[19] *Assembly-line work . . . means increased exploitation, and it works men to death . . . because the quota-times are too short. Renault is using times set by the fastest workers as a basis for its calculations; male workers are being replaced by women and youngsters . . . Assembly-line work means unemployment and wage cuts . . . In shop 4 (brake assembly shop for the 6-CV), it used to take 22 to 24 workers to assemble 120 parts (5 on the housing, 12 or 13 on brake assembly, and 5 or 6 on the gear-box casings). Wages ranged from 576.40 francs to 628.00 francs. All right, they were a bit higher if 5 or 6 skilled men were employed on the job . . . Now that the assembly line has been introduced, the situation has changed. It takes only 16 workers to produce the 120 parts. They earn 3.90 francs an hour, so the wage-cost of producing 120 parts is no more than 499.20 francs. Thanks to Americanization, the individual worker's wage has risen by 5.2 francs a day, but Renault is making an extra 10.70 francs per man per day.* (Le Bolchevik de chez Renault, *January 1927*)

The newspapers often use the term 'rationalization' somewhat indiscriminately to refer to any aspect of capitalist exploitation or of the logic of profit: 'Assembly-line work, timed work, replacing men with machines; the effects are not hard to see: increased output, fewer workers, and unemployment when demand begins to fall' (*Le Jouet vengeur*, February 1931). Figures are often produced to show that there have been cuts in the workforce (SIT, railwaymen in Douai and Toulouse, Citroën and Dinin) or that wage rates have been cut (Talbot, Hotchkiss, Rosengart, etc.) The introduction of new norms has been accompanied by a policy of increased repression (directed against 'hotheads', but also against older or handicapped workers who can no longer keep up with the pace).

We are now in a position to sum up:

1. The term 'rationalization' first appears in literature produced by PCF cells at some point between 1924 and 1927 (probably 1926). It then becomes a major theme, or at least one which is raised frequently.

2. The term has at least three different meanings. Sometimes it is used in its strict sense to refer to structures introduced by management in an attempt to reorganize certain branches from the late 1920s onwards. The obvious example is the assembly line. Usually, it is employed as a synonym for 'the logic of profit' or 'capitalist exploitation' or, more generally, for 'management interference' or 'reformist illusions'. Soviet rationalization ('our rationalization') is sometimes contrasted with capitalist rationalization: 'In the USSR, rationalization benefits the collectivity, and mechanization reduces the need for physical labour; this means that the working week can be shortened, and that our Russian comrades now work a seven-hour day and a five-day week. That is why there is no unemployment in the USSR' (*Le Jouet vengeur*, February 1931).

3. In every case, the appearance of the theme is important; it is not simply a response to circumstances, and has to be seen as an attempt on the part of sections of the labour movement to go beyond the sectional interests they inherited from their traditions of struggle without losing their subjective ability to react, and without losing the historical initiative.

CHAPTER TEN

YESTERDAY, TODAY AND TOMORROW?

We've been kept in a state of dependency for centuries.
We've been moulded by a whole system. It's easier to
brainwash people than it is to de-programme them!
How can you expect people to change overnight when
they've always been used to taking orders?
Shop steward, SEITA factory, Morlaix, cited by
Borzeix

That is the dilemma. It may be too much for us. We
have very little time. If we Poles do not organize, and
if we restrict ourselves to purely economic demands,
the catastrophe may become inevitable.
Jacek Kuron, a leading Polish dissident, August 1980

When he opened the CNPF's [Centre National de Patronat
Français] conference on 'Improving conditions in the factory'
in October 1977, François Ceyrac expressed his surprise at
'the extraordinary profusion, diversity and wealth of initiatives' that had
come to light during recent discussions of 'voluntary reforms in the
factory' (CNPF, 1978). The death of Taylorism is announced at regular
intervals, rather as if its decline were an inevitable process that had been
going on for the last two or three decades. How do things stand today?

Before we turn to that question, we have to agree upon the meaning
of the word. As we have seen, there is a certain discrepancy between the
activities of Taylor himself, those of the Taylor Society, and what is now
understood by 'Taylorism',[1] a term which is used to refer to the most
obvious aspects of the instrumentalization of workers and of the divorce
between the planning of work and its execution (and in that sense, there
is very little difference between Taylorism and Fordism). The 'Taylorism'
discussed below may be defined in the latter sense, but it should be noted

that, given that it is the symbol of the most characteristic structures of a mode of production, we are referring to something which is at once more general and more restricted than the historical Taylorism we have so far been discussing.

Even if we limit the terms of the discussion to French industry, it is obviously difficult to arrive at an overall picture of the organization of industrial work and of working conditions. The publication of the findings of a study of 20,000 wage-earners carried out in October 1978 (Molinié and Volkoff, 1980) is therefore all the more welcome.[2] Let us look for a moment at the findings of this study of the working population.

In 1978, France had a working population of 7,400,000 (5,700,000 men and 1,700,000 women). That figure breaks down as follows:

	%	% of all men	% of all women
Foremen	6.9	8.5	1.5
Skilled workers	40.6	46.6	20.5
Semi-skilled	33.9	30.5	45.1
Labourers	16.4	11.6	32.6
Others	2.2	2.8	0.3
Total	100.0	100.0	100.0

Several of the questions used in this study were designed to evaluate constraints of work rates, and the findings are of considerable interest. They show that 3.7% of skilled workers, 13.4% of semi-skilled workers and 8.6% of unskilled workers 'worked on an assembly line'. These figures are almost identical to those given by the Ministère du Travail on the basis of a factory survey. In round figures, they give a total of 553,000 men and women (excluding apprentices): 111,000 skilled, 337,000 semi-skilled and 105,000 unskilled workers.

Assembly-line work is most common in certain sectors in industry: shoes and clothing (32.8% of all workers), automobiles (17.9%), food, drink and tobacco (16.5%), leather and related trades (12.4%), wood-working industries, including furniture (9.9%), electric and electronic assembly (9%), rubber and plastics (8.3%) and textiles (7.7%). Most of these sectors produce consumer goods. It is not surprising to find that the number of workers on an assembly line is proportional to company size: fewer than 2% of all workers in companies employing under 50 people work on an assembly line; for companies employing between 1,000 and 4,900, the figure is 10.2%.

One of the original features of the questionnaire used by Molinié and Volkoff was the inclusion of two questions relating specifically to work rates:

1. Workers were asked if, at their work station, the speed of work was set by 'the automatic displacement of a product or part'; 3.9% of skilled workers, 10% of semi-skilled workers and 6.7% of unskilled workers replied 'yes'. This gives a weighted total of 450,000.

2. Operatives were asked if they had to 'keep up with the speed set by an automatic machine'; 8.8% of skilled workers, 18% of semi-skilled workers and 12.9% of unskilled workers replied 'yes'. This gives a weighted total of 877,000.

The findings obviously leave certain questions unanswered. It is, for instance, something of a paradox to find that there are more people 'working on an assembly line' than there are people who work at a speed set by 'the automatic displacement of a product or part' (in fact fewer than half of those who said that they worked on an assembly line *also* said that they worked at a speed set by the automatic displacement of a product or part).

A more general question about the repetitive nature of work ('Does your job consist of repeating the same set of movements or operations?') was answered in the affirmative by 23.9% of skilled workers, 44.2% of semi-skilled workers and 39.3% of unskilled workers. This gives a weighted total of 2,227,000 (excluding foremen and apprentices).

The above findings should be compared with the answers given to the question: 'Is your income level unrelated to the speed at which you work?' The authors rightly express some reservations about the lessons that can be learned from a question phrased in this way, but the fact remains that 17.2% of all skilled workers, 21.4% of semi-skilled workers and 16.7% of unskilled workers said that their income level did relate to the speed at which they worked. This gives a weighted total of 1,260,000 men and women, most of them in the following sectors: paper and cardboard (41.7%), textiles and clothing (30.2%), metals and metal-working (20.5%), rubber and plastics (20.5%) and leather and shoes (20.1%).

These figures give some indication as to how many people do repetitive jobs on an assembly line and are paid on a piece-rate basis. They are much more significant if, like Molinié and Volkoff, we look at the nature of the work done by *women*.

What do women workers do? The study identified fourteen areas of 'principal activities'. The findings reveal a broad sexual division of labour: 41.7% of all women (as opposed to 33% of men) are directly involved in production work; on the other hand, 20% of all men and only 3.1% of women are employed on maintenance, machine-setting and product assessment; 4.1% of men and only 2.5% of women operate moving machines; 7.1% of men and only 0.3% of women work on deliveries, door-to-door sales, after-sales service or transport outside the factory. In statistical terms, men have almost total responsibility for transport outside the factory.

The data suggests, in very general terms, that women tend to perform tasks which involve them directly in the manufacturing process, irrespective of whether or not it is mechanized, whereas men's involvement tends to be more peripheral.

Women are more directly involved in the manufacturing process, and if we now look at significant aspects of their working conditions, it becomes quite clear that those conditions display characteristics specific to highly instrumentalized work:

Delimitation of space: 35% of men, as opposed to 3% of women, can 'breathe freely' at work; 7% of men and 13% of women work in air-conditioned premises.

Delimitation of time: almost 30% of all workers in France have to clock on (2,200,000, including supervisory staff and apprentices). For semi-skilled women, the figure is 56%. 68.6% of semi-skilled women and 48.2% of skilled women workers have repetitive jobs. 26.5% of semi-skilled women and 15.1% of skilled women work on an assembly line. Their work load is also subject to norms:

With men, there is little correlation between levels of skill and number and length of breaks; men higher up the hierarchy tend to have slightly fewer breaks. Unskilled women workers are a special case: over 40% get at least one break and 16.6% at least two breaks. This is relevant because of the particular nature of their work load. (Molinié and Volkoff, *p. 113*)

Restrictions on movement and behaviour: 12.8% of the skilled women, 8.7% of the semi-skilled women and 15.1% of the unskilled women interviewed said that they could not talk to their colleagues at work for reasons unrelated to noise levels (isolated work stations, a ban on talking, wearing ear-mufflers, demands of work, work rates, level of concentration).[3]

If by 'Taylorism' we mean the general process of the instrumentalization and subordination of workers described at the beginning of this chapter, the dying man would appear to be still alive and kicking. This is particularly obvious if we look at the overall evolution of work, and especially at office work where, in relatively recent years, the mechanization and then the automation of work has been accompanied by a fragmentation of tasks. Discipline has been tightened up, and rationalization has been used to intensify work to an extent previously almost unknown in this sector. There are also other aspects to Taylorism: the current trend to re-deploy capital goes hand in hand with the relocation of consumer-goods industries such as textiles, clothing and electronics to developing countries.[4] Relocation takes place at an advanced technological level: highly mechanized industries are being relocated to countries where economic, social and political conditions are more conducive to the implementation of the principles of Taylorism and Fordism, which are therefore finding a new field of application.

Finally, the use of much the same principles in countries where the means of production are in social ownership indicates that they are more or less universal.[5]

However, there are also indications that the replication of the Taylorist and Fordist models is now coming up against its historic limitations. And they are so numerous that they cannot be ignored. We may sum up many of them by asking: are these models, whose coherence was established during a period of large-scale mechanization, now technologically obsolescent?

I am not suggesting that we should overestimate the rapidity of technological change or its structural effect on the role of human intervention in the labour process. In many sectors, the main changes relate to the speed and precision of machines. In others, the introduction of systematic mechanization is still an on-going process. As for automation and computerization, Moynot (1975) notes that: 'From a concrete and empirical point of view, and in the majority of cases, automation is an addition to existing processes of production; neither the labour process nor the plant is changing to any great extent at the moment.'

It is, however, true to say that the effects of automation are already making themselves felt. And given that the aim is to replace certain functions of the human brain by machines, automation has far-reaching implications. In general terms, human activity is being displaced from the manufacturing process itself to the process of designing and programming the system. In the present context, we can do no more than outline the main issues; the following remarks rely heavily on Zarifian's (1980) study of automation.

The displacement of human intervention (and the tendency to eliminate direct human labour) is already a reality. Thus, the centralized integration of several numerically controlled machines paves the way for the automated factory in which flexible machine shops can be equipped with special machine-tools, automated conveyors and with automated stock-control systems, and for the unmanned shop in which numerically controlled machines are supplied automatically and can produce complete parts automatically.

In all these cases, human activities take place at a certain remove (in terms of both space and time) from the direct manufacturing process, and the relationship between human activity and the product is modified considerably. The tendency to use sophisticated numerically controlled machines more widely is leading to the de-skilling of preparatory operations. Automation also leads to an increased disproportion between the quantity of industrial goods produced and the amount of direct effort required to produce them. As Dupin (CCEES, 1979) stresses, this technological development also reveals a major contradiction within the mode of production. Given that these automated systems function as capital, they break down the simple ratio between the level of human activity and the quantity of commodities produced. They also reduce to an unprecedented extent the amount of labour time required to produce a given quantity of commodities, even though labour time is an essential precondition for valorization.

This sheds some light on the possibilities that are being opened up by automation and on the issues it raises.

Only two of those issues will be discussed here:

1. The contradiction between the possibility of increased leisure time and the tendency to keep to a long working day. This is one of the most obvious features of the inadequacy of the modes of economic efficiency capitalism has inherited from the machine age, and its effects are now being reproduced in every area of social life.

2. Changes in the levels of skill required are increasingly subordinating execution to conception, but they also represent an intellectualization of manufacturing work and a homogenization of skills; as a result, the basis of the capitalist use of labour-power is changing. This raises major questions. Current solutions – and foreseeable solutions – reveal the capitalist mode of production's limited ability to adapt to the increasing socialization of human labour and to the changing material base of production. Even in the age of automation, Taylorist and Fordist models still influence choices relating to the division of labour (breakdown of intellectual processes, serialization, divisions and de-skilling on the one hand; concentration of knowledge on the other). But, as a coherent system, Taylorism has had its day: there is no longer any simple relationship between the valorization of capital and the immediate forms of the consumption of labour-power which could once be reduced to a mechanical model of the productive human body.

Large-scale mechanization resulted in clumsy ways of programming and controlling tasks; serialization and the direct gearing of living labour to the movement of the line are the most eloquent examples. It now seems, according to Fouet (1980, p. 142), that 'the logic of organization is moving away from the mechanical level, and that it is shifting towards automation, long-distance communication and programming'. She therefore underlines the importance of channelling investment into microcomputers which can be adapted to take direct control of production and which make it possible to achieve 'flexibility in breaking down and combining individual components of the labour process and in recombining them in various ways'.

Michel Aglietta sums up this development:

The new principle of work organization is that of a totally integrated

system in which production operations properly so called, as well as measurement and handling of information, react upon one another in a single process, conceived in advance and organized in its totality, rather than in successive and separate steps of an empirical process of heterogeneous phases. An organization of this kind is made possible by the systematic application of feedback to the functioning machine tools.
    (1979, p. 124)

Zarifian (1979) stresses the effects of the socialization of the content of labour: 'This involves the individual in a very real sense, and it represents a challenge to the forms of commodified individuality we have inherited from Taylorist and Fordist models of work organization.'[6]

This is obviously a major issue, as it implies both a new relationship between conception and execution, and new forms of objective socialization. But it also opens up the possibility of the atomization of the labour process,[7] as it allows control to become 'more abstract and more rigorous' because 'The workers are no longer subjected to a constraint of personal obedience, but rather to the collective constraint of the production process' (Aglietta, 1979, p. 128).

We have to come to terms with all these transformations, and with their implications:

It is quite certain that all these transformations at the level of production represent an immense long-term process; its starting point was a system, a productive model which has been developing in all its material, social and cultural reality since the beginning of the century and which now has a great inert weight. (Moynot, 1979)

The Trilateral Commission stresses that, in the major industrialized countries, this slow change, which extends beyond changes in the production process and which affects our whole way of life, is converging with a change in social consciousness.

During its Washington session, the Commission (CCEES, 1979) referred to Lodge's work on the decline of traditional individualist ideology in the US and on the appearance of a 'community spirit' (in terms of which an individual contract is less important than a consensus, the right to own property is less important than the right to belong, and for which models of consumption and definitions of needs are communal rather than individual). The Commission's own preoccupations led it to conclude that the transition from individualism to a community spirit represents an obvious threat to social hierarchies and wage hierarchies based upon the old ideology. It stressed the international dimension to cultural influences (arguing that Canada might well be less resistant to imported 'European' community policies and practices) and recommended the adoption of conservative but flexible strategies.

The Washington Report continued the work of the Tokyo Session on 'The Crisis in Democracy' (in Western Europe, the US and Japan). The work of the Commission represents, of course, an attempt on the part of the leaders of the major capitalist countries to come to terms with political developments by commissioning numerous concrete studies on such issues as 'loss of confidence in leadership' and 'the rising demand for mass democracy' and by relating their findings to changes at the level of production and ways of life, with all the subjective factors that involves. But, as Moynot points out, its attempts to understand the direction in which contemporary history is moving

> . . . ultimately express a fairly deep pessimism. The tone is obviously not one of panic, but it is certainly not triumphal. To take only one example: the eulogistic account of industrial relations in West Germany and Scandinavia ends by admitting that, in those countries which have pursued the most daring experiments in profit-sharing, the workers and the unions are now demanding more, despite the fact that those experiments took the ideological and institutional line of collaboration within the existing economic system. (1979)

Whilst technical and institutional structures imply certain forms of relations between rulers and ruled, and even a certain style of government in the workplace, there are, in other words, no technological or institutional solutions to social contradictions. This obvious point has to be borne in mind when we look at that current which, because of its coherence, seems to hold out the best hopes for reform: the socio-technical current.

The history and basis of this doctrine have been clearly described by other writers (on France, see in particular Ortsman, 1978a), and only two basic points will be discussed here.

      1. In the original research carried out at the Tavistock Institute between 1945 and 1960, the notion of an 'open socio-technical system' was an expression of a desire to improve 'personal satisfaction and social

relations at work' (Ortsman). It was a reaction against both Taylorism and the compensatory strategies offered by psycho-sociology. As Emery and Trist put it: 'It has been fashionable of late, particularly in the "human relations" school, to assume that the actual job, its technology, and its mechanical and physical requirements are relatively unimportant to the social and psychological situation of men at work' (1960, p. 326). It represents a pragmatic attempt to grasp the social element in technology, but the social itself is defined in technological terms, and it is reduced to immediate practical relations between men at work: 'So close is the relationship between the various aspects that the social and the psychological can be understood only in terms of the detailed engineering facts' (Emery and Trist, p. 326).

2. In one sense, the aseptic reduction of social relations to concrete questions of technology is a prelude to a recognition of the need for the autonomous organization of space, and it is this which makes the doctrine so effective. The notion of an open system (and the biological metaphor of adaptation-functions from which it derives) does break with the Taylorist schema in which 'conception' is seen as something which takes place prior to and at a distance from more general activities. The Taylorist model of a factory organized on the basis of 'command and execution' gives way to a communal model in which articulated sub-systems interact with the environment. Thus, the function of management is 'to guard the frontiers of the system'; its role is to 'regulate' and not to 'apply internal controls' (Ortsman). 'The ability to bring about internal transformations implies an ability to learn, suppleness and a spirit of initiative. This is not a purely executive role; it implies an ability to adapt' (Ortsman). As Provent (1978) suggests, these transformations are so immense that it might, perhaps, be a mistake to see them simply as a 'mutation in the Taylorist mode of organization' rather than as the 'supersession of Taylorism'. But these 'solutions' represent an *ad hoc* response to the socialization of labour, and they leave many questions unanswered. They assume, among other things, that the factory should become an end in itself ('like an organism') and that it can work on the basis of an apolitical consensus. But an apolitical consensus is not something that can be achieved by fiat, particularly as the limitations of 'coherent' Taylorism help to reveal that the various implications of the mode of production are all bound up together: models of consumption,

life styles, moral and cultural values, and so on. Even when they are expressed in limited ways, demands for control over the social use of factory products have to be understood as a reflection of a deep-rooted aspiration for economic democracy in the major industrial countries. They represent a challenge to the age-old division of responsibility which gives managers control over the economy and which leaves 'social demands' to working-class organizations.

Once the aspiration towards mass democracy begins to challenge the structures of the mode of production, the stakes are high indeed. And the Trilateral Commission recognized that when it declared that democracy was in a state of crisis. Edwards puts it in more powerful terms:

> The central problem for our time is whether this relationship will continue. The historical association between capitalism and democracy cannot be presumed to persist automatically, any more than we can expect capitalism's future to be like its past. Indeed the real question now is whether the marriage between capitalism and political democracy was made in heaven and will therefore be eternal, or whether it is merely a marriage of convenience, to be soon discarded. (1979, pp. 209–10)

The other aspect of the 'central problem for our time' is obviously the search for alternatives to this mode of production.

CONCLUSION

In a recent paper Fred Emery (1978), who was one of the historic founders of the socio-technical movement, offers an allegorical representation of the social contradictions of production and describes them in terms of a conflict between 'paradigms'. Thus, the master–slave relationship is central to the traditional paradigm of work. In logical terms, this is an asymmetrical relationship; the slave depends upon his master for work, and whenever he enters into a relationship with his master, he does so as an interchangeable element. This naturally gives rise to managerial privileges. Over the last fifteen or twenty years, a new paradigm has emerged. This is a relationship of symmetrical dependency, a relationship based upon co-operation at work.

This fable obviously pays scant regard to historical reality or to the reality of social facts, but it does contain a grain of truth: the persecutory, reifying and desubjectivizing relationship which characterizes Taylorized work (the master–slave relationship) is determined by a practical relationship of asymmetrical dependency which is at once social and technical.

We can reach the same conclusion by trying to put the development of productive structures into perspective, and by looking at them in terms of the social relations they imply. The co-operation of the age of manufacture, the mechanized factory, the assembly line and standard times are so many significant stages in a general trend towards the socialization of human labour, and that trend is by no means metaphysical. It relates both to the accumulation of humanity's cultural and technical patrimony and to the accumulation of economic value.

If the term 'Taylorist madness' has any meaning, it is because it helps us to see through coherent economic and technical systems and to perceive the contradiction between the objective socialization of labour and the subjective expropriation of the agents of the labour process.

The reason why the assembly line so often appears to be the 'boss' in a mechanized shop, and why machines seem to be the real subject of the collective labour process, is that they are Janus-like entities. They simultaneously isolate the operatives, and articulate, collectivize and socialize their work; like any disciplinary system which imposes rules for socialization but denies those who obey them access to its laws, Taylorism is experienced as a form of persecution.

If something new is 'emerging', it is not really a 'thing', but a new and dynamic expression of the contradiction in the form of industrial sociality imposed by the dominant mode of production.

As we have seen, the question of 'Taylorism' involves our whole way of life: relations of production and of consumption, habits, representations, the relationship between human beings and natural wealth (between human capacities and the resources of the environment) . . . The stakes are so high, and the technical, cultural and political levels are so interconnected that we cannot indulge in over-simplifications or sensational prophecies. The question of what has traditionally been called 'alienated labour' takes on a new meaning within this theoretical field. In this study, we have outlined one possible approach by deliberately emphasizing the role of the productive structures within which work is inscribed. In order to go beyond this stage, we would presumably have to rethink the implications of the articulation between so-called 'social facts' and the subjectivity of social actors. The result might be a new form of 'history', 'politics' and 'psychology'.

NOTES

CHAPTER ONE MANUFACTURE

1 In his introduction to Poulot (1980, pp. 66–9), Cottereau quite rightly points out that the 'bespoke work' carried out by increasing numbers of workers – and especially by women working at home – cannot be regarded as a survival of handicraft forms of industrial labour. The *canut* of the eighteenth century and the female home-worker of the nineteenth century (who, as Cottereau notes, was often paid a wage on piece-rate terms) were not in the same position. Existing forms of home-working had been transformed by the tendency to pay wages. This also indicates that, whilst the enclosure of labour within specific places of production is the dominant feature of the move towards a wage-system, that move can also take other economic and cultural forms. In other words, the inclusion of traces of labour in the cycle of capital can quite easily take place in dispersed or nominally open productive structures.

2 Earlier legislation, which was elaborated from the sixteenth century onwards, centred upon the repression of vagrancy. It was codified primarily by the Act of 1601, which defined 'legal pauperism' and which adopted the parish as the territorial unit for the administration of charity.

So long as the demand for labour was not excessive, factory-owners really had no cause to complain about the ready availability of outdoor relief or about the number of charitable institutions. In a sense, these gave public support to the pauper population from which they drew their industrial labour-force.

3   *English workhouses are vast buildings of good appearance, often with pretensions to architectural elegance, like the example I saw in Greenwich. They are usually built on a smaller scale than the hospitals found in our great cities, but their general appearance is more pleasing, especially when they are built in a rich and gracious landscape. They are usually built of stone and brick, like the most elegant cottages, their only distinguishing feature being their great size. (Buret, 1839)*

4 The political idea that work is both a citizen's right and a duty began to emerge with the philosophy of the Enlightenment. While he was still an *intendant* in Tours, Turgot established 'charity workshops' to complement the measures designed to repress 'idle vagrancy'. The Constituent Assembly asserted the principle of the right to work (La Rochefoucault Liancourt's report to the Comité de Mendacité), and raised the problem of vagrancy from the point of view of public order. The Penal Code of 1801 defined vagrancy as an offence.

5 As Gaudemar notes (1979, p. 30), Jeremy Bentham came up with a scheme for workhouses as early as 1797 and argued forcefully that they should be self-sufficient (the 'self-supply principle'). Buret (1839) describes the workhouses he saw with a mixture of horror and admiration. He viewed the work done in them both as an activity reduced to a purely penal dimension ('the treadmills and cranks are the crudest instruments of barbarism to be found in England'), as something absurd ('shovelling pebbles on a beach') and as an expression of an extraordinary economic utopia ('the crank is the most economical and admirable of machines').

6 From this point of view, the most eloquent example is probably provided by the regulations introduced at the Schneider factory in Le Creusot in 1896. Legislation introduced two years later implied that responsibility for industrial accidents might lie with the employer, but the burden of proof still lay with the victim. The Schneider regulations break down into a series of catch-all provisions ('It is forbidden to do anything that might disturb the peace of the factory in any way'; 'Workers

are constantly reminded not to expose themselves to danger, and to check safety devices and the reliability of their tools') and a host of specific rules applying to individual workshops. As Imbert (1902) notes, 'Many of the regulations are designed to protect the employer. The Management obliged the workforce to take precautions so as to be able to deny all liability if accidents occurred.'

One could also cite the unpublished memoirs of Lucien Moynot, an engineer who worked at the Vieux Jean d'Heurs et Rénesson ultramarine factory in the Doubs *département* between 1899 and 1904. As we shall see, the factory introduced a full set of regulations as early as 1867 but, by the end of the nineteenth century, this excessive legalism simply served to mask a level of exploitation which defied all social laws:

Many workers arrived at five-thirty in the morning and did not leave the factory until seven in the evening. Yet a large number of them lived a long way off and had a long journey to face before they got home. I have seen their bitterness. I have seen them hurrying to heat up scraps of bacon and potatoes at the midday break, eating quickly and then, collapsing with exhaustion, stretching out on the ground to sleep. Yet there were social laws at this time, and the factory inspector did call from time to time. He made no comments, and I have good reason to believe that he was paid to say nothing.

Moynot's comments make it easier to understand the 1867 prohibition on 'falling asleep at work'.

7 The thirty-five sets of regulations discussed here relate to a spectacle-making factory (1800), a clock factory (1873), a corset factory (1867), a printing works and a tile pottery (1868), a mine (1873), a public works department (1863), a screw-cutting shop (1890), a factory producing blast furnaces (1868), a mechanical-engineering works (1871), a refinery (1869), three paper mills (1846, 1852; one undated), eight textile mills (1846–72), nine power mills (1845–88), one ultramarine factory (1867) and two unspecified industries (1853).

8 These regulations may seem archaic. It should, however, be recalled that a study of the 'working conditions of male and female workers' in which 20,000 people in France were interviewed in October 1978 (Molinié and Volkoff, 1980) found that 5% of male workers and 11.6% of female workers could not talk to colleagues during working hours (either because their work stations were isolated, because their work was

too demanding or simply because they were forbidden to do so; cases in which the level of noise made conversation impossible were not taken into account).

9 *Some of you may have seen the feverish activity which reigns in specialist shops where the worker is no more than an automaton working ten, eleven or twelve hours a day, and has no idea of the value of the product he holds in his hands, where he is incapable of remedying the mistakes made by earlier operatives, carries out his skilled task as best he can, and then passes on a product which goes through the hands of ten or twelve men in a day before it is finished. Anyone who has seen that must, we say, ask what effects such a system will have on the future of the workers. By sacrificing men to products, this system destroys the worker's spirit of initiative and enterprise; it stupefies him by stunting his physical development, destroying his mind and, in a word, turning him into a machine.* (leather-workers' delegation to the 1867 Exposition Universelle)

10 Attempts had certainly been made to replace this considerable expenditure of skilled activity by introducing machinery. A revolutionary machine was imported from England; it could do the work of ten women, but a large skilled workforce was still required to operate it. What was more important was that it required experienced workers. All in all, it was cheaper to rely upon the old skills inherited from the age of manufacture.

CHAPTER TWO THE TABLE SYSTEM

1 Such as those carried out by the 'swarm of women' Turgan (1860) describes sorting rags at the Papeterie d'Essonne. Each woman stood in front of a box divided into twelve sections and sorted the pieces of cloth under the supervision of a checker: fine cloth, very fine, average, black, coloured, fishing nets, and so on. Then there were the 'straw pickers' [*épailleurs*] at the Teinturerie Boutardel in Clichy (1870). They sat at tables in groups of twelve, and each group was supervised by two overseers. Sitting side by side with their backs to the windows and equipped with tweezers, they skilfully removed 'all the little pieces of straw, cotton and hair that clung to the dried and dyed cloth and that had been missed during the combing process'.

2 Current methods (such as MTM, which is discussed below) obviously result from the machine's dominance over living labour, but the principles behind them can be seen as a more refined version of the first experiments in timing operations carried out by Jean Rodolphe Perronet, who published his findings in 1760.

3 In that sense, the form of co-operation that developed during the age of manufacture still exists in the contemporary workplace:

What would be nice . . . well, it would be nice to know that this does that, and that this goes there for a reason . . . They tell us nothing, but we'd like to know. The other day, when I was working on tetrode transistors, I thought to myself, 'I do sixteen zone passes a day and not fourteen: why? . . . What would happen if there were no wires?' It might be a stupid question, but basically . . . it's not that stupid [woman soldering base contacts for integrated circuits]. Obviously, the quality of the parts I make [for a transistor or an integrated circuit] represents a form of wealth, and I create that wealth, but it's difficult to see it that way. It's not easy to see the 3,000 parts you make every day as a form of wealth . . . It takes thirty operations to make one part, and even then you don't know what it's for . . . So I just put in the chips [the tiny slivers of silicon which contain the semiconductor circuit; the heart of an integrated circuit]. It takes a lot of imagination to see that what you're making is wealth, that it has a value. (woman in the same plant)

As we shall see below, many modern forms of work involve the collectivization of the labour process and imply responsibility on the part of the operative. But that dimension is usually overlooked by the formal organization of labour; it follows that a considerable amount of real labour appears to find no involvement in work organization or in the conscious mind of the worker.

4 *Oh my God! How can I explain what I do? I'd have to act it out. I do it so many times a day . . . Right. I take two screws, and a screwdriver. I put the screws in there, press them down like that, make sure the wires are not in my way, twist, pick up the iron, and then I solder it there. By the time I've done that, the next lot is already there . . . I put the set there, arrange my gear, and start again.* (transistor assembly worker)

5 *I shall only observe . . . that the invention of all those machines by which labour is so facilitated and abridged seems to have been*

originally owing to the division of labour. Men are much more likely to discover easier and readier methods of attaining any object when the whole attention of their minds is directed towards that single object than when it is dissipated among a great variety of things. But in consequence of the division of labour, the whole of every man's attention comes naturally to be directed towards some one very simple object. It is naturally to be expected, therefore, that some one or other of those who are employed in each particular branch of labour should soon find out easier and readier methods of performing their own particular work, wherever the nature of it admits of such improvement.
(Smith, *1970, p. 115*)

Sulleron (1973) is surprised by Smith's argument and by the claim that the division of labour gives rise to the invention of machines. He argues that 'if we try to establish a link between the division of labour and machinery, the idea that immediately springs to mind is that increased mechanization leads to a division of labour' (p. 26). But ideas that immediately spring to the contemporary mind are not necessarily the best way of coming to terms with Smith's insight. As Marx (1976, p. 468, n. 19) notes, Smith was right to 'assign a subordinate part to machinery' in the age of manufacture.

6 Indeed, the form of the division of labour emphasizes these features. The women perform repetitive but skilled tasks which bring them into direct contact with the object of labour. Supervising the table, supplying it with coffee and empty jars, and removing the full jars is work for men. There is a definite analogy between the team of workers who supply the women with their raw materials and the teams of workers who operate machines.

CHAPTER THREE
SPLENDID VALUE-MACHINES?

1 *Machines have invaded the workshops and have displaced a large number of workers. If, despite their strength and their intelligence, the men do not succeed in supplying the requisite quantity of labour, they are dismissed without pity (leather-workers' delegation). We are faced with competition from immensely powerful steam-engines which take the longest – and most lucrative – jobs away from us and*

which leave us, alas, only the worst jobs of all. (lithographers' delegation)

2 *This machine's sole purpose is to serve the interests of an individual or a company. And so they place it in a small dark room which is as far away as possible from the shop floor and, as though such precautions were not enough, they board it up, as though it had to be kept hidden from the eyes of the multitude, as though it were a holy image. They lock it away, just as they lock money and banknotes away in the company's strong box. Its workings are invisible to the people appointed to serve it. It becomes, in a way, a symbol of the passion, or rather the religion of 'every man for himself'.* (hatters' delegation, *1867*)

3 In 1867, the Godillot factory in the rue Rochechouard was able to supply the Army with one million pairs of boots, thanks to its high level of mechanization. Of the 300 workers employed, only 100 were trained shoemakers.

4 Its forebears are well known: the spinning wheel which refines a skilled activity, the mule jenny which partly mechanizes it (but not to such an extent that human muscular activity was no longer needed, as a mechanical system of winding on had yet to be found; the yarn still had to be stretched and twisted by hand), and Arkwright's water frames and throstle mills.

5 cf. Drapier:
I promised earlier that I would explain   why I added a set of grooved cylinders to the mule jenny. They correspond to the   fluted plates on a loom. Here is the explanation: I noticed   that as they passed over the yarn, both ends of the fibre became   trapped in it. It is undeniable that these threads are   stronger than threads   that are twisted without the friction caused by forcing the yarn through them. (1854)

6 For a long time to come, Monge's programmatic report re-examined an important reference point for teachers at the Ecole Polytechnique, and similar arguments were used by Hachette, Laboulaye and others. Marx uses a similar argument:
Large-scale industry tore aside the veil that concealed from men their own social process of production . . . Its principle, which is to view each process of production in and for itself, and to resolve it into its constituent elements . . . brought into existence the whole of the modern science of

technology . . . Similarly technology discovered [endekte] the few
grand fundamental forms of motion which, despite all the diversity of
the instruments used, apply necessarily to every productive action of the
human body, just as the science of mechanics is not misled by the
immensely complicated nature of modern machinery into viewing this as
anything other than the constant reappearance of the same simple
mechanical process. (1976, pp. 616–17)

The fact that the principal architect of this unveiling of human labour
and of its resolution into its component elements [*Die grosse Industrie*
zeriss den schleier . . .] was a certain Taylor was a minor joke on the part
of history which Marx did not live to enjoy. Curiously enough, he talks
in the past tense about a process which was not to take on its true
dimensions for another fifty years.

7 At the end of the century, Lucien Moynot, the engineer whose
unpublished memoirs have already been cited (p. 169, n. 6),
complained about the abstract nature of the education he received at the
Ecole Polytechnique:

I have always regretted the fact that the lectures given at the X [Ecole
Polytechnique] were so exclusively abstract. I am not, as it happens,
alone in this. I discovered that many of my old comrades thought the
same way when the Société des Amis de l'X tried to have the course on
kinematic geometry replaced by a course on the resistance of metals.

8 In certain particularly eloquent examples, attempts were made to
organize domestic space itself around machines:

Even without using small machines to break down motive power, those
who work at home or in small workshops can, in certain cases, be given
the benefits of mechanical power. Certain entrepreneurs in Paris have
built estates in which a powerful central steam-engine transmits power
to every floor of the buildings via a system of belts and drive shafts. The
buildings are divided up into small workshops in which whole families
or small teams can work. Attempts have been made to combine workshops
and living quarters by devoting part of the living space to mechanical
labour and using the rest for domestic purposes. Combinations of this
kind could help to resolve the problem of reconciling the needs of industry
with the interests of the family. (Eichtal, 1873)

9 In 1837, the old Fonderie Royale was bought by E. Schneider, who
reorganized things on a grand scale: there were five blast-furnaces,

fifty forges, twenty-three steam engines, with railway lines (six kilometres inside the factory and ten kilometres outside it) connecting the plant with the canal. At this time, the factory employed six hundred miners, and a total of twelve thousand smiths, turners, fitters, clerks and 'casual workers'. A recently built extension with forges and foundries opened for the first time in 1866.

10 cf. Marx:
In the paper industry generally, we may advantageously study in detail not only the distinction between modes of production based on different means of production . . . The old German paper-making trade provides an example of handicraft production; Holland in the seventeenth century and France in the eighteenth century provide examples of manufacture proper, and modern England provides the example of automatic fabrication. (1976, p. 503)

According to Turgan, in 1860, there were still 206 traditional vats in England, and 322 paper-making machines. Under the old system, the *ouvreur* [opener] worked the pulp, plunged the deckle into the vat and then removed it. The *coucheur* [bedder] placed each sheet on a piece of felt and pressed it, and the *leveur* [lifter] removed it. 'Amédée' was the finest of the nine machines at the Papeterie d'Essonne; it was named after the director. Other machines were known as Auguste, Georges, Alice, Palmyre, and so on. In fact the whole Gratiot family was represented. The Essonne paper-mill was a successful example of social paternalism: the workers were provided with housing, a shop charging 'cost prices', a free school and orphanage, medical care and a chapel where 'Madame Gratiot was kind enough to install an organ on which she herself accompanied the canticles sung to the Virgin by the young women of the Papeterie . . .' Turgan concludes that: 'The working population of the Papeterie is happy, moral, lives in a charming setting and is bursting with health and activity.'

11 This operation consisted of grinding the outer faces of watch glasses. It was a delicate operation. The twenty-four work-benches faced the windows and were overseen by a foreman. Stocks of glass were kept in the centre of the room.

12 Grevet (1980) stresses that there are two sides to the development of tools and that they are a materialization of a social force:
A. It becomes possible to articulate a great number of tasks on a

*regular basis, to further the division of labour, and to begin mass
production. These possibilities provide the basis for commodity 'mega-
structures', but, in an increasingly contradictory fashion, they are also
eminently collective elements in social life.*

*B. They make it possible for individuals or small work-groups to
acquire a greater autonomy.*

Grevet goes on to criticize the 'tendency to look only at the former aspect'
of the question (a tendency which is particularly strong in Soviet
ideologies).

13 We have already mentioned the example of the Manufacture
Impériale de Tabac, where an automaton did indeed end up on the
scrap-heap because it placed too much responsibility in the hands of the
workforce.

14 The *sublime* expresses his scorn for morality and power by likening
his body to a machine; when he has had too much to drink he has
'downed a telegraph pole', 'his wheels slip' and 'the needle on his
manometer sticks'. He may also describe himself as having 'heated the
furnace', 'blown a valve', 'heated his coil' or 'cleaned out the tubes'. In
other words, the master may well have control over the machines, but
the *sublime* can boast of having mastered the mechanics of his own body.

15 cf. Poulot:
'So, my friends; you want to bankrupt the workshop.'
*'That doesn't matter a damn to us. You have only one workshop.
We have two hundred all over the capital. And we've had enough
of your abattoir. Give us our money, and let that be an end to
it.' (1980, p. 186)*

16 The extraparliamentary commission on workers' combination
(1883–8) reveals something of the employers' motivations. The
following statements are taken from the *Bulletin de Participation* (1916):
*M. Tulen (director of the Deberny factory, which produced metal type
and employed 150 workers): 'The results we have achieved with the
profit-sharing scheme include complete agreement between management
and workers, and a feeling of mutual trust to which we attach great
value. Profit-sharing has attracted the best workers in the country to our
firm.'*

M. Fourdinois (a furniture-maker employing eighty workers): 'By restricting membership of the profit-sharing scheme to those whom the committee considers worthy of that privilege, and by excluding those who have been with me for only a short time and those who serve no useful purpose, I have succeeded in establishing a scheme based upon the élite members of my workforce.'

17 Like those of the old craft workers (the *grosses culottes* described by Poulot), the skills of machine-operators appear to be an almost biological personal attribute. According to the *Journal des Economistes* (1870):

Young men whose fathers were not factory workers are good for nothing but labouring and understand nothing about machines. But a young man who was born in a town or village which has supplied industry with workers for several generations has an almost atavistic aptitude, and quickly learns how machines work. (1870)

18 cf. the statement of the piano-makers' delegation to the 1867 Exposition Universelle:

Steam speeds up the work by driving the cutting machines, the lathes, the circular saws and the drills, but it also fragments the job and subdivides it. And so, one man works exclusively on the circular saw, and another cuts patterns; one man does nothing but drill holes and his neighbour does nothing but add the trimming. And so it goes on until the piano is complete and ready for delivery. This division of labour means that the workers acquire a certain virtuosity because they are always doing the same thing, but it also cuts costs as it means that men who know nothing about the real nature of the work can be employed.

19 The Céramique Bapterosse was a typical example. A hundred or so women and girls sitting at long tables prepared trays of 300 buttons. The male workers at the end of each table had merely to stamp them with the aid of a rudimentary press.

CHAPTER FOUR
MECHANICAL DISPLACEMENTS

1 It was this banal dimension of the assembly line that struck Hyacinthe Dubreuil:

As a result of this constant search for a way to ensure that operations represented a continuous sequence . . . it naturally transpired that handling operations could be eliminated by organizing work around a moving belt which carried parts from one machine to the next . . . The materials that had to be worked automatically came within the operatives' reach. (1929, pp. 173–4)

The assembly-line principle was explained to Renault foremen in similar terms (*Bulletin des Usines Renault*, 1918, no. 4, p. 4); it was claimed that it reduced the need for transport and handling, that it saved on physical labour, and so on. It was also pointed out that: 'The workers themselves have succeeded in reducing the number of movements they make so as to reduce the level of fatigue.' Because it imposes a very rigid structure, 'scientific' management makes it necessary for workers to adopt individual strategies to cut down the number of movements they make. We will return to this point later.

2 Barclay (1936, p. 100) lists the handling equipment used in each of the eighteen buildings of the River Rouge factory. The foundry alone used twenty-five different handling devices, including monorail trolleys, bucket elevators, cranes and hoists, trailers, lift-trucks and iron-pigging conveyors.

3 This point emerges clearly from an English study published by the ILO in 1957, which showed that the introduction of an assembly line into a cylinder-head shop cut production time by 55%, and that the reduction in the total length of the operation was almost entirely due to the elimination of superfluous movements and handling operations (CCEES, 1978, p. 82). Ford's propaganda sheet *Ford Factory Facts* (1917) claimed that the new system produced marvellous results by clearing floor space and eliminating clutter.

4 'They set the machine; we have to keep up with it, and it is constantly being speeded up. All they have to do is turn the knobs a little, and we have to keep up' (CERNUR, 1974). It is this which makes it so difficult to define assembly-line work. In the study carried out by Molinié and Volkoff (1980), 26.5% of all the unskilled women interviewed said that they worked on a line, but only 16.5% said that the speed at which they worked was set by 'the automatic displacement of a product or part'. The only explanation for this discrepancy is that working to keep up with a machine (or working on the line in a very loose sense) is more common than working on a fully mechanized assembly line.

5 A mechanized assembly line was introduced at Renault early in 1915. It was in a small finishing shop employing women.

6 *Ford Factory Facts* (1918) gives the following figures: before the introduction of the assembly line, 1,100 men working a nine-hour day assembled 1,000 engines in a day; when the line was installed, 1,400 men could assemble over 3,000 engines in an eight-hour day.

7 Edwards (1979, p. 117) outlines the history of the assembly line. Car factories were originally seen as a more complex version of the plants where teams (a skilled mechanic and helpers) assembled complete bicycles. When it was transposed to car plants, this model was transformed into a serial structure involving more and more teams. See the brief history of the Csepel cycle factory in Budapest given in Chapter 10, below.

8 Even Hyacinthe Dubreuil was forced to revise his pragmatic and banal views on the assembly line. He began to see it as a spectacle, as a symbol of the new industrial order:

It is one of the most admirable instruments of labour to be found anywhere in the world . . . The main conveyor is the focus of a vast range of activities, just as the vertebral column is the focus of the nervous system. One can literally see the endless flow of production, as this system does more than any other to make it visible. Not only do the surrounding areas bustle with activity; an invisible army of workers on the upper floors provides all the elements that are required to assemble the flood of cars.
(1929, p. 179)

Dubreuil's admiration for the spectacle is less surprising if we recall that his entire book is a populist apologia for American industry, Taylorism and Fordism.

9 *. . . having a liking for fine work and a leaning towards watches, I worked nights at repairing in a jewellery shop. At one period in my early days I think I must have had fully 300 watches. I thought I could build a serviceable watch for around thirty cents and nearly started in the business. But I did not because I figured out that watches were not universal necessities, and therefore people in general would not buy them. Just how I reached that surprising conclusion I am unable to state. (Ford, 1923, p. 24)*

But was it a 'surprising conclusion' or an intuitive realization that there was more money to be made by using a stop-watch as an instrument of power than by using watches as consumer goods?

10 cf. Edwards on the first assembly lines in the meat-packing industry:

From the perspective of control, the benefits of such production were immediate and obvious. By establishing the pace at which hogs were driven up the passages and on to the slaughter platform, managers could set the pace of work for the entire workforce. There were limits, of course, both physical and worker-imposed ones, but supervisors no longer had primary responsibility for directing the workers. Instead, the line now determined the pace, and the foremen had merely to get the workers to follow that pace . . . Struggle between workers and bosses . . . was no longer a simple and direct personal confrontation; now the conflict was mediated by the production technology itself. Workers had to oppose the pace of the line, not the (direct) tyranny of their bosses. The line thus established a technically based and technologically repressive mechanism that kept workers at their tasks. (1979, pp. 116–18)

11 cf. Ford:

About 90% of our equipment is standard, and the conversion into a single-purpose machine is a matter of detail . . . The major classifications of the standard machines are under 250 different headings, each of which is divided and subdivided into types and varieties until the list runs into the thousands. (1926a, pp. 84–5)

12 This attempt to eliminate waste or 'friction' in the human machine obviously relates to Taylor's struggle against 'soldiering', which is a form of resistance to the intensification of labour. Even Dubreuil (1929, p. 139) was struck by the 'barracks-like' atmosphere that dominated the workshops, where 'everything takes place in silence, as everyone is busy with a specific task and is perfectly indifferent to what is going on around him' (p. 180). The picture painted by Ford (1923) gives some idea of the effects this discipline had on the Detroit plant's turnover, despite the many social measures that had been implemented in an attempt to win the Fordman's loyalty. In 1919 30,000 men were dismissed, 10,000 of them because they had been absent from work for more than ten days, and 3,700 because they were not suited to the tasks to which they had been assigned.

13 'Radicalism' is to be understood in its English and American sense. Unlike the AFL, the IWW stood for industrial syndicalism and called for the socialist transformation of society. Its members were subjected to very severe repression.

14 Welfare provision included a Ford School, a Ford Hospital, cut-price shops and a newspaper (*The Fordman*) with a circulation of 50,000; this was a vehicle for the suggestions, complaints, criticisms and compliments voiced by the 'Ford Industry Family'. In some respects, this aspect of Fordism recalls European forms of social paternalism, but there are also differences, notably at the level of Ford's active promotion of productivism. As Gramsci notes (1971, pp. 296–7), puritanism was invoked to 'regulate sexual instincts', and this led industrialists like Ford to take an interest in 'the sexual affairs of their employees' and in 'their family arrangements in general'. Gramsci also demonstrates (pp. 297, 303) that Prohibition had its part to play in the development of the industrial mentality of the Fordman. Ford's own preoccupations with economics and energetics confirm the accuracy of Gramsci's analysis:

It is perhaps possible accurately to determine – albeit with considerable interference with the day's work itself – how much energy the day's work takes out of a man. But it is not at all possible to determine how much it will require to put back that energy into him against the next day's demands. (Ford, *1923, p. 124*)

15 According to Cambon's preface to the French edition of Ford's autobiography, 34,500 cars were sold in 1910, 78,000 in 1911 and 308,000 in 1914. He adds that: 'Thanks to these prodigious feats of organization, Henry Ford cut the number of men employed on chassis-construction month by month; as a result, both the cost price and the retail price fell, whilst wages rose.' In 1924, before the massive lay-offs, the 125,000 workers employed in the Detroit factory were producing parts for 9,000 cars a day.

16 Vialatte (1908) claimed that there was 'no such thing' as an American worker. Most of the 'skilled labourers' who operated the machines were recent immigrants: 60% of all workers employed in New York and 70% of those employed in Chicago at the beginning of the century were born outside the US. Most of those employed in metal-working industries were English, German or Scandinavian. Most labourers were Slav or Italian immigrants; in the South, many of them were black migrants. Vialatte describes the factories he saw as Towers of Babel, where regulations had to be posted in several languages and where workers communicated in sign-language. Dubreuil stresses that Ford's supervisory staff was poorly qualified, particularly at the lower levels of the hierarchy. According to *Ford Factory Facts*, roughly half the workers employed at Ford in 1920 were foreigners; this was slightly below the average for American factories. Even so, fifty-eight nationalities were represented at Highland Park in 1917.

17 Fifteen million Model T Fords were produced between 1915 and 1927. Its successor, the Model A, was available in only a limited number of versions. Advertising material for 1928 (New York Public Library) offered purchasers a choice between five styles of coachwork (the engine, chassis and cab were all standard). There were five variants on the light truck model (with modified chassis).

CHAPTER FIVE THE BODY AS MACHINE

1 A treadmill was a cylinder with a diameter of 1.3 or 1.5 metres with boards on the inside. The following description is from the third volume (*Dynamique*) of Dupin's *Cours normal* (as cited by Poncelet, 1839):

> *A treadmill may be operated by up to twenty men, each leaning on a pole at chest height. The English have discovered a very convenient and advantageous means of using the strength of prisoners by employing them to grind corn or to drive machines for spinning cotton, etc. The daily task of each prisoner is to climb an average of fifty steps (each of them 0.2 metres high) a minute, or 3,000 steps an hour, and to go on doing so for a full seven hours.*

The figures given by Dupin are based on observations carried out in various English prisons. The prisoners climbed the equivalent of between 2,300 and 5,700 metres a day. Buret was not mistaken when he described the similar devices used in workhouses as 'instruments of torture'.

2 cf. Le Chatelier:

> *It is futile to shed too great a light on preparatory operations; the details are sometimes difficult to understand, and may give rise to misunderstandings. Workers should only be shown the final result: the increased wages they can make thanks to scientific methods.*

3 Physiological observations cannot in fact ignore the way in which the biological is conditioned by the social. The way in which norms can vary is obvious from the tables published by Scherrer (1967).

4 cf. Taylor's account of the science of pig-iron handling (1914, pp. 40–61). A certain E. A. Doll provides a further example of non-innocent displacement when he writes in the *Bulletin of the Taylor Society* (Doll, 1926) that it would be of considerable interest to transpose the results of experiments in organizing prison labour to industrial organization. He argues that the observation of prisoners, who are under guard twenty-four hours a day, would provide scientific management with the perfect opportunity to carry out research which could then be applied in industrial life.

5 Flachat (1835) recalls that, according to the 'old science of mechanics' (Bernouilli), every kind of human labour resulted in the same level of fatigue. Coulomb describes a seven-hour day as representing the 'proper utilization' of the human machine, but makes no connection between the quantity of labour performed and its nature.

6 As Canguilhem writes:
The emergent chemistry replaced the mechanical model of the organism proposed by Descartes with a model from antiquity: that of the flame. The organism had yet to be seen as a machine powered by heat, but it was no longer seen as one driven by weights (a clock), by springs (a watch), by air (an organ) or by water (a mill). (1973, p. 38)

7 cf. the dynametric recordings obtained with the capsule developed by Marey, Mosso's ergograph, and the work of Chauveau.

8 Examples include the apparatus designed by Helmholtz in 1850, which made it possible to measure the speed of conduction in a nerve impulse, and Bernstein's differential rheotome of 1868, which made it possible to measure the length of potential nervous action (0.7 of a millisecond).

9 cf. Muybridge (1887). In Muybridge's system, a running horse (or a camel, an ostrich or a tiger) triggered the lenses of a battery of cameras which had been held shut by electro-magnets.

10 Marey and Demeny summarized their recommendations in a report submitted to the Ministère de la Guerre. It could well have been entitled 'Feet, proper use of', and defined the optimal rhythm for a

forced march, a quick march, and for marching with a full pack, and so on.

11 Examples will be found in any medical thesis published after 1825. In his thesis on 'sympathy between organs', Augay writes: *Whilst every part of an inorganic body contains within it an explanation for its mode of existence, the same cannot be said of bodies endowed with life. Here, all the parts are subordinate to one another. The material and inevitable condition of organized bodies is in fact such that they are born and live with their respective parts subordinated to one another; when this law of living matter ceases to apply, they die and re-enter the vast field of inorganic bodies.*

Similarly, Camparan's *Propositions générales* include the following theses: 'VII. All the phenomena of life depend upon organization'; 'X. The purpose of all functions is the preservation of the individual and the species'; XVII. 'Life is a death sentence'; 'XXI. The greater the energy of an organism or system of organisms, the more active its functions, and the more acute and frequent the maladies that attack it; lesions are therefore usually to be observed on the right side of the body.'

12 Lahy is a typical example. Being a co-founder of the journal *Le Travail humain*, he does not challenge the utilitarian recovery of scientific 'discoveries'; in the editorial which appeared in the first issue, he writes: 'We have entitled our journal *Le Travail humain*; it could easily be subtitled: "Understanding man with a view to using human activity as judiciously as possible".' But he does insist that scientific criteria must take priority over economic rationality. In an earlier work (1920, pp. 203ff.), he noted the 'barbaric' effects of the introduction of Taylorism at Renault, attacks it on physiological grounds, and challenges 'the complete assimilation of man to a mechanical motor'.

13 It is, for example, difficult to find any major discovery in the work of Taylor, even though Edouard Herriot (1920), in his enthusiastic attempts to find French precedents for American-style ideas about rationalization, cheerfully compared him to Coulomb, Claude Bernard and even Descartes. Taylor himself admitted (1914, p. 139), with his typical but rather forced modesty, that 'Scientific management does not necessarily involve any great invention, nor the discovery of new or startling facts.' In one sense, Taylor's one real discovery was of a purely technical order, and related to the use of high-speed steel in metal-

cutting. At the time he made his discovery, Taylor was working for the Bethlehem Steel Company, which had diversified its activities considerably. Documents in the collections of the New York Public Library give some idea of just how diverse they were: the 1938 catalogue comprises ninety-five sections relating to ship-building, buildings, cars, railways, hardware, and so on. Writing in the *Bulletin of the Taylor Society* in October 1928, Le Chatelier recalls that he was very impressed by the display of lathes equipped with Taylor's cutting machines which he saw when he visited the 1900 Exposition Universelle in Paris. Taylor's innovation provoked so much discussion that, four years later, Le Chatelier published an article in his *Revue de Métallurgie* defending the inventor against his critics. As a result, the two men eventually met, and Taylor's writings were published in France.

CHAPTER SIX
NORMS, PRODUCTIVITY AND WAGES

1 cf. Marx: 'A commodity appears at first sight an extremely obvious, trivial thing. But its analysis brings out that it is a very strange thing, abounding in metaphysical subtleties and theological niceties' (1976, p. 163).

2 It will be recalled that, in semiological terms, a *sign* is a combination of a signifier and a thing signified. The signifier is that part of the sign which is 'sensuous' (visible, audible, etc.); the thing signified is that part of it which remains 'hidden' but which can be re-presented (through a change in its form) in a conventional form by the signifier.

3 cf. Marx:

Here two different kinds of commodities (in our example the linen and the coat) evidently play two different parts. The linen expresses its value in the coat; the coat serves as the material in which that value is expressed. The first commodity plays an active role, the second a passive one. The value of the first commodity is represented as relative value, in other words the commodity is in the relative form of value. The second commodity fulfils the function of equivalent, in other words it is in the equivalent form.

The relative form of value and the equivalent form are two inseparable moments which belong to and mutually condition each

other; but, at the same time, they are mutually exclusive or opposed
extremes, that is, poles of the expression of value . . . 20 yards of
linen are nothing but 20 yards of linen, a definite quantity of linen
considered as an object of utility. The value of the linen can therefore
only be expressed relatively, that is, in another commodity. The
relative form of the value of the linen therefore presupposes that some
other commodity confronts it in the equivalent form. On the other
hand, this other commodity, which figures as the equivalent, cannot
simultaneously be in the relative form of value. It is not the latter
commodity whose value is being expressed. It only provides the
material in which the value of the first commodity is expressed. (1976,
pp. 139–40)

4 None of this is particularly mysterious or complex, but these propositions do allow us to make great advances at the theoretical level.
They may, for instance, allow us to arrive at a rigorous articulation
between the Marxist theory of alienation (and of alienated labour, which
is discussed below in Chapter 8), questions relating to the fetishism of
norms, and psychoanalytic theory, as exemplified in France by the
contributions of Jacques Lacan. No one can fail to be astonished at the
poverty of current theoretical work in what is obviously an essential field
if we are to understand the implications of the commodity dimension of
social relations at the level of individual subjectivity. My knowledge of
Lacanian psychoanalysis is restricted to the paper on labour read by G.
Haddad to the day school organized by the Ecole Freudienne de Paris on
8 November 1975. Having advanced the view that 'labour is structured
like a language', the author argues that we find in labour the same
figures (nomination, metaphor and metonymy) that we find in rhetoric.
Assembly-line work, for example, effects a displacement of the signifier
(metonymy) because activities become meaningful only at the end of the
line. The only problem with this construct is that it overlooks the
economic dimension of production.

From a Marxist point of view, matters are rather different. Lucien
Sève's pioneering work on the theory of personality (1978) is in many
respects very illuminating, but it overlooks these effects of meaning and
the relationship with the law which is implicit in economic relations. It
appears to me, however, that this is an essential question if we are to
understand what 'happens' in the dialectical history of subjects whose

186

adult personality structures are still marked by their primal relations with the 'symbolic' and the 'law'.

5 Mitchell (in Société Taylor, 1932, p. 320) describes how he selected his best workmen and then spent a week ensuring that production would not be interrupted by non-standard conditions (broken belts, poor transmission, poor-quality wire, etc.). The workmen were thus able to complete their tasks inside the standard times; this proved to them – and to everyone else – that the times could be achieved. Two other workers were then put on the same job, under the same protected conditions for half a week. Four more were then set to work. Eventually, they were all working on the same basis.

6 cf. Taylor:

Every labourer's work was planned out in advance, and the workmen were all moved from place to place by the clerks with elaborate diagrams or maps of the yard before them, very much as chessmen are moved on a chessboard, a telephone and messenger having been installed for this purpose. (1914, p. 69)

7 According to Taylor's theory, when a time-study expert observes a man at work, he watches only eight or ten of the movements he makes; the others have already been studied by watching other workmen. Most of the movements a mechanic makes are already subject to norms, and they therefore do not need to be timed.

8 cf. Karger and Bayha: 'MTM is a method which breaks down every manual operation into the basic movements necessary for its execution, and which sets a predetermined standard time for every movement; the standard time is determined by the nature of the movement and by the conditions under which it is executed' (1957, p. 43). The war effort helped to popularize Taylor's ideas, and by 1919 his disciple Thompson was expressing doubts about the many efficiency engineers who were setting up as consultants; in a lecture given in Paris, he described them as unscrupulous profiteers who were exploiting Taylor's doctrine (*Bulletin des Usines Renault*, 1920, no. 37, p. 14). The Bureau des Temps Elémentaires, a non-profit-making organization established by a group of industrialists in the wake of the inter-war rationalization movement, set itself the task of co-ordinating and simplifying information about these various methods.

9 The basic assumption was that the women with the most highly developed conditioned reflexes would be able to supply the greatest quantity of labour for a given level of fatigue. Psychotechnical tests were used to eliminate those with very poor responses; they were assumed to have a 'low personal coefficient'.

10 There were two sides to this policy towards the handicapped. It meant that 'sub-standard men' could be integrated into production (or kept on the line), but there was no mystery about the fact that it was also a repressive practice. The Detroit factory, for instance, was equipped with twenty medical rooms, each with seven beds; they could be used if the Company believed that it was better for a workman (and the Company) for a man to remain at work and receive medical treatment inside the factory than to be sacked for absenteeism. At one point, bedridden men 'who were able to sit up' were strongly encouraged to work (Ford, 1923, pp. 109–10). Teams of special investigators were employed to look into cases of absenteeism.

11 The practice of establishing files on individual workers was not really new when the Taylor Society discussed it. In an article published in the Bulletin of the Society to Promote the Science of Management (November 1915, vol. 1, no. 6; the Society was later to become the Taylor Society), Richard A. Feiss describes the methods he used in his industrial garment factory. A system of cards was used; one side of each card contained information about the worker's identity, parents, ethnic origins and previous employment; the other contained a certain amount of medico-psychological information ('anaemic', 'nonchalant') and notes on the individual's degree of motivation and way of life ('father out of work', 'mother has agreed to take care of child', etc.). This was followed by his medical record (doctor, optician, dentist) and by basic health advice on the need for rest and fresh air.

12 Mechanical models of human personality were discussed in the Bulletin of the Taylor Society (vol. 15, no. 2, March 1929). For example, punctuality was defined as a combination of caution, stability and reliability, and courtesy as a combination of cordiality, respect, good disposition and a desire for approval. Each primary quality was evaluated on the basis of three characterological questions. In order to determine whether or not he had a 'good disposition', for example, a worker might be asked: 'If you disagree with someone, to what extent are you prepared

to give him the benefit of the doubt?' We shall not be so uncharitable as to criticize this method.

13 cf. the article by Ram (the engineer who was called in by Louis Renault to introduce 'shop management') in Le Chatelier's *Revue de métallurgie* (Ram, 1908). Ram describes how the output of a shop employing fifty people was doubled, and how 'mediocre' workers were eliminated naturally and rapidly (over a period of eighteen months). One quarter of Renault's shops were Taylorized between 1908 and 1914, despite two 'time-study' strikes (1912 and 1913). A mechanized assembly line was installed in a small finishing shop in 1915. By 1918, tanks were being assembled on the line system; the chassis were loaded on to trolleys running on rails and were pushed from one work station to the next. A fully mechanized line was introduced in 1922 for the assembly of the 10-horsepower Renault; there were only twelve work stations, and the line stopped at each of them for forty minutes (cf. Maillard, 1971). The big assembly lines on the Ile Séguin were not introduced until 1930.

14 Cottereau (in Poulot, 1980, p. 73) shows that differential piece-rates are the culmination of a whole series of management innovations designed to replace agreed rates with set rates, and to link wages to productivity. In the case of France, an engineer called Euverte perfected this system at Cail in about 1840, and then introduced it at Le Creusot. He describes it in the *Journal des Economistes* (1870, vol. 19, pp. 364ff.). The method in fact combined elements of collective and individual bargaining between workers and their employers with elements of the set-rate system, as bargaining was based upon a previously agreed rate for each job. Wages began to be linked to productivity when a system of 'progressive bonuses' was introduced in 1851; the introduction of a 'daily accounting system' also allowed the workers to see the results of their labours. As a result, 'The men's actions became faster, and everyone tried to avoid wasting time; output finally rose to a considerable extent, much to the advantage of all' (p. 369). Euverte describes similar incentive methods which were in use in the mines around Le Creusot and in the Gard. He also states that such enormous amounts of capital had been invested in the industry that the question of the intensification of labour was crucial. This meant 'producing as much as possible with the smallest possible number of workers' (p. 348). Euverte's article is virtually the only systematic account of management views on these questions to have been published by the *Journal des Economistes* during this period. For a discussion of all these points, see Mottez (1966).

15 The method used for arriving at a 'scientific' method of paying higher wages for intensified work suggests that this was in fact the case. It was, as Taylor explained to a Congressional Committee of Inquiry in 1912, arrived at after a long series of experiments. Although every effort had been made to establish an atmosphere of mutual trust, a group of six workmen who were offered a 15% bonus refused to extend their contracts beyond an initial six-month period. Taylor explains: 'This experiment showed that an addition of 15% to the workman's pay was not sufficient to compensate him for the bother of having to change his ways and methods of working and to adopt some other man's way of doing things' (1914, p. 266). An offer of 20% was also refused, but half the workmen agreed to accept the new conditions in exchange for 25%; all but one agreed to accept 30%,and general agreement was reached at 35%: 'It was in this way that we arrived at these percentages. I call that a scientific experiment' (Taylor, p. 266).

16 The introduction of individual wage rates and, more generally, the use of individual 'profiles' as a basis for promotion at Ford resulted in the creation of a weighty bureaucratic apparatus which Cestre (1921, p. 29) describes briefly: files on each of the 40,000 workers were held in several different registers, and the personnel department occupied a whole building.

17 Dubreuil's confused thinking and his extraordinary political evolution (which took him from membership of the Fédération CGT des Métaux to militant support for Pétain) mean that he can now be seen as a symbolic figure in the history of 'profit-sharing'. cf. *Bulletin D'Information du Comité Hyacinthe Dubreuil* (1978).

18 The innovations made by Otto S. Beyer, Jr, at the Baltimore and Ohio Company are a typical example (*Bulletin of the Taylor Society*, February 1926, vol. 12, no. 2). Having seen the trench warfare that was going on between unions and management (and in his view it was symbolized by the glass partitions which divided the offices from the shop floor below), he instituted joint committees in each shop and each trade. There was no discussion of 'secondary' issues, such as wages; discussion was restricted to the analysis of standards, the improvement of supplies and raw materials, the rational distribution of teams, and so on. In a period of just over one year, 16,000 meetings were organized, each lasting for at least an hour; 9,000 proposals were accepted. Taylor himself had thought of establishing similar joint committees.

CHAPTER SEVEN SHARING?

1 cf. Lemaire's statement of principle: 'Any worker who, in obedience to the law of labour, nourishes and helps the Society to which he belongs must, in all justice, receive what he needs to keep him while he produces.'

2 On Leclaire's social achievements at Herblay, see Leclaire (1868).

3 cf. the remarks made by J.-P. Drouet, a mechanic and former union representative at Cail:

The reason why we do not produce as much as we could, do not save on raw materials and do not treat the instruments of labour as we should is that we are not interested in the master's prosperity. He pays us as little as possible, and we work as little as possible. How many times a day do we ask, 'What time is it?' What a penance! If we see a mate wasting raw materials or damaging a tool, we are indifferent. A lot of the time, we even laugh. (Faure and Rancière, 1976, pp. 396–426)

4 cf. the account of the Assemblée Générale de la Participation at the Chaix printworks given in the *Bulletin de Participation* (1880): only one man took part in the 1878 strike. Five apprentices went on strike 'despite strict orders from their parents'. Their loss of privileges was an example to all.

5 Sedley Taylor, who taught at Trinity College, Cambridge, published his *Profit-Sharing Between Capital and Labour* in 1884.

6 The comments made by miners to the authors of a study of trade unions carried out before the 1865 reforms give some idea of their attitudes: 'All coal-masters are devils, and Briggs is the prince of devils . . . He would be the devil if he had the horns' (cited by S. Taylor, 1884, p. 135).

7 According to A. Dunoyer, a Versailles contributor to the *Journal des Economistes* (April–June 1871), the International Working Men's Association had 25,000 members in Great Britain in 1866. The 1866 Sheffield Conference's decision to allow unions to join the International

considerably reduced the leadership's control over union lodges and branches.

8 *The amount of capital devoted to production – according to the prevalent strength of the effective desire of accumulation – determines the force of the demand for labour: the number of labourers desirous of employment – in accordance with the prevalent strength of the instinct of population – regulates the supply. All unknown to the capitalist and the labourer, the rate of wages is fixed for them, by the natural adjustment of these antagonistic forces. (Stirling, 1870, pp. 311–12)*

Stirling goes on to denounce wage struggles as 'contrary to natural law' and attacks trade unions for their 'master-bating' and 'intolerable meddling with the daily conduct of business' (pp. 327, 326).

9 According to the 1912 Report on Profit-Sharing and Labour Partnership, these systems operated in only 136 companies, but those companies employed 106,000 people.

10 The Zeiss Foundation is to be compared with the Krupp factory. In 1850, Krupp introduced insurance schemes to protect the workforce from the effects of illness, accidents and old age. In 1877, a life-insurance scheme was added to the existing measures designed to encourage saving. Housing was the object of a particularly active policy: workers were housed in 'colonies', some of which were semi-rural and had gardens where it was possible to keep animals. In 1892, Krupp employed 15,300 workers and housed a total of 25,800 tenants. The housing policy was part of a productivist attempt to rationalize relations between the home and the factory, and to introduce a form of moral and ideological policing (tenants were required to admit the company's investigators to their homes at any time). It was also intended to produce a stable workforce; only those who had worked for the company for ten years could apply for housing. Like Zeiss, the Krupp factory had a hospital, a health service, trade schools, libraries and a network of shops and markets charging 'reasonable prices' (Muller, 1898).

11 cf. Abbe's lecture on 'Shortening the working day':
'If he had more free time, what would the worker do with it?'
Answering that question is none of the employer's business, but it is still of great relevance to him, as the misuse of free time might render the entire system ineffective. The worker must rest all the bodily organs

he uses in the factory, and the Zeiss Company specifically requires him to do so. It is no concern of the Company's whether a worker does nothing at all in his free time, or whether he finds some way of occupying his time. Eventually everyone will find some occupation which comp-lements his primary task; his family and the Company will provide him with an opportunity to do so. (Iena Society for Political Science, *1901; cited by* Auerbach, *1906*)

12 An early official report by Caroll D. Wright (1880) made frequent references to European experiments in organizing life outside the workplace (housing schemes at the Menier factories in Noisel, at mills in Mulhouse, and at Krupp), and in organizing industrial relations (the Guise Familistère, the printworks in Tours, etc.). The report was commissioned in connection with the 1880 census.

13 In January 1917, 144 'advisers' were employed by this department, and *Ford Factory Facts* describes their work in striking fashion. An article on 'Education and profit-sharing' is illustrated by a picture of a traditional Russian family who have just got off the Detroit train. This is followed by a series of pictures: an adviser, catalogue in hand, gives the mother advice on how to furnish the house; first we see an untidy kitchen ('education must have more lasting results than a clean oven') and then a tidy kitchen when the adviser calls a second time.

14 A summary of Wolf's report on individuality in industry was published by the *Bulletin of the Taylor Society* in its May 1915 issue, together with some critical comments on the first part. The comments depart from the *Bulletin*'s usual optimistic tone by remarking that Wolf has nothing constructive to say and that he stresses the weaknesses of the system. The report was then published in its entirety in August of the same year. Wolf's report was in fact originally commissioned by the American Society of Mechanical Engineers in 1912, and it points to the contradiction between concentration in factories and management, and the need for detailed supervision in the factory. Using a neurological model of the human personality, he makes a series of general recommen-dations designed to promote individual initiative (taking into account the development of individuality so as to stimulate creativity; leaving the individual a margin of choice; allowing individuals to express their tastes and talents in a controlled way). In later years, the Society also discussed Person's report on management and the social scientist (Person, 1917),

Kendall's paper on the centralization of authority, Follet's contribution on 'The illusion of final authority' (1926) and Person's (1926) paper on relations between chief executives and associate executives.

15 Bingham's article is based partly upon his report to the first congress of the International Association for Industrial Relations, Cambridge, 1928.

16 In his reply to the criticisms addressed to his 1916 report by Wolf, Thomson, Feiss, Kent and others, Valentine expressed an unusually pessimistic view. His starting point was the notion that industry should be part of a universal system of education, but he feared that, if industry did not try to promote a new kind of industrial citizenship, the effect on industrial reconstruction in the years to come would be cataclysmic. There was, however, nothing inevitable about this.

17 For a summary of Mayo's research and of the major critical analyses that have been made of it, see Ortsman (pp. 21–8).

18 Contemporary developments in scientific management revealed that 'coercive' logic had its limitations and disadvantages. In Germany, Durig found that if 'soldiering' was eliminated, other forms of resistance took its place (sabotage, loss of quality, absenteeism). A new interest began to be taken in the figures for industrial accidents (cf. the 'Safety First' movement in the US, and the survey carried out by the American Engineering Council in 1922–5). In England, the IFBR echoed the fears of industrialists who found that output fell in factories where work was fragmented; studies by Vernon, Wyatt, Bredford, Fraser, Ogden and others helped to challenge the dogma that repetitive work and coercion resulted in maximum efficiency. Systematic studies based on empirical observations showed that shorter working hours could lead to increased output, and experiments with a shorter working week were made in England, the US and Germany.

19 This representation of social life sometimes results in the claim that Marxists 'support' class struggle. Althusser treats this claim with the irony it deserves:

> For the reformists . . . it is not class struggle which is in the first rank;
> it is the classes. Let us take a simple example, and suppose that we are
> dealing with just two classes. For the reformists these classes exist before
> the class struggle, a bit like two football teams exist before the match
> . . . One class may be exploiting another, but for reformism that is not

the same thing as class struggle. One day the two classes come up against one another and come into conflict. (1972, p. 316)

20 Poitou (1972) demonstrates, for example, that the definition of a 'group' given by writers like Cartwright and Zander (1968; the purpose of forming a work group is described as being to carry out a task as efficiently as possible by pooling and coordinating the behaviour and resources of a number of individuals. The prototype for such groups is the small society an entrepreneur founds in order to manufacture a product. Organizing an expedition to explore Antarctica is another example. Work groups of one sort or another are thus found throughout society) cannot be unproblematically applied to a factory. On the one hand, management's objective is not to 'manufacture a product', but to valorize capital; on the other, the workers do not share that objective, and are pursuing their own goals.

21 For both Homans and Skinner, sociality and the feeling of social approbation become a sort of general equivalent to the exchange of goods and services (an equivalent to a social transaction for Homans; to general reinforcement for Skinner). These models, like those derived from the work of Lewin, are basic to the notion of the 'group'.

22 Maslow's (1954) classic schema identifies five levels of needs: psychological needs, safety needs, belongingness and love-needs, esteem needs, and needs for self-actualization. Higher needs cannot be expressed unless these lower needs have already been satisfied.

23 Hartmann's paper was first read to the Vienna Society in 1937; it was first published in the USA in 1939.

CHAPTER EIGHT ON ALIENATED LABOUR

1 *The Mercantile system in fact denies the creation of absolute surplus value – [in opposition to this] the Physiocrats seek to explain absolute surplus value. (Marx, 1969a, p. 66)*

2 cf. Quesnay:
You will agree, I think, that obtaining the greatest possible increase in wealth by reducing expenditure as much as possible represents the highest form of economic behaviour. Not only would I like to reduce expenditure as much as possible; I would also like to do away with the need for hard labour, in so far as it is possible to do so, and to obtain the greatest possible wealth. It appears to me that this is a

universal human desire; those who can legitimately gain this advant-
age profit from it as best they can, and they can even profit from it
without prejudicing the general interest . . . The rich spend their
wealth to pay their workers; they would do themselves a great wrong
if they stooped to labour, as that would deprive them of their wealth
. . . And they would not obtain the greatest possible increase in wealth
by reducing expenditure as much as possible. (1888, pp. 535-7)

3 'For them [the physiocrats] the bourgeois forms of production necessarily appeared as natural forms. It was to their great credit that they
conceived these forms as physiological forms of society: as forms arising
from the natural necessity of production itself, forms that are independent
of anyone's will or politics, etc.' (Marx, 1969a, p. 44).

4 'Agriculture, that most fertile and normal element in commerce, and
the source of the kingdom's wealth, was not seen as a primary fund
of wealth; it seemed to be of interest only to the farmer or the peasant'
(Quesnay, 1888, p. 193).

5 This is why, Denis noted (1966, p. 181), the sovereign, who possesses
both wealth and subjects and who had the right to raise taxes, can in
physiocratic thought be identified with the farmer.

6 cf. Quesnay's article on farmers in the *Encyclopédie*. Quesnay defines
farmers in the English sense (as opposed to the French sense of 'tax
farmer') as 'those who promote and exploit the wealth of the countryside
and those resources which are most essential for the support of the state'.
They are, that is, agrarian capitalists. Quesnay goes on: 'As the labourers
become richer, the more they use their faculties to increase the produce
of the land and the might of the nation. A poor farmer works to the
detriment of the state, because his work does not yield the products that
the earth bestows only on those who have an opulent nature.'

7 How can one be both a labourer and a citizen? This is the contradiction
behind this passage from the *Second Dialogue sur les travaux des*
artisans:

H. *(Contradictor): Is it not preferable to employ our fellow citizens*
rather than foreigners in the fields?

N. *(Quesnay): Yes, it is preferable, as we do not have to reward them*
for their labours. Were that not the case, it would be preferable to use
not only foreigners, but animals or even machines; the profits, which

increase the available wealth, always come back to the population of
the country. (Quesnay, *1888, p. 540, emphasis added*)

8 cf. Denis:
   In 1776 Quesnay published his Analyse du gouvernement des
   Incas du Pérou. *In the same year, he also published a long study
   entitled* Despotisme de la Chine. *He believed that he could find an
   illustration of his political economy in Peruvian or Chinese society,
   as both those societies were based upon age-old principles. This shows
   quite clearly the extent to which political economy was, according to
   Quesnay, independent of history. (1966, pp. 184–5)*

9 It will be recalled that Robinson Crusoe gradually assumes his
   condition and wins economic and political control over the island
which became his after his deliverance from the sea: 'In a word, I had a
dreadful deliverance. For I was wet, had no clothes to shift me . . .
neither did I see any prospect before me but that of perishing with hunger
or being devoured by wild beasts' (Defoe, p. 54). Eventually, he becomes
its sovereign, and his creator's equal. In the meantime, he has become
rich; thousands of miles away, his Brazilian plantations, which his partner
and overseers tended so carefully, have made him 'over £59,000'.
Although man is the weaker sex in this Malthusian vision of nature, his
ingenuity and his ability to save allow him to dominate nature. They are
the true sources of his power. Banfield, for example, argues that when
the forces of nature are put to work instead of slaves, society is spared
the greatest humiliation ever experienced by human nature. He views
the productive powers of primitive man as an affront to the pride of the
human race; being weak and having no capital, primitive man's only
instruments of labour were those supplied by his organism. The same
myths about man's original impotence can be found in Chevalier ((1870):
the author claims that man was cast up naked on to the shore with only
a clump of trees and a hole in the rocks for shelter; he shared his only
resources with the animals; but he was also naked, weak and clumsy, and
was therefore at a disadvantage compared with many of the creatures he
was called upon to dominate) and in Molinari ((1907): 'In the initial
period of its history, a history which has culminated in the colossal
machines of modern industry, mankind was, like the lower species,
reduced to living on what nature provided . . . Although we have no

first-hand accounts, legends tell of the tributes levied by monsters which ate human flesh. The Cretans paid similar tributes to the Minotaur.')

10 cf. Stirling: 'A different force constrains the workman and his master; one is pinched by hunger; the other is racked with care; and who can tell which suffers more? Things so unalike cannot be measured one against the other' (1870, p. 137).

11 *To prevent possible misunderstandings, let me say this. I do not by any means depict the capitalist and the landowner in rosy terms. But individuals are dealt with here only in so far as they are the personification of economic categories, the bearers [Träger] of particular class-relations and interests. My standpoint, from which the development of the economic formation of society can be viewed as a process of natural society, can less than any other make the individual responsible for relations whose creature he remains, socially speaking. (Marx, 1976, p. 92)*

12 Poulantzas (1978) characterizes the 'fundamental ideological mechanism' behind the capitalist mode of production in the following terms:

When it is the cycle of the reproduction of capital itself (and not extra-economic reasons) which governs the extraction of surplus value (surplus labour), and when the sub-symbolizations which cement personal territorial links between its agents are destroyed, the rule of capitalist law is based upon the signifying void which surrounds it. (p. 97)

13 On this dimension of labour, cf. Lainé (1971): 'Man's relationship with work and his relationship with language are two inseparable links in a single chain. Both activities are specific to man . . . they produce man as social being.'

14 According to a study carried out by the Chambre de Commerce de Paris: 'Most cabinet-makers are German; they come to work in Paris for a while and take furnished lodgings in the VIIᵉ *arrondissement*. Over the last twenty years, a considerable number of German immigrants have moved into the area, and they in fact make up the greater part of what might be termed the resident population' (cited by Gaudemar, 1979, p. 59).

15 These were official statements made before the Emperor and fellow craftsmen during the Exposition Universelle (*Rapport des délégations*, 1867).

16 In terms of economic thought, the idea that labour is a purely economic activity gradually took shape on the basis of the distinction between the use-value and exchange-value of commodities. The physiocrats had already developed a conceptual distinction between the two (Quesnay's 'venal value' and 'useful value'; Turgot's 'appreciative value' and 'estimative value'), but not a structural theoretical distinction, as their concept of wealth did not allow them to differentiate between a material increase in agricultural produce or stock-raising, and an increase in exchange-value. Adam Smith made a clear distinction between the two, related them to different dimensions of production, and clearly defined the exchange-value of a commodity as being 'equal to' the quantity of labour it allowed its owner to buy or control. He also realized that labour is therefore the measure of the exchange-value of any commodity. On this basis, it becomes possible to make a distinction, within the process of production itself, between the process of valorization (which is 'purely economic'; this dimension of production is inscribed within a system of economic signifiers) and the labour process, which can initially be defined as a residue which is not directly inscribed within that system of signifiers.

CHAPTER NINE TAYLORIST REALISM AND THE REALITY OF TAYLORISM

1 *The organizer reconstructs the action of soldering: how long does it take to pick up the iron? How long does it have to be held on the solder to produce the right result? How long does it take to put down the iron? All that can be analysed. But, unfortunately, conditions are never standard. The iron becomes worn, and that affects the time it takes to solder something. The women are also well aware of the fact that the quality of the solder itself varies, that the length of time it takes to solder something depends on how much resin there is. . .*
(Durrafourg, *1980*)

2 Durrafourg records the comments made by a woman operating a small press in a toaster factory: 'A defect is not something that either exists or doesn't exist. A defect appears, and then it changes. That's what a defect is.' Durrafourg adds: 'A part is neither good nor bad; it's always in between the two, because a part is a place where faults develop, and where they either get worse or sort themselves out.'

3 cf. Linhart:

I was surprised to see that Georges could leave his place on the line for ten minutes at a time. He laughed: 'Pavel and Stepan are there!' The explanation was that the three Yugoslavs were on adjacent work stations. They all worked on the lock assembly; a delicate job, with lots of little screws to be fitted in the corners. But they were so dextrous and worked so quickly that they succeeded in turning the work of three men into a job for two. One of them was therefore always free to go and have a quiet smoke in the toilets, or to go off and chat up the girls in upholstery. The foreman turned a blind eye to this arrangement and to their mutual aid system because he never had any trouble on that section of the doors line . . . The management had obviously toyed with the idea of doing away with one of the three jobs since the Yugoslavs had managed to turn them into two. But you only had to see them at work to realize that no normal person could keep up that speed. You'd have thought they were conjurors. (1978, pp. 33–4)

4 'The girls have never worked as fast as they do in the present difficult economic climate'; conversation with F. Blanc, a shop steward at Playtex.

5 Observations carried out in a traditional factory where the process of trouser-making is divided up between ninety work stations give the lie to the notion that the assembly line is the only thing that connects work stations. Fourteen stations were observed for 24 minutes, and 61 instances of verbal communication were recorded (in almost every case they were work-related: 'Careful, that's the wrong size'; 'It's not the same colour'; 'There's a belt-loop missing'; 'The side seam has split'; 'The machine's staining the cloth' . . .). In 11 cases, a pair of trousers was used as a means of communication (a fault was noticed; the argument 'went back up the line' to be repaired). In 41 cases, women had to move around to pass messages. The four overlookers were constantly on the move to carry messages backwards and forwards. On average, they changed position at least once a minute. (This research was carried out for a multidisciplinary study on behalf of the CGT. The findings are to be published.)

6 In the first three months of 1927 alone, *L'Humanité* published the following: 'Their rationalization and ours', a long article by P. Semard on the positions adopted by the Executive Committee of Comintern (3 January); an article on proposed wage cuts and rationalizations as a means to 'remedy' problems in the leather-working industry (4 January); a full-page spread entitled 'Rationalization' and reproducing Comintern slogans (11 and 12 January); 'The industrialization of the fishing industry and its effects' (17 January; 'The Leningrad Leather Trust: an example of Socialist rationalization' (27 January); Raveau on 'Capitalist rationalization means job losses and increased exploitation' (3 February); an article by Marty (9 February); articles by Raveau on 'Rationalization and unemployment' and 'Rationalization and wages' (10, 18 and 23 March); 'They want to rationalize Citroën' (2 March) and 'Rationalization and apprentices' (L. Jeanne, 15 March).

7 The exception to the rule is *L'Etincelle de la Thomson* which, in its second issue (September 1924), published an article on piece-rates and on the bonus systems in operation in other factories. It invited 'all comrades to express their views, not only on the life they are forced to live, but also on the organization of labour and on the production methods used in the work teams'. The following issue announced a series of background articles on work organization and on Thomson's profits. Only one of the articles was devoted to explaining the meaning of the terms 'standards office', 'planning office' and 'cost-price office' and to explaining the roles of those offices in economic terms: 'Overheads account for a greater proportion of the cost price than wage-costs (three, five or even ten times more) and overheads are proportional to production time. A speed-up in production means faster circulation. Every effort will therefore be made to cut production time as much as possible.'

8 In the summer of 1920, the newly created Communist International adopted a number of 'theses' on union questions. Most of them were concerned with the criteria on which Communists should participate in the activities of reformist unions and with possible criteria for forming break-away Communist unions. The issues discussed also included 'workers' control' over production.

The positions adopted at Comintern's second congress (July–August 1920) may be summarized as follows:

1. Aspirations towards workers' control represent a dynamic tendency, and they are fairly widespread in the industrialized countries. They find expression in factory councils.

2. Factory councils prefigure the new role the organized working class will play in socialist production and, more generally, in socialist society as a whole.

3. In more immediate terms, factory councils are forward looking and provide invaluable experience. They represent a dynamic element of major importance, and a step towards the seizure of power in either the short or the longer term. It is argued that the workers will be forced to go beyond taking control of individual factories, and that the reaction of governments and employers will transform the struggle for workers' control into a struggle for the seizure of political power.

9 The reasons for its failure cannot be dealt with here. We shall simply note in passing that Gramsci's analysis (1977) obviously raises the question of the potential 'autonomy' of the working class and its ability to acquire permanent control over its own destiny:

> The working class is closing ranks around its machines; it is creating its own representative institutions based on labour, based on its newly won awareness of self-government. The Factory Council is the foundation for its positive experiences and for its appropriation of the instruments of labour. It is the solid foundation for the process which must culminate in the workers' dictatorship and the conquest of State power. (Gramsci, 1977, p. 166)

It also raises the issue of the almost physical structuration of the movement around machines, and of the coherence and discipline that implies.

10 cf. *L'Atelier* (September 1926):

> *This Congress [the 1920 London Congress of the International Trades Union Federation] was quite extraordinary . . . The main questions discussed were changes in the international distribution of raw materials and in the socialization of the means of production. The decisions taken on the basis of reports from Jouhaux, Mertens and Oudegeest provided the basis for the general economic programme which the International has since tried to promote and which, we can say with some pride, also provides the basis for the solutions we have adopted in dealing with post-war problems.*

The article is entitled '25 années d'action internationale'. *L'Atelier* was the CGT's theoretical journal. The National Committee's report of October 1926 on 'Problems of production and the working class' is reproduced in issue 35 under the title 'Organisation scientifique du travail'. It was this report which launched the campaign for 'economic reorganization'. The report is fairly comprehensive, and is a reminder that the CGT had been following the same line since 1918. The international context is outlined, but the International Federation's ability to intervene and to co-ordinate action is clearly overestimated. The report recommends the adoption of a National Plan for Labour, and of co-ordinated programmes ranging from the exploitation of hydroelectric power to putting a halt to the pillaging of the wealth of the colonies. It argues the case for rationalization, and makes much of its positive effects (one section deals with the shorter working week introduced at Ford). It also proposes social criteria which will allow the specific objectives of the union movement to be reconciled with 'the general interest' and with the stated aims of rationalization (better wages, job security, a 'normal' working day, housing, leisure . . .).

11 In this sense, the evolution of Merrheim, the Secretary of the Fédération des Métaux, is particularly spectacular. After the 'time-study strikes' that took place at Renault and Arbel, he published a virulent article in *La Vie ouvrière* (Merrheim, 1913) entitled 'L'Homme-outil: La Méthode Taylor'. He denounces Taylorism as a 'bestial method' which results in physical and moral decadence. A few months later, in the spring of 1914, he changes his tone completely. When interviewed by Vielleville, Merrheim states:

In my view, the rational organization of work is absolutely necessary if we are to bring the industrial revolution we are experiencing [sic] to a successful conclusion; the revolution will speed up, and we are now experiencing only its initial effects. For my part, I believe that, when it has been adapted to the French mentality, the Taylor system will be introduced more widely in industry. It therefore seems to me that it is in the best interests of the workers themselves to take control of its introduction and to do all they can to encourage it in so far as it does not come into conflict with their moral, financial or physical interests. (Vielleville, 1914, p. 139)

12 In 1927 the Fourth Congress of the Fédération Unitaire de la Métallurgie adopted the following resolution:

We are in favour of the principles of scientific management, including assembly-line work and production norms. This is something which corresponds to a stage in the development of the capitalist regime. To attempt to block technical progress would not really be revolutionary; revolutionaries understand that the working class is capitalism's heir, and that scientific organization will allow the working class to build socialism much more quickly when it takes power.

13 There is a high degree of ambiguity here. The discourse of the papers published by PCF cells (and CGT sections) describes rationalization as the science of exploitation and as a pure expression of the aims of the boss class. But it is also assumed that in other contexts (in the USSR, in the future or after the seizure of power, or even in the present context if the struggle is pursued) rationalization can lead to a better standard of living. Basically, this implies an instrumental representation of science. That representation is, for example, implicit in Pouget's (1914) famous book. Having attacked the 'pedantic nonsense' talked by intellectuals (this is a reference to Amar), Pouget wholeheartedly adopts a mechanical/energetic model of the workings of the human body and even extends it by correcting what he sees as the 'ineptitude' of Amar's observations ('Brain work does not involve any measurable expenditure of energy'). He adds that 'Refuting this so-called experiment and demonstrating the absurdity of its frightening results is simply a matter of common sense.' Scientific experiments should, that is, be conducted on a common-sense basis and should reflect the conditions under which labour-power is sold as a commodity. Taylor makes a symmetrical error when he attempts to discover his law of fatigue. It is scarcely surprising that, at the end of his book, Pouget should adopt the same position as the man whose 'ridiculous discoveries' he mocked at the beginning. He even attempts to defend what he terms Taylorist orthodoxy against the distortions introduced by 'French panegyrists' such as Le Chatelier.

14 Although Soviet Taylorism has serious implications, it cannot be dealt with in any detail here. The reader is referred to the analysis by Linhart (1976, part 2, chapters 2 and 3) of 'the complexity of Lenin's "Taylorist" position' and, for later developments, to Bettelheim (1977, pp. 228–49). A succinct account of the doctrine of Soviet Taylorism will be found in Lapidus and Ostrovitianov (1929, chapter 6, 'The productivity of labour'), where it is argued that Scientific Management can play an important role if it is applied rationally and if its negative features can be overcome. The 'positive/negative' duality implies something very close to the idea of 'proletarian science', which was being developed by Nikolai Bukharin at this time.

Bettelheim describes the debates that developed around the notion of Soviet Taylorism and draws upon material cited by Carr and Davies (1974, p. 510). At one extreme, Chaplin, who was the Komsomol delegate, claimed that for the Central Institute of Labour, the worker was 'an adjunct of the machine, not a creator of socialist production'. At the other, Gastev, the director of the Institute, was quite happy to contribute an article to the *Bulletin of the Taylor Society* in August 1929. The meaning of the debate can of course only really be understood in terms of the alternative models of industrial development which the USSR was forced to choose between at this time.

15 It is, for instance, quite obvious that, although the most blatant expressions of the anarcho-syndicalist tradition of defying the foremen disappear from these newspapers in the period 1924–31, this does not reflect any real change in working-class mentalities. It is the result of self-censorship, but not everyone accepted the new line. In a forthcoming history of the Renault plant at Boulogne, Depreto cites an eye-witness account of the 1936 strike. At the time, *L'Humanité* was practising self-criticism and arguing that the struggle against 'Mr Stopwatch' tended to make workers forget 'who the real exploiters were'. Costes found it very difficult to win support when, acting in the name of the union leadership, he tried to get the strikers to throw coffins representing the foremen into the Seine. He was told: 'The boss is the real enemy.'

16 In 1923, a major strike occurred at the Dietrich factory in Bourgoin; it lasted for two months, and the strikers received some support from the local population. The workforce walked out over the introduction of a system of arbitrary checks, enforced by a squad of 'spies' who were not qualified metal-workers and whose activities included making systematic inquiries into the private lives of the workers.

17 The Bedeaux system used 'points' both to evaluate tasks and to determine wages.

18 These 'slogans' were painted on the walls of the Ile Seguin plant in 1931. Photographs in two publications entitled *Renault 1897–1931* and *Renault 1899–1934* (Bibliothèque Nationale: Wz2334) show small posters pasted up at regular intervals alongside the assembly line. They read: 'Always put your tools in the same place'; 'Do not drop spray-guns on the floor; put them on the special stands provided'; and 'Win your foreman's confidence: trust him'.

19 In his forthcoming history of Renault, Depreto points out that although *L'Humanité* devoted many articles to Renault during this period, there was almost no mention of assembly-line work. The newspaper cited above appeared a few months before the Congress of the Fédération Unifiée de la Métallurgie; as we have seen, the Congress refused, after a lively debate, to condemn assembly-line work as such. Subsequent issues of *Le Bolchevik* describe the effects of 'Americanization' on individual shops in some detail (wages, profits, and job-cuts are all discussed, and the paper adds: 'Renault wants to destroy our minds; it is trying to turn thousands of workers into idiots').

CHAPTER TEN
YESTERDAY, TODAY AND TOMORROW?

1 cf. Spryopoulus (1978):
Although doubts have long been expressed about the application of management principles deriving from Taylor's writings, it was really only in the 1950s and 1960s that there was widespread dissatisfaction with waged labour in industrial societies.

2 The initial findings were published in full in a supplement to the *Bulletin mensuel de statistiques du travail* (1979, supp. 71) in December 1979. A summary appeared in *Economie et statistiques* in January 1980 (Molinié and Volkoff, 1980).

3 In order to prepare a report for a conference on health organized by the CGT in February 1978, the author investigated women's working conditions in a factory producing telephone equipment (with the assistance of the Comité d'entreprise). This was a much more modest study than the one described above, but the hundred or so replies received did provide certain information which would repay further study. Half the women who filled in the questionnaire stated that they never had to move around the factory while they were at work; 60% said that the only part of the factory with which they were familiar was their work station; 48% said that they had 'total responsibility' for their work; 47% said that they had 'partial responsibility', but the phrasing of the question left some room for ambiguity. It is interesting to note that 39% of all women with 'total responsibility' for their work said that they did not know the origins of the parts they worked on; 38% did not know what happened to them, and the same number did not know what they were used for; 32% of all the women answered these three questions in negative terms.

4 On the specific effects of relocation on working conditions, see Wisner (1976).

5 Many studies of assembly lines in Eastern-bloc countries have been published. Only two will be quoted here:

1. A study of the Csepel motorcycle plant in Budapest (as summarized in Kemeny, 1978), based upon interviews with men and women on the assembly line (the assembly of a motorcycle involves fifty-eight people) and upon biographical interviews. This is a fascinating piece of work in that it provides an informal picture of relations of production under a different mode of production. Even the history of the line itself provides food for thought. When the factory was nationalized in 1948, each 'Csepel' motorcycle (or motorized cycle, to be more accurate) was assembled by a single worker; the parts needed to build two motorcycles were delivered each day, but no real technical instructions were provided. A foreman was on hand to give advice as required. The suggestion that work should be carried out by specialists and that it should be collectivized around twenty or thirty work stations came from the workers themselves, and reflected increased demand for the product. At this stage, between two and five people worked more or less simultaneously on each cycle; eventually assembly came to involve eight to ten people. Finally, the factory began to work on an assembly-line system; the workers were still responsible for organizing their own work, but the teams were now defined more strictly. In 1952, the factory management introduced a system of trolleys running on rails, and the work became completely fragmented. Relatively empirical norms were introduced ('We divided up everything that could be divided up and when things began to work smoothly, we established a system'). The authors stress that 'It was the workers themselves who divided the assembly process

into phases, and they did so on a purely anthropomorphic basis. Initially, one worker had full responsibility for each phase. At a later stage, personal work relations were ignored, but the personal aspect was still the starting point.' It seems that, in this factory, the contradiction between the technical socialization of labour and the isolation of individual workers (which is inherent in the structure of the line) led the workforce to make real technological innovations.

2. A study of the Voljky car plant in Togliatti, USSR (*Informations BIT*, 1978). This short study stresses the reduction of the work load, the role of training programmes for assembly-line workers, of attempts to develop multiple skills and the importance of social measures to improve life inside and outside the factory. The general measures described in this study confirm my own observations on work at the Dacia car plant in Piteski (Romania) in 1975; again, the emphasis was placed on the need to offer workers on the line 'skill' programmes, to develop multiple skills and to provide theoretical training. The line stopped for four and a half minutes at work stations 'manned' by mixed teams of four or five men and women, and it was possible for them to organize their work to a certain extent on a collective basis. Despite these differences – and they are by no means negligible – it is still true to say that there was no basic difference between these assembly lines and a line in a Ford plant. The assembly line necessarily generates a certain type of management–worker relationship, and it necessarily produces a contradiction between the practical socialization of labour and the collective worker's inability to intervene in the labour process.

6 Echoes of the subjective effects of this objective socialization of labour can be heard in the comments made by a UAP typist working at a computer terminal console when she was interviewed by *Antoinette* (the CGT women's paper) in January 1980: 'The work might be interesting if I knew its purpose. If I knew how the machine worked . . . and how insurance worked!' The many men and women who spoke at *Antoinette*'s conference on automation in December 1980 also gave the impression that the objective socialization of labour does not necessarily make the overall process any clearer to its agents.

7 cf. Fouet:
  A line of serial or complementary work stations can be reorganized as a star, with orders coming from the centre. Sub-systems can process

and generalize the experience of autonomous work-teams, and the productive equipment can thus become mobile. Each operational satellite receives a production programme with very detailed norms, and organizes its own work. (1980, p. 142)

BIBLIOGRAPHY

Aglietta, Michel (1979) *A Theory of Economic Regulation: The US Experience*, David Fernbach, trans. London: New Left.

Althusser, Louis (1972) 'Reply to John Lewis (self-criticism), Graham Lock, trans. *Marxism Today* October: 310–18.

Amar, J. (1909) 'Le Rendement de la machine humaine', Université de Paris, Thèse de sciences.

—— (1914) *Le Moteur humain et les bases scientifiques du travail professionnel*. Paris: Dunod.

—— (1927) *Organisation et hygiène sociale*. Paris: Dunod.

Ampère, H. (1935) *Essai sur la philosophie des science*. Paris: Bachelier.

Arnold, H. L. and Faurote, L. F. (1975) 'Ford methods and Ford shops', *New York Engineering Magazine*.

Audiganne, A. (1860) *Les Populations ouvrières et les industries de la France*. Paris: Musée Social.

Auerbach, F. (1906) *Etudes sur les procédés techniques et les institutions sociales de la Fondation Carl Zeiss à Iéna*. Paris: Giard et Brière.

Babcock, G. (1928) 'Research on production', *Bulletin of the Taylor Society* 13.

Banfield, T. C. (1884) *Four Lectures on the Organization of Industry. Being Part of a Course Delivered in the University of Cambridge in Easter Term 1884.* London: Richard & John E. Taylor.

Barclay, Hartley W. (1936) *Ford Production Methods.* New York/London: Harper.

Barros, J. F. and Virnot, P. (1975) 'Architecture industrielle et autogestion', *Aujourd'hui* (CFDT) 4.

Bernstein, I. (1970) *Turbulent Years: A History of the American Worker, 1933–1941.* Boston, MA: Houghton Mifflin.

Bertrand, M. (1978) *Histoire des théories économiques.* Paris: Editions Sociales.

Bethlehem Steel Company (1936) *Bethlehem Alloy and Special Steels, Bars, Billets, Blooms and Slabs.*

Bettelheim, Charles (1977) *Les Luttes de classe en URSS. Deuxième époque: 1923–1930.* Paris: Seuil et Maspero.

Beynon, Huw (1973) *Working for Ford.* Harmondsworth: Penguin Education.

Bingham, W. V. (1928) 'Industrial psychology', *Bulletin of the Taylor Society* 12.

Blau, P. (1955) *The Dynamics of Bureaucracy.* Chicago: University of Chicago Press.

Borzeix, A. (1980) *Syndicalisme et organisation du travail.* Paris: CNAM, Laboratoire de sociologie du travail et de relations industrielles.

Bour, E. (1865) *Cours de mécanique et machines professé à l'Ecole Polytechnique.* Paris: Gauthier-Villars.

Bouvier-Ajam, M. (1969) *Histoire du travail en France depuis la Révolution.* Paris: Librairie générale de droit et de jurisprudence.

Braverman, Harry (1974) *Labour and Monopoly Capital.* New York: Monthly Review.

Brown, J. C. (1931) 'Workers' participation in management', *Bulletin of the Taylor Society* 14:1.

Broy, A. (1972) 'Automation in high gear', *Dun's* November.

Bruhat, J. (1952) *Histoire du mouvement ouvrier français.* Paris: Editions Sociales.

Bruno, P., Pêcheux, M., Plon, M. and Poitou, J.-P. (1973) 'La Psychologie sociale, une utopie en crise', *La Nouvelle Critique* March.

Bulletin de la Fondation André Renard (1977) Numéro Spécial: 'Est-ce la fin des temps modernes?'.

Bulletin d'information du Comité Hyacinthe Dubreuil (1978) 'H. Dubreuil, F. Taylor: deux précurseurs, deux destins parallèles' October.

Buret, Eugène (1839) *De la Misère des classes laborieuses en Angleterre et en France*. Brussels: Paulin.

Cailleux, A. (1901) 'Les Questions des règlements d'ateliers en France', *Revue d'économie politique* August–September.

Canguilhem, Georges (1973) 'La Constitution de la physiologie comme science' in C. Kayser, *Physiologie*. Paris: Masson.

Carnot, L. (1811) *Traité des machines*. Paris: Hachette.

Carpenter, C. U. (1909) *Comment organiser les entreprises et les usines pour réaliser des bénéfices*. Paris: Béranger.

Carr, E. H. and Davies, R. W. (1974) *Foundations of a Planned Economy. 1926–1929*, vol. 1, Harmondsworth: Pelican.

Cartwright, D. and Zander, A. F. (1968) *Group Dynamics in Research and Theory*. London: Tavistock.

Caspard, P. (n.d.) 'La Fabrique au village', *Le Mouvement social* 97.

CCEES (1977a) 'Questions sur le procès de travail et ses transformations récentes', *Note économique* 145: March–April.

—— (1977b) 'Une opinion sur l'évolution des conditions de travail dans l'industrie par ceux qui la subissent', *Note économique* 151: October.

—— (1977c) 'La Presse patronale d'entreprise', *Etudes et documents économiques* October.

—— (1978) 'Des manufactures à la crise du taylorisme', *Etudes et documents économiques* November.

—— (1979) 'La Commission Trilaterale dans les textes', *Note économique* 178: October.

—— (1980) 'L'Automatisation de la production, premières réflexions', *Note économique* 184: May.

CEE (1974) *Conférence sur l'organisation du travail, évolution technique et motivation de l'homme*. Brussels: CEE.

CEREQ (1976) L'Organisation du travail et ses formes nouvelles', *Bibliothèque de la CEREQ* 10: November.

CERNUR (1974) *Noyautage-fonderies de moteurs d'automobiles*. Enquête Service Economique.

Cestre, C. (1921) *Production industrielle et justice sociale en Amérique*. Paris: Garnier.

CGT (1926)'L'Organisation scientifique du travail', *L'Atelier* 35.

Chevalier, M. (1870) *Discours au Collège de France*.

Cita futura (1959) 'Il movimento operario torinese durante la prima guerra mondiale'.

Clément, C., Bruno, P. and Sève, L. (1973) *Pour une critique marxiste de la psychanalyse*. Paris: Editions Sociales.

Clément, J. (1877) 'Le Congrès des trades unions', *Journal des économistes* 37.

CNAM (1972a) 'Textes généraux sur l'ergonomie', *Rapport* 34.

—— (1972b) 'Etude du poste de conducteur de machine Trio', *Rapport* 32.

—— (1974) 'Contenu des tâches et charge de travail', *Rapport* 41.

—— (1976) 'Pratique de l'ergonomie et pays en développement industriel', *Rapport* 52.

CNPF (1978) *Portes ouvertes sur l'entreprise (4e Assises nationales)*. Paris: Editions Techniques Patronales.

Combe, M., Chombart de Lawe, H. and Ziegler, M. P. (1980) *Effets traumatisants d'un licenciement collectif. Tome 2: Etude médicale*. Centre d'Ethnologie Sociale et Psychosociologie.

Comegno, C., Mottre, B., Warin, C., Doray, B. and Suchet (1980) *Conséquences du chômage sur la santé*. Paris: CNRS and CCEES-CGT.

Congrès International de Mécanique Appliquée (1890) *Compte rendu*. Paris: Bernard.

Cooke, A. (1917) 'Individual, group, leadership: their relationship to content, and the ideals of democracy', *Bulletin of the Taylor Society* August.

Coriolis, G. G. (1826) *De Calcul de l'effet des machines*. Paris: Carilian-Guery.

Corrado, S. (1955) *I Consigli di fabrica comme organi institutionali di un futuro stato*. Milan: Instituto Feltrinelli (roneo).

Cuvilliers, A. (1954) *Un journal d'ouvriers: 'L'Atelier'*. Paris: Editions Ouvrières.

Dawson, W. (1911) 'Le Nègre sudiste sous son aspect économique', *Journal des économistes* 30.

Déclarations des délégations ouvrières à l'Exposition Universelle de 1867 (n.d.) Paris: Morel.

Defoe, Daniel (1719) *Robinson Crusoe*. New York: Airmont.

Delamotte, Y. and Walker, K. F. (n.d.) *L'Humanisation du travail et la qualité de la vie de travail, tendances et problèmes*. ILO.

Denis, H. (1966) *Histoire de la pensée économique*. Paris: PUF.

Desbrousses, H. (1975) *Le Mouvement des masses ouvrières en France entre les deux guerres d'après 'La Vie ouvrière'*. St Germain-de-Calberte: Centre de sociologie historique.

Doll, E. A. (1926) 'Psychology in the organization of prison industries', *Bulletin of the Taylor Society* 11:4.

Doray, Bernard (1978) 'Les Pratiques scientifiques dans le champ du travail industriel: la crise du modèle taylorien', *La Pensée* 199: 44–57.

Drapier, D. (1854) *Cours complet et pratique de filature de coton*. Rouen: Lanctin.

Dubreuil, Hyacinthe (1929) *Standards*. Paris: Grasset.

Durrafourg, J. (1980) 'Produire autrement', *Economie et politique* March.

Edwards, Richard (1979) *Contested Terrain: The Transformation of the Workplace in the Twentieth Century*. New York: Basic.

Eichtal, E. (1873) 'Du travail des femmes', *Journal des économistes*.

Emery, F. (1978) 'Designing socio-technical systems for green-field sites', unpublished paper.

Emery, F. E. and Trist, E. L. (1960) 'Socio-technical systems' in F. Emery, ed. *Systems Thinking*. Harmondsworth: Penguin, 1981, pp. 322–38.

Engels, F. (1892) *The Condition of the Working Class in England*. London: Panther, 1969.

Faure, A. and Rancière, J. (1976) *La Parole ouvrière*. Paris: UGE 10/18.

Feiss, R. A. (1915) 'Personal relationships as the basis of scientific management', *Bulletin of the Society to Promote the Science of Management* 1:6.

Flachat, S. (1835) *Traité élémentaire de mécanique industrielle*. Paris.

Follet, M. P. (1926) 'The illusion of final authority', *Bulletin of the Taylor Society* 11:5.

Ford, Henry (1923) *My Life and Work*. London: Heinemann.

—— (1926a) *Today and Tomorrow*. London: Heinemann.

—— (1926b) 'Progressive manufacture', *Encyclopaedia Britannica*.

Ford Motor Company (1917, 1918, 1920) *Facts From Ford*. Detroit.

Fouet, Monique (1980) 'Les Etats-Unis, une économie dominante dans une période de transition', *Notes et études documentaires* 4573–4.

Fourier, Charles (1830) *Le Nouveau Monde industriel*. Paris: Bossange Père.

Friedmann, Georges (1946) *Problèmes humains du machinisme industriel*. Paris: Gallimard.

—— (1964) *Le Travail en miettes*. Paris: Gallimard.

Gaspard, P. (1976) 'La Fabrique au village', *Le Mouvement social* 97.

Gaudemar, J.-P. de (1979) *La Mobilisation générale*. Paris: Le Champ Urbain.

Godard, Jean-Luc (1980) *Introduction à une véritable histoire du cinéma*. Paris: Editions Albatros.

Godelier, Maurice (1971) 'L'Anthropologie économique', in J. Copans, S. Tornay, M. Godelier and C. Clément, *L'Anthropologie, science des sociétés primitives?* Paris: Denoël.

—— (1972) *Rationality and Irrationality in Economics*. Brian Pearse, trans. London: Verso.

Gogol, N. (1923) 'The nose' in *The Overcoat and Other Stories*. Constance Garnett, trans. London: Chatto & Windus, 1923, pp. 177–216.

Gramsci, Antonio (1971) *Selections from Prison Notebooks*, Quintin Hoare and Geoffrey Nowell-Smith, trans. and ed. London: Lawrence & Wishart.

—— (1977) *Selections from Political Writings (1910–1920)*, Quintin Hoare, ed., John Matthews, trans. London: Lawrence & Wishart.

Grevet, Patrice (1980) Contribution to Colloque de l'Institut de Recherches Marxistes sur l'Autogestion, May.

Guérin, Daniel (1968) *Le Mouvement ouvrier aux Etats-Unis*. Paris: Maspero.

Hachette (1828) *Traité élémentaire des machines*. Paris: Corby.

Hartmann, Heinz (1958) *Ego Psychology and the Problem of Adaptation*. D. Rapoport, trans. New York: International Universities Press.

Hatry, G. (1971) 'La Grève du chronométrage', *Bulletin de la section d'histoire des Usines Renault* December.

Heron, A. (1975) 'Le Taylorisme hier et demain', *Les Temps modernes* 220–78, 349–50.

Herriot, E. (1920) *Créer*. Paris: Payot.

Herzberg, F. (1971) *Le Travail et la nature de l'homme*. Paris: EME.

Imbert, P. (1902) *Des rapports entre patrons et ouvriers dans la grande industrie*. Thèse de droit de Paris.

Informations BIT (1978) 'De la chaîne de montage à de meilleurs emplois' 14:4.

International Council for the Quality of Working Life (1978) *Working on the Quality of Working Life*. Hingham: Martinus Nijhoff.

Izart (1918) 'Méthode économique d'organisation des usines'. Paris: Dunod.

Jardillier, P. (1973) *La Psychologie industrielle*. Paris: PUF.

Kafka, Franz (1925) *The Trial*, Willa and Edwin Muir, trans. Harmondsworth: Penguin, 1953.

Karger, D. W. and Bayha, F. H. (1957) *Engineered Work Measurement*. New York: Industrial Press.

Kellenbenz, H. (1970) 'Les Industries dans l'Europe moderne, 1500–1750', in *Colloque sur l'industrialisation en Europe*. Paris: CNRS.

Kemeny, I. (1978) 'La Chaîne dans une usine hongroise', *Actes de la recherche en sciences sociales* 24: November.

Laboulaye, C. (1849) *Traité de cinematique, théories des mécanismes*, Paris.

Lacan, Jacques (1966) *Ecrits*. Paris: Seuil.

Lahy (1920) *Le Système Taylor et la physiologie du travail*. Paris: Gauthier-Villars.

Lainé, T. (1971) *L'Agir*. Paris: CEMEA.

Laing, R. D. (1965) *The Divided Self*. Harmondsworth: Penguin.

Lapidus and Ostrovitianov (1929) *Précis d'économie politique*. Paris: Editions Sociales Internationales.

Lavoisier, A. L. (1862–93) *Oeuvres complètes*. Paris: Editions Officielles.

Le Chatelier, H. (1928) 'Courtesy of H. Le Chatelier: sa correspondance avec Taylor', *Bulletin of the Taylor Society* 12:5.

Leclaire, Godin (1868) *Causeries d'un maire à ses administrés*. Paris.

Lefort, J. (1875) *Intempérance et misère. Etude sur la moralisation et le bien-être des classes ouvrières*. Paris: Guillaumin.

Le Guillant, L. (1958) 'La Névrose des téléphonistes', *La Raison* 2–21.

—— and Desoille, H. (1957) 'Les Effets de la fatigue sur la santé des travailleurs', in *Conférence internationale sur l'influence des conditions de vie et de travail sur la santé*. Paris: Privat.

Leloutre, G. (1883) *La Transmission par courroies*. Lille: Danel.

Lequin, Y. C. (1979) 'La Rationalisation du capitalisme français a-t-elle eu lieu dans les années vingt?', *Cahiers d'histoire de l'Institut Maurice Thorez* 31.

Linhart, R. (1976) *Lénine, les paysans, Taylor*. Paris: Seuil.

—— (1978) *L'Etabli*. Paris: Minuit.

MacGregor, D. (1966) *Leadership and Motivation*. Boston, MA: Massachusetts Institute.

Maillard, P. (1971) 'Le Montage à la chaîne de la 10 HP Renault', *Bulletin de la section d'histoire des Usines Renault* December.

Maltese, F. (1975) 'Notes for the study of the automobile industry', in *Labor Market Segmentation*. Lexington, MA: D. C. Heath.

Marey, E. J. (1873) *La Machine animale*. Paris: Masson.

—— (1894) *Le Mouvement*. Paris: Masson.

Marglin, S. A. (1973) 'What do bosses do? The origins and functions of hierarchy in capitalist production', in André Gorz, ed. *The Division of Labour*. Hassocks: Harvester, pp. 13–61.

Marx, Karl (1969a) *Theories of Surplus Value*, vol. 1. London: Lawrence & Wishart.

—— (1969b) *Theories of Surplus Value*, vol. 2. London: Lawrence & Wishart.

—— (1975) 'Economic and philosophical manuscripts (1844)', in *Early Writings*. Harmondsworth: Penguin, in association with *New Left Review*.

—— (1976) *Capital*, vol. 1. Harmondsworth: Penguin, in association with *New Left Review*, pp. 279–400.

Masini, P. (1951) *Anarchici e communisti nel movimento dei consigli a Torino*. Milan: Gruppo Barriera.

Maslow, A. H. (1954) *Motivation and Personality*. New York/London: Harper & Row.

Maury, L. (1967) 'L'Actualité de Taylor', in F. W. Taylor (1967).

Merrheim, A. (1913) 'L'Homme-outil: la méthode Taylor', *La Vie ouvrière* 20 February.

Miles, E. (1965) 'Human relations or human resources?', *Harvard Business Review* 43:4.

Molinari, Gustave (1907) 'Théorie de l'évolution', *Journal des économistes*.

Molinié, A. F. and Volkoff, S. (1980) 'Les Conditions de travail des ouvriers . . . et des ouvrières', *Economie et statistiques* January.

Monge, Gaspard (1792) *Rapport devant la Convention nationale: 3 vendémiare An III*. Paris: Imprimerie Nationale.

Monmousseau, Gaston (1922) 'Problèmes révolutionnaires: Contrôle syndical et conseils d'usine', *La Vie ouvrière* 3 February and 3 March.

Mottez, B. (1966) *Systèmes de salaires et politiques patronales. Essai sur l'évolution des pratiques et idéologies patronales*. Paris: CNRS.

Moynot, J. L. (1975) 'Déterminations sociales et individuelles des besoins', *La Pensée* 180.

—— (1979) 'Base sociale et rôle révolutionnaire d'une démocratie de masse', *La Pensée* 205.

Muller, F. C. (1898) *Krupp's Steel Works*. London: Heinemann.

Murard, L. and Zylberman, P. (1970) 'Naissance du petit travailleur infatigable', *Recherche* 25.

Muybridge, E. (1887) *Animal Locomotion*. Philadelphia, PA: University of Pennsylvania.

Ortsman, O. (1978a) *Changer le travail*. Paris: Dunod.

—— (1978b) 'Organisation du travail: le refus d'une recette', *Hermès* 2: June.

Paton, Stewart (1922) *Signs of Sanity and the Principles of Mental Hygiene*. New York/London: Charles Scribner's.

Perrot, M. (1972) *Enquêtes sur la condition ouvrière en France au XIXᵉ siècle*. Paris: Microéditions Hachette.

Person, S. (1917) 'The manager, the workman and the social scientist', *Bulletin of the Taylor Society* 3:1.

—— (1926) 'The relations of the chief executive to his principal associative executive', *Bulletin of the Taylor Society* 11:2.

Peters, R. S. (1973) *Le Concept de motivation*. Paris: ESF.

Platone, F. (1951) *L'Ordine Nuovo*, Special issue of *Rinascità: 30 Anni di vita e lotte del PCI*.

Poitou, J.-P. (1972) 'Hierarchie et solidarité dans les groupes', thesis, Départment de psychologie, Université de Provence.

Poncelet, V. (1839) *Introduction à la mécanique industrielle*. Metz: Thiel.

Pouget (1914) *L'Organisation du surménage: le système Taylor*.

Poulantzas, Nicos (1978) *L'Etat, le pouvoir, le socialisme*. Paris: PUF.

Poulot, D. (1980) *Le Sublime*, A. Cottereau, ed. Paris: Maspero.

Pratiques et folies (1981) Dossier Playtex, 1, February.

Prévenir (1980) *Chômage et santé* 1.

Provent, Denise (1978) 'Travailler en France aujourd'hui, *2,000 Avenirs* September.

Quesnay, F. (1888) *Oeuvres économiques et philosophiques*. Paris: Peelman.

Ram (1908) 'Quelques notes sur un essai d'application du Système Taylor dans un grand atelier de mécanique français', *Revue de métallurgie*.

Rankine, William John MacQuorn (1872) *A Manual of Applied Mechanics*, sixth revised edn. London: Griffith.

Rapport des délégations (1867) Paris: Morel.

Report on Profit-Sharing and Labour Partnership in the United Kingdom (1912) London.

Ricardo, David (1817) *The Principles of Political Economy and Taxation*. London: Everyman.

Robert, C. (1870) 'Discussion à la Société d'Economie Politique sur la participation aux bénéfices', *Journal des économistes* 18.

Roethlisberger, F. and Dikson, W. (1939) *Management and the Worker*. Cambridge, MA: Harvard University Press.

Rouet, H. and Cotto, F. (1918) *Le Contrôle technique à l'usine*. Paris: Dunod.

Saint-Germain, P. (1976) 'La Chaîne et le parapluie', *Révoltes logiques* 2.

Scherrer, J. (1967) *Physiologie du travail*. Paris: Masson.

Sève, Lucien (1978) *Man in Marxist Theory and the Psychology of Personality*, John McGreal, trans. Hassocks: Harvester.

Smith, A. (1970) *The Wealth of Nations*, Andrew Skinner, ed. Harmondsworth: Pelican Classics.

Société Taylor (1932) *L'Organisation scientifique dans l'industrie américaine*. Paris: Dunod.

Spyropoulus, G. (1978) 'L'Evolution des conditions de travail dans le monde', *2,000 Avenirs* September.

Stirling, J. (1870) 'Mr. Mill on trades unions: a criticism', in *Review Studies*, Sir Alexander Grant, ed. Edinburgh: Edmonston and Douglas, 1870, pp. 309–22.

Sulleron, L. (1973) *Profil d'une oeuvre: 'La Richesse des nations' d'Adam Smith*. Paris: Hatier.

Taffe, A. (1835) *Application des principes de méchanique aux machines*. Brussels: Meline, Cans et Cie.

Taylor, Frederick W. (1911) 'Taylor's testimony before the Special

House Committee', in *Scientific Management*. London: Harper & Row, 1964.

—— (1914) *The Principles of Scientific Management*. New York/London: Harper.

—— (1967) *La Direction scientifique des entreprises*. Paris: Marabout.

Taylor, Sedley (1884) *Profit-Sharing between Capital and Labour*. London: Kegan Paul, Trench.

Trist, E. L. and Bramforth, K. W. (1951) 'Some social and psychological consequences of the longwall method of coal-getting', *Human Relations* 6:1.

Turgan, J. (1860–85) *Les Grandes Usines de France*. Paris: Michel Lévy Frères.

UIMM (1974) *Evolution dans l'organisation du travail*. Paris: UIMM.

Unwin, G. (1904) *Industrial Organisation in the Sixteenth and Seventeenth Centuries*. Oxford: Clarendon.

Ure, Andrew (1835) *The Philosophy of Manufacture: Or an Exposition of the Scientific, Moral and Commercial Economy of the Factory System of Great Britain*, third edn. London: H. G. Bohn, 1861.

Valentin (1972) *Introduction à l'histoire de l'ergonomie*. Paris: CNAM.

Valentine, R. G. (1915) 'Scientific management and organized labor', *Bulletin of the Society to Promote the Science of Management* 1:1.

—— (1916) 'The progressive relation between efficiency and consent', *Bulletin of the Society to Promote the Science of Management* 3:1.

Valleroux, P. H. (1885) *Les Corporations d'art et de métiers et les syndicats professionnels en France et à l'étranger*. Paris: Guillaumin.

Vialatte, A. (1908) *L'Industrie américaine*. Paris: Alcan.

Vielleville, A. (1914) 'Le Système Taylor', thesis, Faculté de Droit de Paris.

Villermé, L. R. (1971) *Tableau physique et moral des ouvriers employés dans les manufactures de coton, de laine et de soie*. Paris: UGE 10/18.

Walker, Charles and Guest, Robert (1952) *The Man on the Assembly Line*. Cambridge, MA: Harvard University Press.

—— (1956) *The Foreman on the Assembly Line*. Cambridge, MA: Harvard University Press.

Ware, N. (1964) *The Industrial Worker 1840–1860*. Chicago: Quadrangle.

Williams, J. H. (1926) 'Top control', *Bulletin of the Taylor Society* 11:2.

Willis, M. R. (1841) *Principles of Mechanism*.

Wisner, A. (1976) 'Pratique de l'ergonomie et pays en développement industriel', CNAM, *Rapport* 52: September.

Wolf, R. B. (1915) 'Individuality in management', *Bulletin of the Society to Promote the Science of Management* 1:3 and 4.

Wright, C. D. (1880) *Manufactures, the Factory System: The Future of the Factory System*. Census.

Yanouzas, J. (1964) 'A comparative study of work organization and supervisory behaviour', *Human Organization* autumn.

Zarifian, P. (1979) 'Crise de la production et émergence aujourd'hui de l'individualité sociale', *La Pensée* 207.

—— (1980) 'L'Automatisation de la production, premières réflexions', CCEES, *Note économiqe* 184: May.

INDEX

This first edition of
From Taylorism to Fordism:
A Rational Madness
was finished in July 1988.

It was set in 10/13pt Plantin
on a Linotron 202, and printed
by a Miller TP41 offset press
on woodfree Supreme book wove 80g/m² vol. 18.

The book was commissioned by Robert M. Young,
edited by Les Levidow,
copy-edited by Roger Wells,
indexed by Sue Ramsey,
designed by Wendy Millichap,
and produced by David Williams and Selina O'Grady
for Free Association Books.

by a Crabtree SP56 offset press

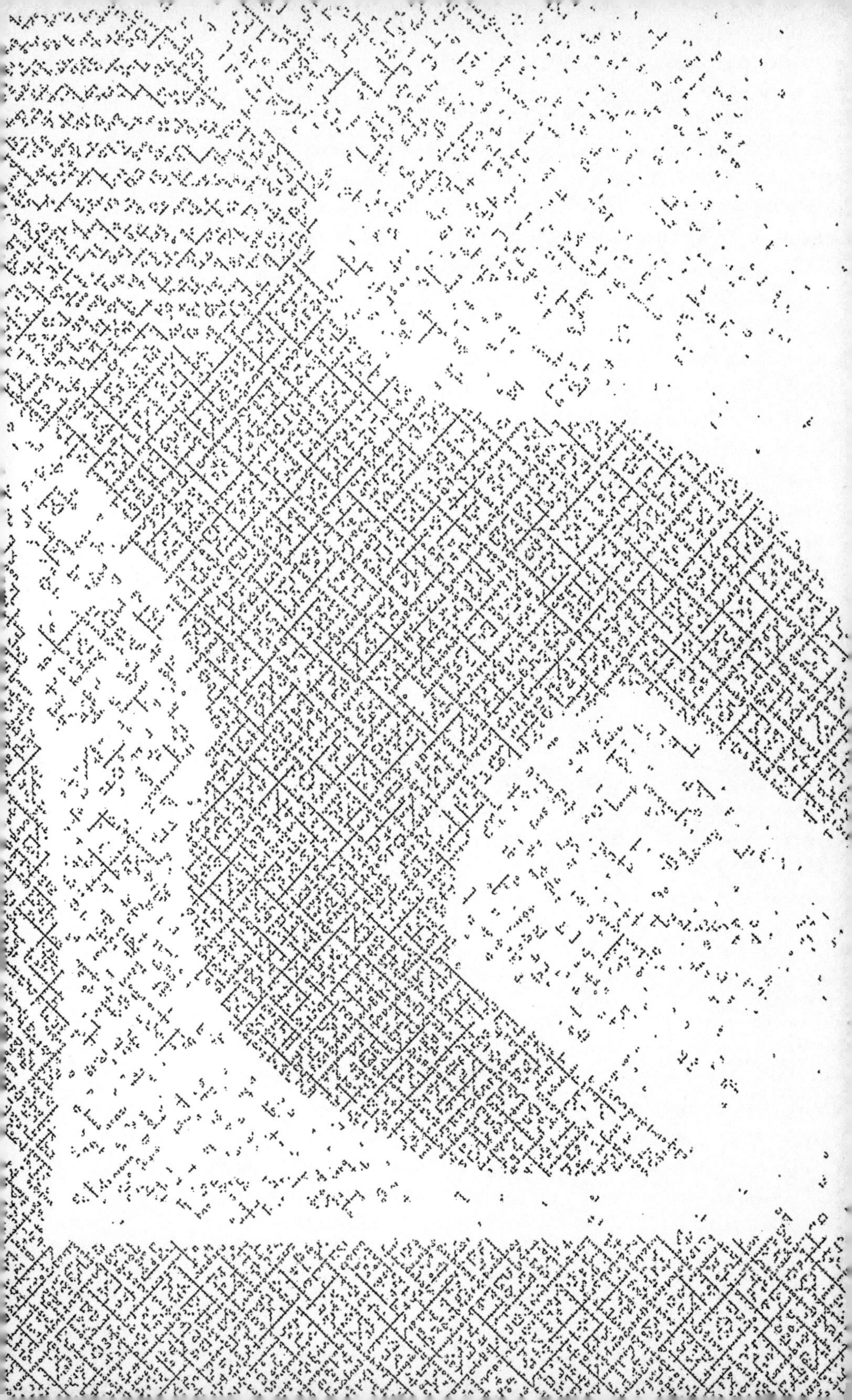

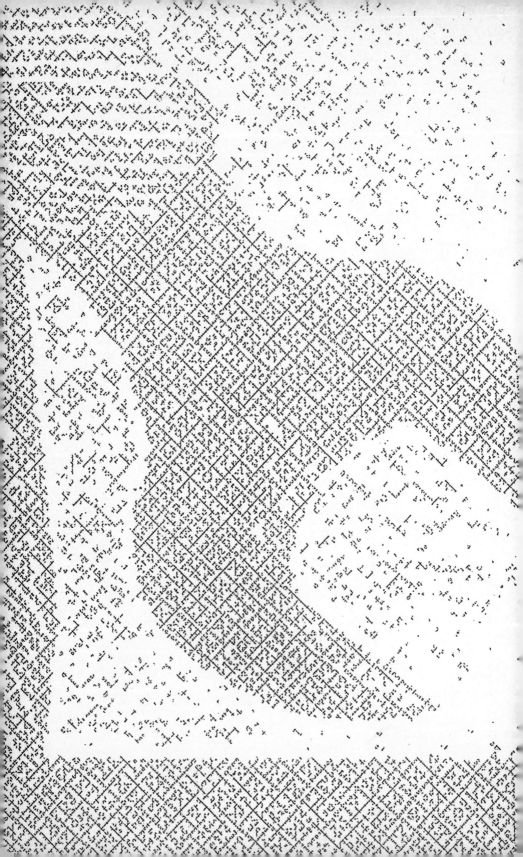